THE MASTER OF SANTIAGO AND FOUR OTHER PLAYS

Queen After Death, or *How to Kill Women*

Malatesta

No Man's Son, or *More than Blood*

Tomorrow the Dawn

The Master of Santiago

TRANSLATED FROM THE FRENCH,
WITH A PREFACE, BY

Jonathan Griffin

Henry de Montherlant

THE MASTER OF SANTIAGO AND FOUR OTHER PLAYS

Alfred A. Knopf: New York

1951

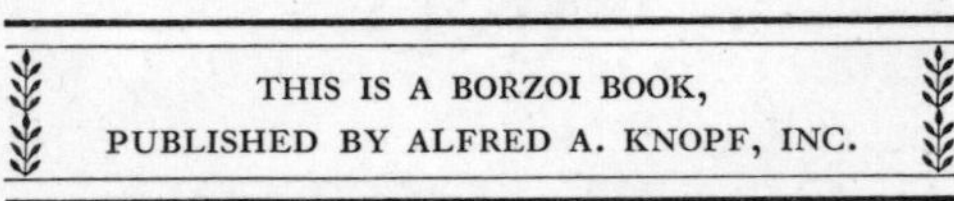

Manufactured in the United States of America. Published simultaneously in Canada by McClelland & Stewart Limited.

FIRST AMERICAN EDITION

ORIGINALLY PUBLISHED IN FRANCE AS *La Reine morte, Fils de personne, Le Maître de Santiago, Malatesta,* AND *Demain il fera jour.* COPYRIGHT BY LIBRAIRIE GALLIMARD RESPECTIVELY IN 1942, 1944, 1947, 1948, 1949.

PREFACE

BY JONATHAN GRIFFIN

IT WILL BE A long time before I forget what I felt as the curtain came down for a moment after the first act of *The Master of Santiago* in that Paris theater: a feeling of having been inside a painting by El Greco and having actually heard the people whom he painted talk; also that this was clearly the finest newly written play to be staged in Paris since the Liberation. At the end of the last act, as Montherlant himself remarks proudly in an article on "Playwriting and Bullfighting," the public went out haggard, "having followed, where he meant to lead them, an author they did not like, who had fought them as you fight a bull, with a play of which they understood damn all, and a character whom they detested."

Montherlant, still hardly known in England or in the United States, is in France generally accepted as a great writer, even by most of those—and they are many—who intensely dislike some of his work. In the summer of 1949 the weekly review *Carrefour* put to its readers the question: "Which of the contemporary French writers will be the most read in the year 2,000?" and in the many replies it was Montherlant who most often came first—more often than Gide, Malraux, Colette, or Claudel. (A measure, of course, not necessarily of merit, but certainly of influence, though not among the very young or the very Left-wing.) Montherlant's reputation, which was already great twenty years ago, was based then on novels and essays. With two exceptions—*L'Exil* and *Pasiphaé*, both special cases—it was not till 1940 that he began writing for the stage.

This is curious, for there is in Montherlant's temperament and philosophy a major element that marks him out to excel in the theater and makes it an inevitable form of expression for him. He himself has remarked this. In an essay on his still unpublished play *Port-Royal* he discusses the peculiar difficulties of its subject (the religious revival known as Jansenism), and then says:

> On the other hand, I was helped by that natural disposition of mine to tip easily over from one extreme to the other, or rather to find myself at one and the same time at both extremes. . . . If, as a thinker, you proclaim the principle "All is true," you are treated as a frightful dilettante and skeptic. If, as a playwright, you are soaked in that principle, you will be congratulated, or at least you will congratulate yourself, on being able to set all your characters talking with equal force (the Greek tragedians did so, perhaps indeed because they had the same disposition . . .).

And he adds: "I have always been filled with Baudelaire's saying: 'It would perhaps be delicious to be by turns the victim and the executioner.' "

And, again, he tells how in 1928 a terrible crisis of unhappiness, through which he had been passing for two years, began "for no apparent reason" to unravel itself; and he comments:

> I suppose it had worn itself out, as love wears itself out, that it had worked out its time. Why does one stop loving a woman? I suppose it is because the organism feels confusedly that it must pass on to something else, that it must not go to sleep in one condition when a thousand other conditions are calling us, including the opposite condition. I suppose that crisis passed because I was tending to go to sleep in it."

"Alternation" is a fact. Happiness comes—at least has come to him—through understanding and accepting it. To do so makes life rich and varied. ("Reason allows of great things. The darkening of reason allows of some great ones also.") And at the same time there is in it an ideal. "I persist," he says, "in believing that being human means understanding all the movements of men." And he calls the poet "limitless lover," because "there is nothing sublime that does not tighten his throat, there is nothing horrible of which he does not feel himself the accomplice and the brother."

There is a parallel, I think, between Montherlant's outlook and Goethe's. Goethe, as a talk by Elizabeth M. Wilkinson on the BBC put it, "could make enormous demands of himself, take on burdens of responsibility, but he was quite certain when to let go, when to run away"; and, again, he "moves easily" between conserving and revolting, "not only because it is natural to him to do so, but because reflection taught him that flexibility is the condition of life and rigidity the condition of death." These words apply admirably to Montherlant—who, indeed, when I showed them to him, quoted to me Goethe's saying: "People always think I am at Jena when I am at Weimar, and at Weimar when I am at Jena," and reminded me that Goethe's symbol for nature was Proteus.

Montherlant's hedonism is not that of the conventional libertine. He is frank enough about the pursuit of pleasure: "To hell with happiness, give me greatness," is, he says in one place, something he felt when he was listening to music; "that is to say, it was someone else's thought"; and he insists that he was "made for happiness," gifted with "a keener and more exacting sense of happiness than is common," and that his good star let him become aware of it in time. But the places where he seeks it are determined by his individual nature—chiefly, it seems to me, by three factors. First—and here he is so much a man of his own time that the experiment of his search and the characters who reflect it in his plays are of universal and intimate interest—he has found, often, his happiness "veiled, as the desert sky is veiled by a mist of sand, by the consciousness of some great thing which was not as it should have been," by, for instance, the injustice between classes or between races, and by both the colonial blemishes and the sufferings of his country: these evils annihilated his lightness and his liberty of spirit. Secondly, pride—a tremendous pride, a heraldic sense of honor—has canalized his search, both in life and in art. It has made of him a brave soldier, then an athlete (the hundred meters, football, and bullfighting—the real thing, in Spain), and then a solitary. It marks his style and technique at all points (of this, more later; but note the way he uses emblems in his plays); and few writers, if any, have put pride on the stage as Montherlant has done: indeed, four out of these five plays are, very largely, studies of pride. Pride governs, too, the special quality of his satire. And thirdly, love of poetry, the poet's wide love already mentioned, takes him well beyond the libertine's limits. It makes him—to give one example from the essays—after saying of the gypsies that he is afraid they deserve the bad press they get, go on to say this of them soon afterwards:

"What is remarkable is that it should be in this godless people that there appears a *quid divinum*, as if the mission of this people was to show that the divine is man." Readers will find for themselves many instances of this sympathy—one is tempted to call it "Christian" and then hesitates because that seems to narrow it—in each of these plays.

But making "alternation" a principle of his life and art, Montherlant has drawn upon himself, in France, violent hostility. It comes in part from those who cannot bear to see his gifts not engaged in the service of their own faith. Claudel for instance—great Catholic poet and playwright—reproached Montherlant (about thirty years ago!) with his "demobilized and aimless force"; to which Montherlant replied:

> Yes, doubtless, for the moment. I shall come out of this condition the day I wish. I have within me all the contradictory conditions, as the cook has, under his hand, cold and burning heat, fire and water. And if I judge that that is better, I shall know how, at the right moment, to paralyze some of them for the sake of cultivating and expressing the others alone. . . .

More generally, Montherlant's freedom pushed to extremes was shocking to a public to whom the appearance of consistency is the test of value, who hate in literature a mixture of forms, who like, more than any other public, to know where they are, who require a tragedy to be only a tragedy, a comedy only a comedy, a hero an unmixed hero, and whose dislike of Shakespeare is none the less deep for being smothered by lip-service or reluctant admiration. To many of them consistency in the pursuit of freedom, or a work of art in which harmony dominates a ranging liberty, is shocking. Rationalizing this traditional distaste, to which is added in many cases a reaction against what is taken to be blasphemous hedonism, they attack Montherlant as insincere. Also, many French people accuse Montherlant of being insincere because they wish he were. Most of those who do so are, I believe, Catholics or women. Many Catholics cannot abide Montherlant because it disturbs them to see basic problems of religion in action treated so searchingly by an unbeliever. Many women cannot abide him because in a group of his novels he treated women with sweeping cynicism (but here "alternation" has been at work, that crisis has worn itself out like others, and in these plays the women have human dignity). Even in England, already, that charge of insincerity has been leveled at him: the talk with which the BBC introduced *The Master of Santiago* to British listeners included the statement that Montherlant in his plays "cynically" adopts one point of view after another.

I believe that that is untrue: Montherlant has, I think, a sincerity more searching than that of most ordinary people, and wholly worthy of an artist; there is a world of difference between being "all things to all men" and being many things in turn because one really is so and because it is an honest and a proud adventure to accept this and see what happens. To prove this is not easy, partly because people mean different things by "sincerity." But if one compares sayings and doings of the characters in the plays with what Montherlant says in the essays in his own person, any impression of cynicism soon fades. Here one example must do. The first act of *The Master of Santiago* presents a devastatingly direct expression of the moral problem of colonial imperialism. Is it a mere "tour de force"? Surely not: for already in 1935, in the autobiographical introduction to his book of essays called *Service inutile*, Montherlant wrote of how, having cut loose from his ancestral property in France and from all the binding temptations of wealth and fame there, he went to Morocco in 1925, "neighing after" some chivalrous exploit, but once in Africa, he "recognized that, if duty there was, it did not lie in harassing the 'infidels,' but in defending them. That was where justice, that was where even courage lay." And he then spent "two hard years" writing a novel called *La Rose de sable*. They were hard "above all because I was torn: the conflict between country and justice, what a horrible thing!" And in the end *La Rose de sable*, the book of his to which, he says, he attached most value, was not published. Montherlant suppressed it—"like a nation that sinks one of its warships to prevent the enemy from using it" (prophetic simile!)—because he felt that to publish at that moment a searching attack on French colonialism would weaken still more the will of the French to face up to the renewed danger from the east.

There is another test of his sincerity: the characters in the plays—and each of the plays creates at least one unforgettable character of major stature. In France the very people who throw doubt on Montherlant's sincerity often identify him with the chief characters of his plays—with Malatesta, with Ferrante, with Georges Carrion, and with Alvaro. Montherlant himself strenuously denies this, because the philosophy of alternation intensifies in him the normal tendency of a creative artist to leave each of his creations behind and pass on to the next. Indeed, he pushes this to the extreme of taking up again the hero of *No Man's Son* and dragging him in the mud in its sequel, *Tomorrow the Dawn*. But the public go on, in spite of his denials, believing that one or other of his main characters is Montherlant himself—and with some excuse, it seems to me.

Montherlant has obviously been impelled to imagine Malatesta by the whole of his preoccupation with "alternation" over many years, and has felt profoundly every one of Malatesta's multitudinous facets. As for Georges Carrion and Alvaro, a few details of the author's life will show from what a convergence of experiences important to him they have sprung.

In 1924 Montherlant found himself famous. He was also handsome, athletic, well off, and of noble family. He had to choose between the life of a successful man of letters—in a country where a man of letters has a prestige unimagined in England—and happiness. He chose the quest of happiness, sold the family place and heirlooms, and left France. (Strangely enough, that other great French writer, Claudel, having passed into the diplomatic service with brilliance, chose the consular service and spent the greater part of his youth, on the whole his most creative time, outside France.) At first, for Montherlant, it was an unbridled pursuit of pleasure, chiefly of the libertine's pleasures, and "alternation" naturally brought satiety—a problem on which he has a great deal to say, but chiefly this: "I had put myself into the conditions for a spiritual life, and later something like that life had come." And he quotes with approval the saying that "one can only detach oneself from the good things of this world if one has indulged in them to excess."

A disaster completed the process: he was badly gored by a bull, his war wounds started to give trouble, and after many months in hospitals he, the athlete, was forbidden to run or ride for some years. From that time he lived for years a strange life: about three months of the year in Paris, the rest in North Africa, "drinking my fill of the sort of hatred I have for everything in the nature of distractions; always under adopted names . . . staying for periods of three weeks at a time without once having anything to do at a fixed hour . . . without any cares except work, reading, and reflection, tempered by the respiration of life, and the possession of human beings, in a part of the world where nature and creature please me. . . ." A solitude very different from the monk's in some ways, but like it, or surpassing it, in the systematic avoiding of distractions. One thinks of T. E. Lawrence—and with fresh surprise when one reads that in 1929 Montherlant had an impulse to join the army in Algeria. All this produced a curious state of mind: he had already a conviction that action "is laughable, except when it is charity"; the idea of marriage he rejected chiefly because "a certain serious way of having the philosophic spirit, a certain serious way of having the religious spirit, a certain serious way of understanding artistic creation" did not fit in with it, "at least for certain natures," and because he "wanted to remain free" for all the possibles "suspended over him"; and, while no longer claiming to have the faith of a Christian, he had "in a great measure" the Christian's sentiments. On this last point he wrote, already in 1929, that he took from the Church that which fitted his spiritual life and his poetic life, "including a certain religious practice," and added:

> If it happened to me one day to be thunderstruck by "grace," I should put myself in the line that I am tempted to call the line of the heart of Christianity, because I seem to see it running, like sap in a tree, through the heart of Christianity: it is a tradition that goes from the Gospel to Port-Royal by way of St. Paul and St. Augustine (and does it not skirt Calvin?). The motto I give it is Bossuet's cry: "Doctrine of the Gospel, how severe you are!" and its form is that of the ever narrowing way.

That is enough to show that deep personal experiences impelled Montherlant to create the two "men of rigor" who are the central figures of *The Master of Santiago* and of *No Man's Son*. Ferrante in *Queen after Death* and even the Pope in *Malatesta* say many things that rise from the same source.

These plays are essentially simple, for all their agility and subtlety. They aim at presenting simple human feelings: the sadness of age, a mother's love for her son, the affection between Isotta and Malatesta, which sings in a sudden hush at the center of his restless machinations, the page-boys playing when the King's back is turned. Often, too, their means of expression are extremely simple: the images used at a climax, for instance, may be the oldest images and the words some of the most worn. In this they carry out Montherlant's ideal of art, which is, as he says in an essay called "*Pour le chant profond*," "only the authenticity and good quality of the soul revealing themselves in a word or a gesture." He has also clearly had the simplicity of Greek tragedy before him as an ideal, especially in *No Man's Son* and in *Tomorrow the Dawn*. He himself compares Georges Carrion's silence in the last act of that play to Agamemnon's silence as Iphigenia is led to the sacrifice, and there are other resemblances of the sort. But he is always on guard against a simplicity untrue to life, against making human beings seem consistent when they are not: * he clearly loves his creature Alvaro, but has no mercy for his faults; and at the end of Act III of *Malatesta*, how fine it is when the Pope very humanly spoils his own good action!

All the five plays are crammed, yet with no apparent effort, no hindrance of their flow, with memorable lines, striking generalizations. Sententiousness, in Shakespeare's time and in Periclean Athens, was thought essential to a fine play, and many plays of our time owe a great deal of their success to it. Shakespeare owes his lasting hold not only to his poetry, his characters, and his stagecraft, but also to having filled his plays

* One of his notes to *No Man's Son* says: "I thought at first that Marie must not be jealous of the demonstrations of affection between Georges and Gilou, because it seemed to me that she ought only to be thinking of her Roger. I saw later that those were two quite separate orders.

"I wanted her to be at some moments rather jealous of these demonstrations, at others . . . happy about them, because this disparity is one of those that are normal in a human character, although authors never like to show them in their works (assuming that they see them in life).

"In the same spirit—to loosen, in order to get in touch with life, which is so loose—I have softened Georges in the fourth act, which at first I had meant to make entirely hard."

with quotable saws that apply to innumerable situations in real life. Webster, in his two great tragedies, achieved something of this by digging chunks out of Florio's Montaigne and chipping them into dialogue. Montherlant is his own Montaigne. He is essentially, as a friend of his remarked to me, a moralist—meaning a writer of maxims in the tradition of Montaigne and La Rochefoucauld, a type of writer in which French literature is richer than ours. His notebooks, like his essays, are full of thoughts in maxim form, and when a character has begun to live in his imagination he has only to dig in them to find many striking things which that character can quite naturally say. This helps to give his plays that continuous liveliness they have in the theater, with each character constantly casting flies and each member of the audience finding himself flicked by some fleeting aphorism that belongs to his own experience or aspirations. It helps, too, to give them unity of style in their diversity; and it fills the characters, for all their individuality, each with something of the author's inner life.

In the dramatic craftsmanship there is a bullfighter's pride—it does not feel to me like the common virtuoso's vanity. He himself has drawn attention to an extraordinary aspect of this. In the article on "Playwriting and Bullfighting" he points out that his plays are of two quite different types: the long, thickly wooded ones, with digressions and embellishments, like *Queen after Death* and *Malatesta;* and the short, economical, tightly knotted ones, like *No Man's Son* and *The Master of Santiago*. In the latter group he came to notice a likeness to the *faena* (the series of passes with which the matador prepares the bull for the stroke of the sword) of the Cordovan or austere school, as opposed to the *faena* of the Sevillian or romantic school. The maximum effect with the minimum of means, and simple means; part of the play's power made up of what it denies itself; no intermission, but the curtain lowered twice (or three times in *No Man's Son*) for a few moments; and "the curtain falls finally on a double kill: that of the play and that of the public . . .

for, in all that, the play and the public, as in the arenas the bull and the public, are in reality one." He noticed also, at rehearsals, an astonishingly close parallel, detail by detail, between the last scene of *The Master of Santiago* (Alvaro preparing Mariana to renounce the world) and a Cordovan *faena*. At the end of it "the work of fascination accomplished by Alvaro upon his daughter is one with the work of fascination accomplished by the author upon his public; and this work of fascination is the same as that which the matador accomplishes upon the bull."

Montherlant has been reproached with opposing only mediocre characters to Alvaro and to Georges Carrion. I do not find this entirely true, for at least Mariana, if perfectly cast, is extremely powerful (*The Master of Santiago* succeeds perfectly with a middling actor as Alvaro, but requires a wonderful actress of a special type as Mariana). But in so far as it is true, it is compensated—as a French critic, Jacques de Laprade, has pointed out—by the part that Montherlant makes the public play, by the fact that Alvaro and Georges Carrion have against them not only the other characters but—invisibly—the normal public opinion of our time with its full weight. This pride of Montherlant's has led, perhaps, to one fall. In a program note for the Paris production of *The Master of Santiago* he wrote that in that play he had gone to the utmost limit of the pared-down, of economy of means. But *Tomorrow the Dawn* is even more pared away: is it perhaps too much so? Is that one of the reasons why—unlike *Santiago*, *No Man's Son*, and *Queen after Death* (*Malatesta* has not yet been staged)—it was not a success with the public in Paris? Or is this simply because the performance was not good enough and the subject was too horrible, too near the bone, for an audience of people who had themselves lived through the German occupation?

The style is very much the man: taut and yet easy as the nostrils of a Lipizzaner horse; no lack of poetic images when these are needed (and they are always placed just where they are really needed); long sentences and words in effectively strange order sometimes, at others spare simplicity or a popular expression used without squeamishness. His sixteenth-century Spaniards speak French, yet somehow speak as, one is sure, sixteenth-century Spaniards spoke; Malatesta and the Pope talk the language of Renaissance Italy, and Gillou's jargon is simply that of a present-day schoolboy; yet all this exists within a single pure style. I hope that something of this comes through translation's more or less creased gauze curtain.

CONTENTS

QUEEN AFTER DEATH

or

HOW TO KILL WOMEN

⚜

A Play in Three Acts

CHARACTERS

FERRANTE, *King of Portugal, aged 60*
PRINCE DON PEDRO, *his son, aged 26*
EGAS COELHO, *Prime Minister*
ALVAR GONÇALVES, *councillor*
DON CHRISTOVAL, *the Prince's former tutor, an old man*
THE GRAND ADMIRAL AND PRINCE OF THE SEA
DINO DEL MORO, *page to the King*
DON EDUARDO, *private secretary, an old man*
DON MANOEL OCAYO
THE INFANTE OF NAVARRE
CAPTAIN BATALHA
TWO OF THE KING'S PAGES
LIEUTENANT MARTINS
INES DE CASTRO, *aged 26*
THE INFANTA OF NAVARRE (*Doña Bianca*), *aged 17*
THREE LADIES-IN-WAITING TO THE INFANTA
OFFICERS, SOLDIERS, COURTIERS, *etc.*

In Portugal, in the past.

ACT I

First Setting: *A hall in the royal palace at Montemor-o-Velho.*

SCENE I

King Ferrante, the Infanta, the Infante, Don Christoval, Three Ladies-in-Waiting of the Infanta, Several Grandees

The Infanta: I cry out to you, I cry out to you, my lord! I cry out to you, I cry out to God! I go about with a sword plunged in my heart. Each time I move, it tears me.

First Lady-in-Waiting [*in a whisper, to the other ladies-in-waiting*]: Poor thing! Look! How it is hurting her!

Second Lady-in-Waiting: She is utterly steeped in pride. And it's her pride that that sword is piercing. Oh, how it's hurting her!

Third-Lady-in-Waiting: Ah, she is from Navarre!

The Infanta: You came, my lord, to my Navarre (God protect it!) to converse with the King, my father, about the affairs of your realms. You saw me, you spoke to me, you believed that an alliance between our crowns, through the instrument of the Prince your son, and of me, might be made for the great benefit of those crowns and for that of Christendom. You, the kings, decided between you upon a journey to be made by me to Portugal, accompanied by the Infante, my brother, not long after your return. We come, we are received magnificently. The coldness of the Prince toward me neither surprises nor saddens me. I had been looking farther; beyond him, I saw the work to be accomplished. Three days passed. This morning Don Pedro, alone with me, makes a confession. He pleads that he did not know your intentions till your return from Navarre, when it was too late to countermand our journey. He declares to me that his heart is bound forever to a lady of your country, Doña Ines de Castro, and that our union will not take place. I believe that if I had not restrained him he would have told me the tale of his love from end to end and in detail: such a mania have those afflicted by the amorous disturbance for believing themselves the object of admiration and envy of the whole world. So I am made to come, like a servant girl, to be told that I am disdained and to be flung back into the sea! My mouth dries up at the thought. My lord, do you know that in our country, in Navarre, people die of humiliation? Don Guzman Blanco, reprimanded by King Sancho, my grandfather, developed fever, took to his bed, and passed away within a month. Father Martorell, my father's confessor, when he was suspended, had an outbreak of boils all over his body and expired after three days. If I were not young and vigorous, My lord, after the affront I have received from the Prince I should be dead.

FIRST LADY-IN-WAITING: To die of wounded honor is certainly the death that befits our Infanta.

SECOND LADY-IN-WAITING: She is always crucified upon herself and she scatters about the blood that flows from her honor.

THIRD LADY-IN-WAITING: Ah, because she is of Navarre, our Infanta!

THE INFANTE OF NAVARRE: I have let the Infanta speak. Her wisdom is great, and her restraint. I shall only add that it is with us as with a bush from which someone wants brutally to tear off a leaf. He tears off a single leaf, but the whole tree shudders. In the same way, with the outrage done to the Infanta the whole of Navarre is shaken. Out of respect and

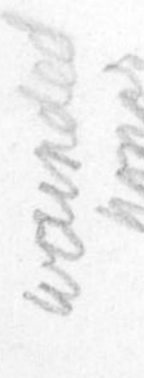

true affection for Your Majesty, we prefer to limit ourselves to stupefaction, for fear of spilling over into fury.

FERRANTE: If I, the King, say to you that I understand your pain, and if by that your pain is not softened, you in your turn will have offended me. Your pain is mine: I cannot say more than that. When I arrived back from Navarre and announced to the Prince my intentions, I certainly saw in his countenance that to him it was a blow; but I thought this meant no more than reluctance at tying himself down and at entering a life of seriousness that is not to his taste. Doña Ines de Castro was not named. He hid his obstinacy from me. And it is at you that he flings it, with a discourtesy that overwhelms me.

THE INFANTA: It's not the woman that is insulted in me, it's the Infanta. Little I care about the Prince!

FERRANTE [*to Don Manoel Ocayo*]: Don Manoel, go and warn the Prince, and bring him in when Their Royal Highnesses have left.

THE INFANTA: My lord, allow me to return now to my country. To my country, where I have never been insulted. Navarre is what I love. The east wind that brings me the snow-mist of my country is sweeter to me than the fragrant wind of Portugal and its orange trees. The wind that comes from Navarre—

FERRANTE: Leave! Think of all we should be losing! All you would be losing!

THE INFANTA: Better lose than acquiesce.

FIRST LADY-IN-WAITING: The Infanta was not so fond of the Navarrese when she was in Navarre!

SECOND LADY-IN-WAITING: Nor of the cold, nor of the snow-mist.

THIRD LADY-IN-WAITING: What a wonderful change in favor of our Navarre!

FERRANTE: Please, Infanta, stay a few days more. I am going to speak to the Prince. His folly may pass.

THE INFANTA: If God were willing to give me heaven itself, but wished to put it off till later, I should rather hurl myself into hell than have to wait on God's good pleasure.

FERRANTE: You like suffering, it seems to me.

THE INFANTA: I like a suffering that comes to me from myself. Besides, Navarre is a hard country. The bulls from our lands are, of all Spain, those that have the toughest hoofs, because they are always walking on rock. . . .

FERRANTE: Stay till the end of the festivities given in honour of Your Highnesses. If Don Pedro were irreducible, you would leave then, but all scandal would be avoided.

THE INFANTA: I shall not come to life again until our ships begin to move toward my country.

FERRANTE: Is it, then, too hard for you to control your face for a few days?

THE INFANTA: Too hard?

FIRST LADY-IN-WAITING: *Mira! Mira!* How she tosses her head, with the roughness of a bird of prey!

SECOND LADY-IN-WAITING: Oh, the proud little creature!

THIRD LADY-IN-WAITING: God be praised! She is of Navarre!

FERRANTE: Can you not constrain nature for a few days?

THE INFANTA: There is something that I could not do?

FERRANTE: To sustain for long the line of conduct that's most opposed to one's character: how tiring! But how honorable! You are as great as you are noble. Don Pedro is there: he is going to hear what I have to say. Perhaps this evening destiny will have changed course.—Live long years, my young princess! Your exaltation was like that of the wave raising its crest. By it you have raised us all.

THE INFANTA: Say rather that I should live eternally, to have the time to accomplish all the great things which are in me, and which, now as I speak, make me tremble.

FERRANTE: You will live, and you will live washed free of all stain. One thinks one is dying of humiliation and rage, and nothing is so transient as an insult.

The Infanta: If God wills, if God wills, I shall be healed by my great things. It is they will wash me free of all stain.

SCENE II

The King, Don Manoel Ocayo

Ferrante: The Prince is there?

Don Manoel Ocayo: He awaits Your Majesty's orders.

Ferrante: Let him wait a little longer, till my anger has cooled down. I've turned pale, have I not? My heart, which in the thick of battles has never lost its royal rhythm, is ragged and palpitating like a cock when its throat is slit. And my soul has fallen into my boots.

Don Manoel: The worst anger of a father against his son is more tender than the tenderest love of a son for his father.

Ferrante: I'm ashamed. I do not wish my son to know the power he has over me, a power my worst enemy could not have. But good heavens! He is one of my acts, and all our acts master us, one day or another. Ah! why, why did I beget him? And why am I forced to reckon with him, why am I forced to suffer because of him, since I don't love him?

Don Manoel: Magnanimous Ferrante—

Ferrante: There I must check you. I don't know why, each time someone praises me, it fills me with a sudden wave of sadness. Each time someone praises me, I smell my tomb.

Don Manoel: Must my devotion then be silently—

Ferrante: At the Day of Judgment there will be no sentence against those who have kept silence. Bring in the Prince. I never know what to say to him; but today I know.

SCENE III

FERRANTE, PEDRO

FERRANTE: The Infanta has told me of the monstrous things you have said to her. Now listen to me. I am tired of my throne, of my court, of my people. But there is also someone of whom I am particularly tired, Pedro, it's you. For just thirteen years I have been tired of you, Pedro. As a baby, I confess, you scarcely held my attention. Then, from five to thirteen years old, I loved you tenderly. The Queen, your mother, had died, very young. Your elder brother was on the way to dullness, and to holy orders. You alone were left to me. Thirteen was the year of your great glory; you had at thirteen a grace, a gentleness, a delicacy, an intelligence that you have never recovered since; it was the last, marvelous ray of the setting sun; only one knows that, within twelve hours, the sun will reappear, whereas the genius of childhood, when it goes out, has gone forever. They always say that the butterfly comes from a worm; with man it's the butterfly that turns into a worm. At fourteen it was all over, you had gone out; you had become mediocre and coarse. Before then, God forgive me, I used sometimes to be almost jealous of your tutor; jealous at seeing you take seriously the things said to you by that old fool Don Christoval, more so than the things I said to you myself. I used to think, too: "Because of the business of the State, I shall be forced to lose my child: I haven't time to devote myself to him." From the moment you were fourteen, I was delighted for your tutor to relieve me of you. I no longer looked for you, I avoided you. You are now twenty-six: for thirteen years I have had nothing more to say to you.

PEDRO: Father—

Ferrante: "Father": all through my youth that word made me tremble. It seemed to me—apart from any idea of political expediency—that to have a son must be something tremendous. . . . But why don't you look at me? Your eyes shift unceasingly to hide from me all there is in you that does not love me.

Pedro: They shift to hide from you the pain you are causing me. You know very well that I love you. But what you blame in me is my not having your character. Is it my fault if I am not you? Never, in how many years, never have you taken an interest in what interests me. You have not even pretended. Yes, once—when you had your attack of recurring fever and thought you were going to die; while I was saying something to you by your bedside, you asked me: "And the wolves, are they giving you good sport?" For my passion then was wolf-hunting. Yes, once only, when you were reduced to utter weakness and despair by illness, did you speak to me of what I like.

Ferrante: You think that what I blame in you is your not being like me. It is not altogether so. I blame you for not breathing the air of the heights at which I breathe. One can be indulgent toward the mediocrity one sees foreshadowed in a child. Not for that which spreads out in a man.

Pedro: You used to talk to me with interest, with gravity, with kindness, at an age when I couldn't understand you. And at the age when I could have, you never again talked to me like that—to me, whom in the public proclamations you call "my well-beloved son"!

Ferrante: Because you could not understand me at that age either. My words seemed to pass through you as through a phantom, to die out in God knows what world: the game had long been up. You are empty of everything, and, above all, of yourself. You are little, and you reduce everything to your stature. I have always noticed how you abased the motives of my undertakings: how you believed that I was doing from greed what I was doing for the good of the realm; how you believed that I was doing from personal ambition what I was doing for the glory of God. From time to time you would throw at my head your fidelity. But I looked at your actions, and they were always pitiable.

PEDRO: Father, if I have behaved badly to you, I ask you to pardon me.

FERRANTE: I pardon you. But what a vain thing pardon is! What's done is done, and what's not done is not done, irremediably. And besides, I've done so much pardoning, all my life long! There's nothing so worn out for me as pardoning. Others take pleasure in pardoning; not I. Anyhow, this time the matter is one in which you can repair a great deal of the harm. I shall not hark back to your incredible conduct, in refusing for years to adopt the spirit and point of view that befit your position; in evading the issue every time I spoke to you of a marriage that is necessary to the throne; in continuing, these last days, to conceal from me your determination, only to reveal it brutally to the Infanta, at the risk of an explosion of the worst sort, with unheard-of lack of decorum. I hardly know Ines de Castro. She is of good birth, though a natural child. She is well spoken of, and I wish her no ill. But she must not put me out. A king may put himself out, but does not let himself be put out.

PEDRO: What do you mean to do against her?

FERRANTE: I shall be gentle with you. Because it is the best way, in my opinion, to get what I want. I could exile Doña Ines, or forbid you to see her again. I shall not do so. Since the Moors have brought to our country something of their own customs and even at the court it is now established usage that a man may have a regular mistress as well as his legitimate wife, marry the Infanta, and do not deny yourself the pleasure of meeting Ines, with suitable discretion. The Infanta, well warned, will not object, especially since in

Navarre concubinage is formally authorized by law. She will have the kingdom, and the kingdom is well worth this little vexation. And she doesn't love you, any more than you love her, which is the best condition for making your union a happy one for the State, and even a happy one quite simply. You understand? I *want* you to marry the Infanta. She is the son I should have had. She is only seventeen, and already her virile spirit is capable of supplying the defects of yours. In your view, the State is always going along nicely when it gives you license to do whatever you want; governing is hateful to you. The Infanta— In short, I love her. She did daze me a little with the cries of her pride, when she was dancing before me the dance of honor (by my faith, she hardly touched the ground). But she is sudden, profound, singular. And that energy full of innocence— Her face is like those faces of adolescent genii one sees carved on breast-plates, crying eternally with wide-open mouth their vexed cry. It's she, yes, it's she that is needed at the head of this realm. And think of the strength it means for us: Portugal, Navarre, and Aragon gripping Castile as in a vice! Yes, I am passionately set upon this marriage. When everything so clearly converges to make a thing good, there must be no mistake about it: God is behind it. I am the King, and to contradict me is to contradict God. But to contradict me in this affair is to contradict Him twice over.

PEDRO: Live partly with the Infanta and partly with Ines. . . . Live torn between obligation and affection. . . .

FERRANTE: I do not see it in terms of being torn, but of a sensible sharing.

PEDRO: I have not your facility for being double. I owe myself to her whom I love and who loves me, and I do not owe myself to her by halves.

FERRANTE: So there exists only your pleasure in the world?

PEDRO: My pleasure? My love.

FERRANTE: Unfortunately they are the same.

PEDRO: There is another reason why I cannot marry the Infanta.

FERRANTE: What reason?

PEDRO: . . . In any case no, even if I could, I will not sacrifice us—myself and a being whom I love—to duties whose importance I do see, but to which I've the right to prefer others. For there is private life, and it too is important, and it too has its duties. A woman, a child, the business of forming them, making them happy, helping them to come through this ordeal of life with a joy they would not have had without you, isn't that, too, important?

FERRANTE: Strange words, among which God and the kingdom are conspicuously absent, though you are Christian and will tomorrow be king.

PEDRO: Christian, yes; the destiny of one being matters as much as the destiny of a million beings; a soul is worth a kingdom.

FERRANTE: What a lot of ideas to justify a vice!

PEDRO: A vice!

FERRANTE: You have a mistress and can't bear the sight of another. Thereupon the whole world must arrange itself so as to prove you right.

PEDRO: I have perhaps forty years to live. I do not propose to be mad. I do not propose to render them, of my own free will, unhappy, when they need not be so.

FERRANTE: There you are at last utterly sincere! It's you all this is about. And your happiness! Your happiness! . . . Are you a woman?

PEDRO: Leave the throne to my cousin Bragança. He relishes such morsels. Let 'em be given to those who like 'em. Not to one who abhors them.

FERRANTE: That's enough absurdities. In you are my succession and my memory. Even if you do not want them. Even if you are not worthy of them. Give the matter more thought. The Infanta, who is so attentive to what is due to her, has nevertheless, after a first heated movement, agreed to dissemble. She will remain here during the festivities organized in honor of her brother and her. You have therefore five days to decide. In five days' time you will tell me if you are marrying the Infanta. If not—

PEDRO: If not?

FERRANTE: Pedro, I am going to remind you of an incident from your childhood. You were eleven or twelve years old. I had given you, for the New Year, a marvelous tiny astrolabe, the work of the good craftsman Estevan, who used to begin every piece of work with prayer and purification. That toy had not been in your hands for more than an hour or two when you appear, your face all to pieces, as if on the point of tears. "What's the matter?" At first you won't say anything; I press you; finally you confess: you have broken the astrolabe. I say all the things that such an act of folly deserves, for the object was a real masterpiece. For a long while you let me storm. And suddenly your face clears, you look at me with eyes full of malice, and you say to me: "It isn't true. The astrolabe is quite all right." I am nonplussed; "But in that case, why?" And you, with an innocent smile: "Sire, I love it when you are angry. . . ."

PEDRO: It was to see—

FERRANTE: To see what?

PEDRO: To see what you would say.

FERRANTE: Well, my dear son—and this is the point to which I was leading—if at twelve you were so insensitive to my anger, I swear to you by the blood of Christ that at twenty-six it shall make you tremble.

PEDRO: Ah! You are not kind, Father!

FERRANTE: Yes, I am kind when I want to be. I tell you, sometimes my heart comes into my mouth from kindness. Look, I have had the experience, when I have just tricked somebody marvelously, of finding myself sorry for him, seeing him so tricked, and of wanting to do something for him. . . .

PEDRO: To leave him a little of what doesn't matter to you, having despoiled him well and truly of what does matter.

FERRANTE: Exactly.

PEDRO: And if you punish me, will you spare Ines?

FERRANTE: Once more, I do not blame you and Ines for your liaison. It was known to me: I had nothing against it. I blame you—you—for not being willing to marry the Infanta: that is all. There, I've finished what I had to say to you. You may withdraw.

PEDRO: Father, after such grave words am I to withdraw without your embrace?

FERRANTE: Let us embrace if you wish. But these kisses between parents and children, these kisses which make one wonder why one receives them and why one gives them—

PEDRO [*who had advanced toward his father, drawing back*]: In that case, no use.

FERRANTE [*suddenly hard*]: You are right: no use.

SECOND SETTING: *In the house of Ines, at Mondego, not far from Montemor-o-Velho. A room giving on a garden.*

SCENE IV

PEDRO, INES

PEDRO: Judge me severely: I didn't dare confess to him either that we were married or that this marriage was going to bear its fruit in you. His anger paralyzed me.

INES: Since we cannot be unbound, even if we wished to be,

the Pope being at present so stiffened against your father, since therefore it is useless for the King to insist on your marriage with the Infanta, go back and see him again, Pedro, and tell him all. Better that he should see that he is checked by a fact against which he can do nothing than that he should believe he is checked by obstinacy of yours. Better his anger today than tomorrow.

PEDRO: It will be terrible. It will envelop us like a flame.

INES: I believe I shall find it easier to bear than our present uncertainty. Strange as it may appear, it seems to me that when it bursts, there will be something in me that will cry: "Land!"

PEDRO: He will separate us.

INES: Isn't it as if we were so already? And I like to think, yes, I like to think he'll not separate us for long. For when he sees that he is facing something done and irremediable, then there'll only be one way out: to persuade him to recognize our union. And why should you not succeed? If the King is so anxious for you to marry the Infanta, it's because he sees in her a woman of government, whereas you are so little that sort of man. Learn to govern, my friend, accept the peril and the boredom of it, doing it from now on for love of me, and perhaps the King will in his turn accept that the future queen should be only a simple woman, whose sufficient reason for living is to make you happy. But, for God's sake, when you are laying siege to him, find a way of convincing him that to be a queen is to me a cup of bitterness, and that I have only been willing to drink it for the sake of drinking it mouth to mouth with you. I believe I should die of humiliation if he took it into his head to think me ambitious, when my whole dream would be to spend my life withdrawn in the nook of tenderness, lost and forgotten in the depths of this garden.

PEDRO: You are right, I shall speak to him like that. We are in the hand of destiny like a bird in a man's hand.

Sometimes it forgets us, it looks elsewhere, and we breathe. And suddenly it remembers us, and it tightens its grasp a little, it throttles us. And again it relaxes the embrace—if it has not throttled us once for all. The embrace will relax, Ines. And I should like to think, I too, that we shall spend many hours yet withdrawn in this garden, and that we shall chatter away there as we have done so often, sitting by the edge of the basin, with the fountain that sometimes sent us drops, and sometimes sent us none, according to the wind. And I breathed in dust of water. And I reflected that you were making of me what every being makes of the one who desires and loves him: you were making me into that basin continually overflowing, ceaselessly filled and continually overflowing. And a song as sweet as sadness came now and then from the road, the song of the stone-breakers, it too coming and ceasing, like the water's dust, according to the wind's caprice.

INES: That sweetness mingled with sadness is certainly the taste of our love. You have given me nothing but joys; none the less, always, when I thought of you, if I had wanted I could have started to cry. For two years, hanging over us, this menace, this feeling of black rain ceaselessly ready to fall and yet not falling. The destiny one feels piling up in silence. How many times, in our house, with you, I have imagined to myself the time when these hours would belong to the past. I was regretting them at the very moment I was living them. And they were doubly dear to me, because they were present and I could enjoy them; and, already, because I could no longer enjoy them. Look, I am like that old Captain Orosco, who had fought for seven years, here and in Africa, with a lion's bravery, and then, when he was put on the retiring list, told me: "I'm very pleased! I'd had enough of risking my life every day." With the same simplicity I'll say to you: I've had enough of being every day afraid. Of finding again every morning this fear, on awaking, like a thing left on the table the evening before. Fear, always fear! Fear that makes your hands go cold. . . .

PEDRO: It's true, those gentle, cold hands of yours. . . . But consider the way the whole world lives under the empire of fear. My father has passed his life in feeling fear: fear of losing his crown, fear of being betrayed, fear of being murdered. He knows his crimes better than we know them, and knows that each one of them creates the threat of a reprisal. I've many a time seen his face at the moment when he had just scored a point against an adversary; what was on that face then was never an expression of triumph, it was an expression of fear: fear of the counterstroke. Wild beasts, too, are dominated by fear. And look at the motes in this ray of sunlight: I've only to advance my hand a little here, at the bottom of the ray, and up there, at the other end, and they go mad, mad with fear.

INES: Often, at sunset, I am invaded by a sort of anguish. For instance, when I see the shopkeepers closing their shutters. A lance-stroke pierces me: "At this very moment something frightful is being decided against me. . . ." Or else (how silly it is!) it's at night, when I'm undressing, at the moment when I unbind my hair.

PEDRO: Do you know that each time you move your head, you send me the fragrance of your hair? And that that fragrance is never quite the same? One time impregnated with air and sunshine, and smelling of flame; at another cold and smelling of cut grass. O dear head, so well shaped for my hands! Ines, dear woman, my love with the name "woman," Ines of the clear face, clearer than the words that lull it, you who are the bond uniting me to all beings; yes, all beings attached to you, and to you alone, as fruits are attached to the tree. . . . And today I do not only love you: I admire you. I find you braver than I.

INES: By dint of worrying without anything happening, one becomes almost calm on the day when the bolt falls. Besides, today I feel as if I were supported by our child. He carried on a ferocious struggle inside me, and I—I'd be ashamed if I were not as strong as he is, to save him by saving us. When you came the first time, two years ago, I had no power of resistance in front of you. A single cruel word from you, and I'd have fallen, yes, fallen to the ground. I cannot defend myself. But to defend him I feel I have all forms of courage. Even to telling myself that to bring him into the world easily would be a diminution. Even to telling myself that the fact of his being formed in tribulation is somehow happy. You I found already created, and later you created me. He, this thing that is being fashioned every moment, this material and immaterial thing that makes you live in the feeling of a perpetual miracle, is made by that into my wealth, Pedro! Pedro! yes, in a way I think you yourself could never— But I'm mad, am I not? No, what I give him is merely not taken from you, but in giving it to him, I give it to you. I hold you, I clasp you to me, and it's him. His neck has not quite the same fragrance as yours, he smells of child. . . . And his breath is that of the doe fed upon violets. And his little hands are warmer than yours. And his arms are around my neck as water is, in summer, when you dive into it and it closes over your shoulders, all full of sunshine. And he makes about my neck a sweet humming, like doves cooing. Adored child, thanks to whom I shall get more power of loving!

PEDRO: You think of him, and, in the middle of all our miseries, there you are as if surrounded with a mist of happiness.

INES: That happiness on whose summit I can still for a moment stay motionless. . . . What is it? Why leave me in this sudden way? You shouldn't have taken me in your arms if it was to let me go like that.

PEDRO: Horsemen are drawing up at the end of the garden.

INES: Here at last is the moment I have always dreaded.

PEDRO: It's he!

INES: Moment so like that I expected.

PEDRO: Withdraw. I shall tell him everything, as you advised me. You were right. This is a sign: destiny has come to meet us.

INES: Perhaps, for years, I shall have to live on this minute I have just lived. I knew it, but not well enough.

A SERVANT [*entering*]: Sire, the King!

PEDRO: I am his servant.

THE SERVANT: It is Doña Ines de Castro that His Majesty wishes to see. And he wishes to see her alone.

PEDRO: It is well. Ines, may God inspire you!

INES: I pass my hand over your face, as the blind do, to carry it with me twice over.

SCENE V

FERRANTE, INES

FERRANTE: So here you are, then, Doña Ines, before me. Your renown had predisposed me in your favor. Your expression, your bearing, even your way of dressing, everything confirms that you are well bred. And so I have no doubt that you will find in yourself the qualities to raise you to the height of the circumstances in which you have placed us.

INES: I am Your Majesty's servant.

FERRANTE: I am glad that you are partly Portuguese, through your mother, while your father was a nobleman from one of the oldest families of Galicia. You were brought up at Santiago de Compostela, were you not, at the court of the Duke of Peñafiel? And you came here, two years ago, to accompany your aged uncle, the Count of Castro, whom I summoned to my side. By ill luck, he returned to God, too soon for all of us. And especially for you, I think. For you were left alone at the Mondego. The situation was a rather strange one for a young girl. Perhaps one should be sorry that I did not know you better. I saw you hardly ever at the court or not at all.

INES: Having no intrigue to carry on there, I should not have felt at ease. I think I should have asked myself without ceasing: "But what am I doing here?" And they say that at the court whoever is at a loss is always in the wrong.

FERRANTE: The court is a place of darkness. In it you would have been a little light.

INES: And besides, I should have had sometimes to hide things from Your Majesty. And I should not have been able.

FERRANTE: Lying is, for my grandees, second nature. Just as they prefer getting by threats what they could get by persuasion, getting by fraud what they could get by straightforwardness, so they prefer getting by hypocrisy what would easily be theirs through frankness: that's the ordinary spirit of courts. And you yourself, come, come! you would very quickly have got a taste for it. Besides, not to lie to others is less important than not to lie to oneself.

INES [*smiling*]: If I lied, I should soon become tied up in my lies. Perhaps that's all that stops me.

FERRANTE: I wanted to make you smile. When one is in doubt whether an unknown person is dangerous or not, one has only to watch that person smile: his smile is an indication, even if not an infallible guide. Yours completes the revelation of what you are. Well, Doña Ines, I was joking: always be truthful with me; you will have no need to regret it. And be truthful, first of all, in speaking to me of my son.

INES: The day I first knew him is like the day I was born. That day my heart was taken away and there was put in its place a human face. It was during the throne feast, in the gardens of Montemor. I had gone a little apart, to breathe the fragrance of the wet earth. The Prince came up to me. One could no longer hear any sound of the festivities, no longer anything except the little cries of birds changing branches. He told me that as soon as he had heard my voice, he had started to love me. That made me sad. I saw him again several times, in the countryside around Mondego. He was always full of reserve, and I, I was always sad. At length I said to him: "Let me simply place my mouth against your face, and I shall be healed eternally." He let me do so, and he placed his mouth upon mine. Later his face was not enough for me, and I desired to see his breast and his arms.

FERRANTE: All that is long ago?

INES: Two years come the 13th of August. For two years we have been living in the same dream. Wherever he is, I turn toward him as the serpent always turns its head in the direction of its enchanter. Other women dream of what they have not; I dream of what I have. And not a single time have I wished anything not to his profit. And not a day have I missed saying to him within myself: "May God bless the happiness you have given me!"

FERRANTE: These sentiments will facilitate my task: I am at home everywhere where there is gravity. And it would be a sin to try to diminish your image of the Prince, even though, in my view, it is a little embellished. In my view, the Prince is—how shall I put it? The Prince is not very deep. A sin, also, to tell you too much about the way I conceive what men and women call love—going into dark houses to the depths of alcoves sadder than themselves, to mingle there in silence like the shadows. No, let's leave that and come to the heart of my anxiety. I am not asking you to break with Don Pedro. I am asking you to use your power over him to make him accept a marriage on which the fate of the realm depends. That may be hard for you, but it is necessary. I have no need to set out for you the reasons for it: the Prince's marriage is an event for which, during two years, you had ample leisure to prepare yourself.

INES: Alas, my lord, you are asking of me the impossible.

FERRANTE: Doña Ines, I am ready to give to human emotions the share that is due to them. But not more. Do not force me to argue the State's case all over again for your benefit—it would be boring for you. [*Leading her to the window*] Look: the road, the cart with its mule, the olive-carriers—it's I that maintain all that. I have my crown, I have my land, I have this people which God has entrusted to me, I have hundreds and hundreds of thousands of bodies and souls. I am like a great tree that has to give shade to hundreds of thousands of beings. And all that requires that this marriage, which serves my policy marvelously, be made. Don Pedro has given a brutal no, and he has been mad enough to say it to the Infanta herself. But that is only a first impulse, on which I wish him to go back. It is for you to help him do so. You have no call to resent his sentiments for the Infanta: between them there is no question of love. And you will be fulfilling the wishes of your King, who is declining toward the tomb and needs his affairs to be in order. Do it, then, on pain of my displeasure, and remembering that any obedience yielded to me magnifies the person who yields it.

INES: My lord, if I would I could not put asunder what God has joined together.

FERRANTE: I don't understand.

INES: Nearly a year ago, in great secret at Bragança, the Bishop of Guarda—

FERRANTE: What?

INES: —united us, the Prince and me—

FERRANTE: Ah, terrible! Terrible! Married! And to a bastard girl! Criminal folly and irreparable harm, for never will the Pope annul this marriage: on the contrary, he will exult in seeing me at his mercy. Marriage? You had the bed: wasn't it enough? Why marry?

INES: Well—to be more happy.

FERRANTE: More happy! Happiness again, like the other!

It's an obsession! Do I worry about being happy? If your answer had even been: to come clear of sin. And for a year my son has been hiding that from me. For a month he has known my intentions about the Infanta, and he has said nothing. And it's to you he leaves it to face my anger, like those miserable tribes that in battle make their women march in front to protect them!

INES: He was afraid of that anger of yours.

FERRANTE: He knew perfectly well that one day he would have to endure it, but he preferred putting it off to the morrow, and he's no less a coward than a cheat and a fool. He's no longer a child, but he has kept the deceitfulness of children. Unless—unless he was counting on my death. I understand now why he argues against all marriage. I die, and at once you are queen! Ah, I was perfectly right when I thought that a father, when he lies down to sleep, should always slide a dagger under his pillow to defend himself against his son. Thirteen years of being strangers to each other, then thirteen years of being enemies: there's your paternity. [*Calling*] Don Felix! Have Don Christoval brought in, with three officers. Madame, you are not the one to blame, go back to your apartments; no harm will be done to you. Don Felix, escort Doña Ines de Castro and see she does not meet the Prince.

INES: But Don Pedro? Oh, my lord, be merciful to him!

FERRANTE: Enough!

INES: God! it is as if a blade were cutting away from me my child.

SCENE VI

FERRANTE, DON CHRISTOVAL, THREE OFFICERS OF THE PALACE GUARD

FERRANTE: Don Christoval, I am entrusting to you a mission that you will find painful. With these three good men, you will arrest at once the individual whom I have for son. You will take him to Santarem Castle, and you will detain him there until I have indicated who is to guard him.

DON CHRISTOVAL: My lord! Not me! Somebody other than me!

FERRANTE: Oh yes, you, and nobody but you. That hurts you? Well, the time has come for people to begin to be hurt a little around me.

DON CHRISTOVAL: Him whom I've brought up—

FERRANTE: And nicely brought up, with a vengeance! A worthy pupil! And a worthy son!

DON CHRISTOVAL: I call the living God to witness that Don Pedro reveres you and loves you.

FERRANTE: If he despised me, if he had my effigy painted on the soles of his shoes to trample me when he walks, or if he loved me so much that he was ready to give his life for me, that would still be indifferent to me. Pedro is married to Doña Ines.

DON CHRISTOVAL: Alas! After what he said to me!

FERRANTE: What did he say to you?

DON CHRISTOVAL: That he would never make a marriage like that. Already he knew he was being laughed at a little for having as mistress—only as mistress—a natural child. One day when I mentioned this tactfully, he said to me: "Never again speak to me of this."

FERRANTE: That is him all over. Go, go, to prison! To prison for mediocrity! [*He goes out.*]

SCENE VII

PEDRO, DON CHRISTOVAL, THE OFFICERS

PEDRO [*coming in*]: The King has gone?—But what's this? Ah! I see!

DON CHRISTOVAL: In the King's name, Prince, I arrest you. [*Going onto one knee*] Don Pedro, forgive me.

PEDRO: Rise, Don Christoval. The day will come quickly enough when I shall have to see men on their knees before me.

DON CHRISTOVAL: I shall not rise until you have given me your blessing.

PEDRO: I give it you. And Ines?

DON CHRISTOVAL: Free.

PEDRO: I wish to be sure of that. I wish to see her. For a moment only.

DON CHRISTOVAL: Sire, you shall not leave here!

PEDRO: Wretched old man! You dare! Ah, you have it at last, your hour of glory!

DON CHRISTOVAL: Kill me, and then I'll no longer have to dare.

PEDRO: I fear the worst for Ines.

DON CHRISTOVAL: I repeat she is free, free!

PEDRO: And tomorrow? Ah, I have been too bold. I ought to have put Ines in safety a year ago: there are three hundred convents in Portugal where she would have found asylum, even against the King. But one would think oneself cowardly for taking precautions. Ines is in danger because I was not afraid. Dear child, how guilty I am toward you, for not having managed to protect you better. You were leaning on me, and I have failed you!

DON CHRISTOVAL: There is always gain in having courage.

PEDRO: Don Christoval, it is waste of time shoving your nose up against reality, you persist in your optimistic commonplaces: they make you drunk. You were a tutor. You thought that that was the food to give to poor young people, although they have already all too much of a tendency to love commonplaces. And you go on. One sometimes gains by being courageous. And sometimes one loses. That is what you should say. But that's too simple. That's too true. You are a tutor and moralizer: you aren't made for the simple and true. And you will never perceive how serious it is to preach courage, above all to young people. [*Holding out his sword*] Come, disarm me. It's time for me to leave a world where I was a man for a world where I shall be an object of contempt. And among my countrymen, of course: the fact that the Moors took me prisoner wasn't interesting. It's curious, men of real value always end by getting arrested. Even in history one can hardly imagine a great man who doesn't find himself at some moment before a judge and before a jailer; it's part of the character. And those of them who haven't gone through prison look in a way like deserters. Gentlemen, what you are really is a guard of honor, for in my father's prison I shall join the flower of the kingdom. But tell me, isn't there one among you who has been put in prison by the Portuguese? What, not one? Ah, you, Lieutenant Martins! Prisoner! And for what?

THE LIEUTENANT: Oh, Prince, for something very modest: for debt.

PEDRO: Whether it's for debt, or for robbery, or for rape, or for murder, anyone who has been made prisoner by his own people is from now on my brother. Lieutenant Martins,

I shall remember you. And now, guard of honor forward, to prison! Or rather no, better say: forward, to the other side of prison! [*They go out.*]

CURTAIN

ACT II

First Setting: *The King's working-room in the palace.*

SCENE I

Ferrante, Egas Coelho, Alvar Gonçalves, Don Eduardo [*seated at a large table*]

Ferrante: Here is the dispatch for the Catalonian Cortes.

Alvar Gonçalves [*after reading it*]: It seems to me that in it Don Eduardo rather exaggerates the poverty of the kingdom. [*He passes the paper on to Egas Coelho.*]

Ferrante: On a directive from me. What is the point? To get something. And to complain is one of the ways of getting something. Pity brings in wonderful returns.

Egas Coelho: May I venture an observation? Since in this letter we are using methods that are legitimate as between princes but would between individuals be considered horrible treachery, I should like Your Majesty to make mention in it of our honor.

Ferrante: You are right. It is when the thing is not there that one should put in the word. Don Eduardo, you will begin this letter again and you will introduce the word "honor." Once only. Twice, nobody would take it seriously.

Alvar Gonçalves: We are all lost in admiration of Don Eduardo's phrase about last year's wheat harvest. Under Don Eduardo's pen an untruth becomes a real intellectual treat.

Don Eduardo: Lying by itself is not enough. One must lie

efficiently. One must also lie elegantly. Alas, what obligations are laid upon poor mortals! One has to live and move in bad faith like a fish in water.

FERRANTE: One should not live and move in bad faith like a fish in water, but like an eagle in the sky. And now, gentlemen, I am going to tell you some news that will surprise you: I have decided to negotiate with the King of Aragon.

EGAS COELHO: After all that you have said! Your doubts! Your apprehensions!

FERRANTE: What I have said never counts. The only thing that counts is what I write. Even that, of course, is a manner of speaking. Alas, at that game there is no beating Ferdinand of Aragon. I don't know at what point his villainy will manage to slide into our agreement and turn it against me, but I know it will get there. I look in vain for the chink in the armor, but I am sure that it exists, and that Aragon will find it.

EGAS COELHO: In that case, don't sign! Let's examine it again.

ALVAR GONÇALVES: We have already been four months examining it.

FERRANTE: Since I had to give in to him, at least I've kept him waiting.

EGAS COELHO: Sire, I beg of you: having such fears, do not sign!

FERRANTE: I am aware of a great mistake; nevertheless I am irresistibly impelled to make it. I see the abyss, and I seek it.

ALVAR GONÇALVES: After those words shall we still be indiscreet enough to offer advice to Your Majesty?

FERRANTE: I command it.

ALVAR GONÇALVES: On no matter what subject?

FERRANTE: I see: you mean Doña Ines. Not only may you speak to me of that, but I invite your suggestions and your views.

EGAS COELHO: There are two guilty parties: the Bishop of Guarda and Doña Ines.

FERRANTE: And Don Pedro. I do not like your being afraid to name him.

EGAS COELHO: The Bishop is in prison: if all goes well, we shall have his head. The Prince, your son, is under guard. Doña Ines is free.

FERRANTE: Doña Ines is the least guilty. There would be nothing against her without Don Pedro and without the Bishop.

EGAS COELHO: Obviously there would be nothing against them without Doña Ines. Your Majesty asks us for our views. In our soul and conscience we form the wish that Doña Ines may no longer have the power to be in future a cause of trouble to the realm.

FERRANTE: That she be imprisoned? Exiled?

EGAS COELHO: That she pass without delay from the King's justice to the justice of God.

FERRANTE: What! Put her to death! What an incredible excess! If I kill someone for having loved my son, what then should I do to someone who had hated him? She has returned love for love, and she has done so with my consent. Love rewarded by death! That would be great injustice.

EGAS COELHO: Injustice consists in not inflicting a deserved punishment.

ALVAR GONÇALVES: And public offenses do not allow of pardon.

FERRANTE: The Prince and Incs are equally guilty. But Ines alone would be killed!

ALVAR GONÇALVES: Tacitus writes: "Both were guilty. Cumanus alone was executed, and order reigned once more."

FERRANTE: Is it not frightful cruelty to kill someone who has done no wrong?

ALVAR GONÇALVES: No wrong! She has been the occasion of wrong.

EGAS COELHO: When a decision of this kind does not arise

from a movement of anger but from the counsel of reason, it is not an act of cruelty, but an act of justice.

FERRANTE: Oh, the impossible position into which reason and justice have got!

EGAS COELHO: Besides, even if there were injustice in this case, God's creation is a heap of innumerable injustices. Should the society of men have the infernal arrogance to claim to be more perfect?

FERRANTE: I am ready to put Doña Ines into a monastery.

EGAS COELHO: From which the Prince, imprisoned or not, will have her kidnapped within three months.

FERRANTE: I can exile her.

EGAS COELHO: Wherever she is, she will be a center of sedition. The Prince will group around her all your enemies. They will wait for your death, or perhaps hasten it, because your death is all that is needed for Ines to become queen. No: all or nothing. Either pardon with its mad consequences, or death.

ALVAR GONÇALVES: Not to mention that—monastery or exile—people would think Your Majesty had been afraid of shedding blood. And that would fit in badly with the idea people ought to have of a king.

FERRANTE: If I were the sort to boast of the blood I've shed, I should recall that I have shed enough, in war and otherwise.

EGAS COELHO: Blood shed in war does not count.

FERRANTE: I said: and otherwise. It seems to me that, in my reign, executions have not been lacking.

EGAS COELHO: People will say that, this time, you had the courage to kill a minister of God, but not a woman, simply because she is a woman.

FERRANTE: Doesn't nature revolt at the idea of taking life from her who gives it? And Doña Ines, besides, is a very pleasant woman.

ALVAR GONÇALVES: Any number of women are pleasant.

EGAS COELHO: More than one monarch has sacrificed his own child—that is to say, the most pleasant thing he had in the world—for the good of the State, and Your Majesty would hesitate to sacrifice a foreign woman, a bastard who has turned your son aside from all he owes to his people and to God! But the question is on a higher plane still. Hundreds of thousands of men from this country have died to prevent the Moors from setting foot in Portugal. And you would be stopped by the death of one human being!

FERRANTE: Ah, there's no proportion!

EGAS COELHO: No, you are right, there is no proportion! And it's always the men that are killed, never the women: that is not just. What is more, when their crime is equal before the law, a woman is not put to death: that is not just. A woman, by treachery, delivers up the army: she is imprisoned for life, and adapting herself little by little, because it is part of nature that everything hard relaxes, she comes in time to draw from this a life not devoid of all amenities. But a man, for the same crime, is cut down at a blow. If Doña Ines said to you: "Why are you putting me to death?" Your Majesty could reply: "Why should I not put you to death?"

FERRANTE: I cannot believe that posterity will reproach me for not having put to death a woman who is more or less innocent.

EGAS COELHO: Posterity would call that an act of clemency, if it took its place in a series of energetic acts. As things stand, it will call it a weakness.

FERRANTE: What are you insinuating?

EGAS COELHO: I am not insinuating, I am speaking openly, covered by my loyalty. Your Majesty, at present, not only is in reality weak on certain issues, but on others is obliged to feign weakness, the better to deceive your antagonists. Hence, in part rightly, in part wrongly, the country appears weak, and this situation is destined to last for a long time yet.

ALVAR GONÇALVES: I would add that the habit of feigning

weakness can easily lead to real weakness. When one has begun swallowing some insults, even though from policy, one ends by swallowing them all. One has got used to it: the fiber is loosened.

FERRANTE: It is, all the same, the greatest proof of strength—accepting disdain while knowing one does not deserve it. But what is all this? Do I really appear so weak?

EGAS COELHO: Look at the facts: it can't be denied that on all hands Portugal is in retreat.

FERRANTE: O humiliated Infanta, I am more like you than you think!

EGAS COELHO: And that faith in the Crown is compromised here and there.

FERRANTE: My daughter in the horror of bitterness.

EGAS COELHO: One gesture pulls you out of this abasement. You strike terror and respect into the realm. The rumor of it swells and crosses the sea. The desert is amazed by it.

FERRANTE: And I raise up against me my son, forever. Between him and me I destroy all possibility of remission, of reconciliation or any forgiveness, irrevocably.

EGAS COELHO: No. With Ines alive and banished, the Prince would rebel because he would be sustained by hope. Once she is dead, he who is unwilling to give himself the trouble of governing will not give himself, either, the trouble of a revolt with no object but vengeance. All will pass away together, love and grievance. What is frightening about the death of a beloved person is not the death, it's the way one gets over it.

FERRANTE [*aside*]: O God, never forgive him, for he knows what he is doing.

DON EDUARDO: And if I may be allowed to venture a modest opinion, I will say that, if Your Majesty is afraid of a sensation, it would be much to Your Majesty's advantage to have Doña Ines at liberty but have her given some food that would not agree with her.

FERRANTE: Alas, we are a long way here from the kingdom of God.

EGAS COELHO: Which has, in fact, nothing to do with our subject.

FERRANTE: That was simply a passing sigh which escaped me.

EGAS COELHO: A single act, my lord, will deliver you from all sighs.

FERRANTE: To be sure. The tragedy of acts. An act is nothing at the moment. It's an object you throw into the river. But it follows the course of the river, it is still there, in the distance, right in the distance, always there; it passes through countryside after countryside; you come on it again when you were no longer thinking of it, and where you least expected it. Is it fair, this interminable existence of acts? I think not. But so it is.

EGAS COELHO: That's all wrong, my lord. The death of Doña Ines, which torments you now, is what will set you free. In this instance the woman is like a chicken; kill her and she feeds you. Acts don't last as much as one thinks. What a lot of your acts, after having fulfilled their expected object, have dried up, have lost their poison, are henceforward as harmless as a dead serpent that the ants are nibbling!

ALVAR GONÇALVES: Besides, after a certain age it no longer pays to do things by means of slow intrigue: one might not see the end. Hurrah for a prompt act, which one can savor fully.

EGAS COELHO: And is it not senseless, the way men are content to sigh, to suffer, to be bound hand and foot by an inextricable situation, merely because one human being is alive, when it would be enough to suppress that being for the whole to be untied, while millions of beings are dying, whose death is useless, or even deplorable? You kill, and the sky clears. Truly, it is stupefying that so many human beings continue to obstruct the world by their existence when a murder is a thing relatively so easy and free of danger.

FERRANTE: If that is how it is, that ease is a form of weakness, a weakness that in the present case would have to be added to the others that you believe you see in me. It is weakness to do what is quickest, most brutal, what demands the least expenditure of the individual. For instance, there are gallants who would rather force a kiss from an unknown woman, at the risk of a slap in the face, than speak to her: they are taken for strong fellows and are really cowards. However that may be, I am glad that you have spoken to me so openly. I shall reflect upon all this. [*He rises.*]

EGAS COELHO: May God assist Your Majesty and guide your heart. [*All rise.*]

FERRANTE [*calling*]: Ho there! A page! [*Aside, to the page Dino del Moro, who has come in*] Go and summon Doña Ines de Castro and let her wait in the audience chamber. [*To Egas Coelho*] You, stay a moment. [*The others go out.*]

SCENE II

FERRANTE, EGAS COELHO

FERRANTE: Why do you want to kill Doña Ines?

EGAS COELHO: But—for all the reasons we have just told Your Majesty.

FERRANTE: No, there is another. You are too keen on this business. You put too much edge into it. Why do you want to kill Doña Ines?

EGAS COELHO: May my mouth be filled with earth if I have spoken with anything in view but an increase in Your Majesty's glory!

FERRANTE: That's enough honey: I want to reign over men who stand up, not over men who are prostrate. And besides, the honey that is offered to me always has on it a bee to sting me. Why do you want to kill Doña Ines? You have a secret. I want to see what you are, after seeing what you display.

EGAS COELHO: My lord, what can I say more than—

FERRANTE: There is a secret! There is a secret! A man of your age doesn't demand the death of a young and beautiful and gentle woman without some secret. Doña Ines has rebuffed you? You are handsome, though, you too. Elegance, ease, you've only too much of all that. You are undulating like a flame, like one of those wicked flames one sees wandering over rotting pools, and they go out when one tries to touch them.

EGAS COELHO: Let Your Majesty inquire of his spies if I have seen Doña Ines more than three times in my life, and if I care about her.

FERRANTE: Well then?—it's not a secret directed against me, is it?—I want to know what you are hiding. I give chase to you and cannot track you down. Look me in the eyes.

EGAS COELHO: I am looking you in the eyes, and my face is clear.

FERRANTE: Yes, you are looking me in the eyes, but do you think I can't see you clenching your fists, from your tense effort to stop your eyes from shifting? And your face is clear. But do you think I don't know what there can be behind a clear face?

EGAS COELHO: Will Your Majesty give me his hand to kiss?

FERRANTE: Let us kiss the hand we cannot cut off.

EGAS COELHO: Great King, our head and our father—

FERRANTE: I'll have your tongue burned out if you go on fawning on me. The wash of the waves brings down in the end the walls it has fawned on too much. One of my grandees, who came to the court late in life, told me that on the day when he discovered hypocrisy he grew ten years younger, so good it was. Is it true?

EGAS COELHO: I don't know.

FERRANTE: Ah! it is good, isn't it?—being a knave. You feel alive. Don't you? [*Gesture meaning: "I don't know," from Egas.*] There is in you something that escapes me, and this irritates me. I like a man to be disarmed before me as a dead man would be. There is in you some ignoble motive, and I want to pierce it. Of course, I like people to have a little mud in them. It cements. In Africa whole cities are built only of mud: it makes them hold together. I could not get on for long with anyone altogether limpid. And besides, every vice that the King approves is a virtue. But when there is an ignoble motive, even if I do not blame it, I want to know it. It belongs to me. I want to know yours.

EGAS COELHO: I was born to punish.

FERRANTE: There's something else.

EGAS COELHO: What Your Majesty believes, I too will believe, since it cannot be mistaken.

FERRANTE: Stand up! Man, stand up! One spends all the time making you rise to your feet. You are all the time on your knees, like the camels of the Moors, which kneel at the gates of each city. Ah, when I look at this people of dulled adorers, I sometimes say to myself that respect is a horrible sentiment. Come, speak. Why do you want to kill Doña Ines de Castro?

EGAS COELHO: If Your Majesty drives me so, I shall say anything that comes into my head: is that what Your Majesty wants? I repeat, I have spoken.

FERRANTE: That is all? [*Silence.*] Well? [*Silence.*] One day you will be old. You'll relax. Your secrets will come out in spite of you. They'll come out through that mouth of yours sometimes, too loose and sometimes too set, through those too mobile eyes of yours, always flying to right and left to look for something or to hide something. [*Silence.*] You fawn on me and trick me at the same time: the two together is too much. [*Silence.*] I know that in everything you have your motives and look only to them, rather than my service, and that they are ignoble motives, but I place confidence in you all the same. That is strange, but there are only strange things throughout the world. And so much the better, for I like things to be strange. Or rather I know very well why I like you: because you have managed to capture my confidence without deserving it, and I like clever people. I place confidence in you, yes, except on this point. I shall not kill Ines de Castro. [*Silence.*] You heard me? I shall not kill Doña Ines.—You may go out through my private room. You will take from there my sentence against the Bishop of Guarda. You want someone to die? You have the Bishop. Glut yourself on him. [*Calling*] Pages! [*To the pages, pointing at the council table*] Take away that table. It gets on my nerves. [*Aside*] O kingdom of God, toward which I drag, I drag, like the ship dragging at its anchors! O kingdom of God!

[*Ferrante goes out in the direction of his private room with Egas Coelho. Left alone, the pages busy themselves with removing the table.*]

FIRST PAGE [*sitting down at the table and clowning*]: We, by the grace of God, sublime monarch, taratata, taratata . . .

SECOND PAGE [*likewise*]: May His Most Grandiose Majesty be pleased to agree that taratata taratata . . .

THIRD PAGE (DINO DEL MORO) [*likewise, making the sign of the cross*]: *Dominus vobiscum adjutorium nostrum* . . . taratata taratata . . .

FERRANTE [*having come back alone and seen them*]: So our proverb is true: "The little boys play behind the altar." You can't, then, stay one moment without being up to some folly?

FIRST PAGE: No, may Your Majesty forgive us, we can't.

FERRANTE: What! You can't!

FIRST PAGE: God made us like that.

Ferrante: All right! Then, if God— No doubt one must consider it good. [*The pages remove the table.*] At any rate, don't upset the inkstand: God does not insist on that.

First Page: And what would happen if we did upset the inkstand?

Ferrante [*watching the table*]: Will you look what you're doing!

First Page: Would we be hanged? [*With farcical gestures*] Oh, we're going to be hanged! Ekk! Ekk!

Ferrante: My poor children, you are even stupider than the monkeys, and of them too much good is spoken. Bring in Doña Ines de Castro.

SCENE III

Ferrante, Ines

Ferrante: Praise God, Doña Ines: my pages have not upset the inkstand over your dress—over your lovely dress. You heard them, how they laugh: a day of their life goes by and they don't know it. They have no more fear of me than my son had at their age. They annoy me sometimes by their frankness, but when they are men—that is to say, hypocrites —I shall miss the period of their frankness. Their function here is not what people think: it is to cure me of my grandees. I have just been in council with two of those. The Moors say that the man who has many servants around him has many devils around him. I would say as much of ministers. They are there, living off my aged strength as an ivy plant lives off the trunk of a gnarled tree. Rogues who will live to bury me! My Prime Minister is a wonderful devil. He has played several tricks even on me, but with infinite art. Oh, what art! For its sake I've forgiven him. Only, on whom can one lean? On my enemies' enemies? They too are my enemies. Only the idiots manage to serve and to be devoted: the only ones who are devoted to me are incapables. Matters of weight dealt with by frivolous people, opinions asked for with the firm intention of not following them, meetings for information at which nobody knows anything, discussions adjourned without reaching any conclusions because it is time to go and sup, decisions taken at random to save someone's idiotic self-esteem, indignation that is just but is expressed by men quite as corrupt as those who have made them indignant—there you have what, for thirty-five years, I have seen in government.

INES: If that is how it is, my lord, it is surely not peculiar to our country.

FERRANTE: No. Thank God, one says to oneself that it must be the same over the way. That's what makes one able to go on. And ruling is like charity: when one has begun, one must go on. But it is hard, sometimes. [*Pointing to the window*] Look at this spring. How like it is to last year's! Isn't it enough to make one die of boredom? And God created that! He is indeed humble.

INES: It is always the same thing, and yet it seems to me as if it were always the first time. And there are also acts that are always the same, and yet each time one performs them it's as if God were descending upon the earth.

FERRANTE: For me, everything is repetition, refrain, ritornello. I spend my days beginning again what I've done already, and beginning it again less well. I've been governing for thirty-five years: it's far too long. My luck has grown old. I'm tired of my kingdom. I'm tired of my acts of justice, and tired of my good deeds; I've had enough of giving pleasure to people who do not matter. The things in which I've succeeded, the things in which I've failed, all have for me today the same taste. And men, too, seem to me far too much alike. All those faces together make up for me now only one face, with shadowy eyes, watching me curiously. One after the other, things are deserting me; they are going out, like those candles one extinguishes one by one, at regular intervals on Holy Thursday at the midnight service, to symbolize the successive desertions of the friends of Christ. And soon, at the hour of death, the contentment of saying to oneself, thinking of each of them: "There's something else I don't regret."

INES: "Soon!" But Your Majesty has long years of life to come.

FERRANTE: No. Soon my soul will have reached the extreme of its flight, like a great eagle hungry for depth and light. In an instant I shall appear before my God. I shall know at last all things. . . .

INES: Sire, if it is your privy council that has put into Your Majesty's head these funereal thoughts, I should like to throw myself on my knees to thank God for never having mixed me up with those men.

FERRANTE: Do you know what they want? A policy of intimidation against Don Pedro and against you. The Infanta, alas, goes away tomorrow. She will be leaving me alone, the prey — in the rooms buffeted on all sides by her genius—to my remorse at not having been able to keep that falcon here because of you and your sentimentality. And yet I do not blame you. The Infanta is an inspired and feverish young woman: she was cradled on a brazen buckler; you, one would say you were born of a smile. . . . But it is not written that she is escaping me forever. The marriage of Don Pedro with the Infanta could take place in a few weeks or a few months if the Pope agreed to grant the annulment, and if Don Pedro consented. And my grandees would like me to gain this consent by letting fly against the Prince and against you. If they dared—which of course they do not—they would ask me for your head. They are hot at my heels like dogs after a bull. I resist; then they accuse me of being faint-hearted. As though by chance, the Dominican who preached yesterday evening in my chapel gave a sermon on firmness! It is true that there's nothing I esteem so much in a man as moderation in the exercise of any sort of power. It is sometimes less admirable to use one's power than to restrain oneself from using it. Added to which the sensation of a power one doesn't use is certainly one of the most exquisite in the world. But all that is taken for weakness, and one has to put up with being disdained unjustly, and that is of all things in the world the most painful to endure.

INES: Sire, severe as the punishment inflicted on Don Pedro seems to me, I understand better now that it could be more so, and I thank you for your kindness.

FERRANTE: No gratitude! Stay natural. And besides, I beg of you, don't talk to me of my kindness. Sometimes there passes over my spirit a breeze of kindness, but it is always short-lived. I am not kind, get that into your head. I am like the rest of them: at times, even, I see a serpent darting its brilliant head out from me. It is not from kindness that I am not punishing the Prince more harshly, it's from reason; because an ass has made a misstep, should one cut off its leg? It is not from kindness that I'm doing nothing to you. Some people think gallantry forbids that we should punish women. That is not at all my view: if a man and a woman have committed an equal crime, their punishment should be identical. For example, a woman betrays the army: she is imprisoned for life, and this allows her still some amenities. But a man, for the same crime, pays with his head. That isn't just.

INES: In that case, Sire, I ought to be put in prison like Don Pedro. And it's true that feeling myself free, when he is captive—

FERRANTE: Oh, you'll be there one day, in prison, you too. And prison is so becoming to women! Once there, they stop painting, get thin, wear decent clothes at last, together with a languid paleness that sets them off to great advantage. Yes, if I treat you gently, it's not from kindness, it's above all from policy. Understand my situation. I have to obtain two things. First, that the Pope annul your marriage. At Rome everything's for sale, granted; but the Pope is in a passion against me, and he is like the rest of men: he puts his passions before his interests. In spite of everything, naturally, I shall seek to negotiate. Next, I have got to bring Don Pedro to agree to marry the Infanta, if Rome annuls. Can you help me?

INES: Oh, Sire, how hard that is for me! So much tenderness offered up before God, only to be—

FERRANTE: Don't talk to me of tenderness. Long ago those emotions ceased to interest me. Be reasonable; you have everything to gain by it. Go and see Pedro, and try to persuade him.

INES: See him?

FERRANTE: Yes, I authorize you.

INES: Ah, Sire, thank you! What joy you are giving me! What joy you are giving me!

FERRANTE: Moderate yourself. One should never rejoice so quickly.

INES: When? Tomorrow? My whole life is opening again, like the tail of a peacock unfolding.

FERRANTE: Tomorrow. At the gates of Santarem Castle. Guards will be there at a distance.

INES: May I not enter the castle and stay a moment alone with him?

FERRANTE: No. Outside. And guards within sight. Ask him if he is prepared to engage himself solemnly to marry the Infanta, should Rome give the dispensation, and if so, I'll relax my severity altogether. I regret to have to make conditions. The necessities of the kingdom have forced me to hold to this language.

INES: But do you not want to see him?

FERRANTE: Face to face with him, my patience would ooze

away through all my pores. Besides, he and I live in different worlds. His presence bores me and weighs on me. Oh, do not imagine it is bitter, losing affection. On the contrary, you have no idea how good it is to feel one no longer loves. I don't know which is better: to break away, or to have someone break away from you.

INES: To break away from one's child!

FERRANTE: Yes, yes, why not? You will experience it one day with Pedro, you too. Our loves are like those immense armies which yesterday covered the plain. Today one looks for them: they have vanished.

INES: Not ours.

FERRANTE: Most affections are only habits or duties that people have not the courage to break.

INES: For one's son!

FERRANTE: What do I care for the bond of blood! There is only one bond, the bond one has with the people one esteems or loves. God knows I did love my son, but there comes a moment when one must make an end with what one loves. One ought to be able to break abruptly with one's children, as one does with one's mistresses.

INES: But you love him still, after all!

FERRANTE: He doesn't deserve it.

INES: Oh, if one's to start calculating what human beings deserve!

FERRANTE: Everything I have done for him comes home to roost in my heart. Let's say I love him enough to be sorry that I don't love him more. He makes me ashamed of myself—of having at one time believed in my love for him and of not being capable of keeping that love. Go now, Doña Ines. When you have seen Don Pedro you will come and see me again. You will tell me if he is very sad, if he is really feeling the edge of the punishment I am applying to him. Unless you tell me that he consents, and in that case you would be bringing me an immense joy. Bring it me: I have great need of it. Good-by.

SECOND SETTING: *Outside the gates of Santarem Castle. It is out in the country.*

SCENE IV

INES, PEDRO

INES [*throwing herself into his arms*]: Don't speak! Don't speak! Let me drink of you. I was so thirsty. My God, sustain me in this supreme happiness! It seems to me as if from now on I shall never again be able to taste any happiness that is not near to madness. . . .

PEDRO: Ines, if you—

INES: Don't speak, I said! This moment which perhaps will never come again. After it I can bear anything. Only let this moment not be taken away from me. A moment, a little moment more, let me rest on the man's shoulder, the place where one does not die. [*Pause.*] To be there, and to be allowed that, and to say to oneself that the earth can hold such things, and that none the less evil and death go on existing, and that one will have to die in one's turn!

PEDRO: Those soldiers watching us—

INES: So like a man: always afraid of ridicule, and afraid of it where there is none. The soldiers are watching us? Very well! Let them watch us, let them take their fill. Let them watch and let them say if they too can love like that. [*Pause.*] Is it your heart beating so hard, or mine?

PEDRO: Ours.

INES: I'd like to give my life for you. You are laughing! How can you laugh?

PEDRO: To see you so in love. You threw yourself on me like the wolf on the lamb!

INES: And to think I stayed for an hour stretched on my bed before coming here, to be mistress of myself when you appeared! What days I have just lived through! Your name spoken in my solitude, spoken in my dreams. Nailed there as by an arrow. And I kept looking at the sky and I kept crying: "Ah, a little less blue sky, and the body of the man I love!" I kept getting up to go to the fountain (that water, so cool, my only support all through the day), or else to pick a flower and bring it back into my room, to keep me company. And now I've found you again. And I've found again the smell of your clothes. . . . When I saw you my heart burst. Ah, let me drink of you again. Let me hold you in my mouth as the fierce birds do when they possess each other rolling in the dust.

PEDRO: Those soldiers always edging nearer—

INES: All right! Let them shoot with their blunderbusses! For I'd gladly die, I and the life I'm carrying in me, yes, I'd gladly die if death was going to fix me forever in a moment such as this. No, you cannot know what these four days have been. There's a brave and almost defiant way of receiving the first onslaught of fate. And then, little by little, it wears you down. It's on the third day that one should see a person who's been stricken. After three days I began to be bathed in sweat at night, and to realize that in those three days I had got thinner. And when I was in the presence of your father, I was as weak as you had been. You hadn't dared to tell him of our marriage. I didn't dare tell him of our child. And I don't know how I managed to say nothing of that, seeing how much I love talking about him.

PEDRO: How is that famous little boy?

INES: In the daytime he doesn't worry me too much. It's at night. . . . He is in the warm place of my heart, and I should like to make myself warmer still to give him better shelter. Sometimes he moves, hardly at all, like a boat in calm water, then suddenly a sharper movement hurts me a little. In the great silence I wait again for his small sign: we are accomplices. He knocks timidly; and then I feel myself melting with tenderness, because all of a sudden I had thought he was dead, he is so fragile. I wish he would never cease moving, to spare me those anguished moments when I imaginc he will never move again. And yet it is those moments that make possible the divine joy of finding him again alive.

PEDRO: May the hard world on which he is going to disembark not treat him as enemy; he is enemy to no one. May the deep earth welcome him with gentleness; he knows nothing yet of its terrible secrets. But tell me, how is it the King let you come to see me?

INES: He wishes—but I do not wish it!

PEDRO: What?

INES: That I should get your promise to marry the Infanta if the Pope grants the annulment. But I don't wish that, I wish you still to be mine alone. Do you love me?

PEDRO: I love you as the sun loves the sand. I love you, and also I love loving you.

INES: So you missed me?

PEDRO: Oh, foolish woman! Let us be serious. Did my father treat you gently?

INES: Very gently. He spoke to me with an extreme lack of reserve. He was bitter because there are always people urging him against us, and also because he is weary of the throne. All those great deserted halls one passes through to get to him, how well they call to mind the loneliness there must be in power! And how much more loudly a man's inner lamentation must resound there—it must ring like steps on the stone floors! He asked me to look carefully and see if you seemed sad, but I have a feeling that when he's harsh, he is forcing himself and that by nature he's benevolent and generous.

PEDRO: He has, all the same, done horrible acts.

INES: No doubt there were reasons.

PEDRO: Oh, there are always reasons. But to try to portray the King is like trying to carve a statue out of sea water.

INES: He also said some bad things about you. But when people say bad things about you to me, it gives me no pain. On the contrary, it's as if because of it I love you more, as if because of it you belong more to me alone. No, it's not of him that I'm afraid. Our whole fate depends on him, and only on him. And yet the fear I feel is a confused fear, and one that doesn't come from him in particular.

PEDRO: What dread is there which that sad heart of yours will never have harbored? What, even now, in my arms!

INES: I'm thinking of the moment when I shall be leaving you.

PEDRO: Ines, always in the past or future! Always busy looking at me as if it were the last time. Hello, what's this? Our guards are moving. . . .

INES: Truly, you think of nothing but them! If you really loved me you would not see them.

PEDRO: You heard? A sound of horses on the road.

INES: Ah, that's enough! That's enough! So two people cannot embrace without there being men who rise up and say to them: "No"? I shall not move.

PEDRO: The soldiers are returning in our direction. . . .

INES: Wait, my death, wait. Let me first have my fill. I shall not move. Even if it were God Himself appearing in this bush.

PEDRO: The Infanta!

INES: She! Here! Doubtless urged on by the King, she is coming, before leaving, to ask you herself for that promise. She's coming to tear you from me. Don't speak to her. Go back into the castle and refuse to receive her. Besides, if necessary I'll bar her passage. [*The soldiers surround the Prince and take him back into the castle.*]

SCENE V

Ines, the Infanta

The Infanta [*into the wings, to her attendants*]: Stay some way off, please, and wait for me. [*To Ines*] Doña Ines de Castro?

Ines [*with claws out*]: Your Highness!

The Infanta: You think I've come to see the Prince. Not at all, it's you I'm looking for. You saw the King yesterday?

Ines: Yes, Princess.

The Infanta: What impression did he make on you? [*A vague, prudent gesture from Ines.*] Well, I am going to tell you. Your necklace of medals has pressed upon your neck and has left a red mark. That is the place where you will be beheaded.

Ines: God!

The Infanta: Princes put lions on their coats of arms, on their oriflammes. And then one day they find one in their heart. Did you see the green pallor of his face? Like someone who has forgotten to get buried. And with all that, the heavy eyes that lions have. The King has the dying sickness: well, it's at the end of the bullfight that the bull is wickedest. Oh, I'm not saying the King has the clear intention of having you killed. He is as men are: weak, variable, and not very sure of what he wants. But a dangerous thought like a blade has been slid into his mind, and he has not repelled it as violently as he should have.

Ines: How do you know?

The Infanta: One of the pages has talked.

INES: One of the pages!

THE INFANTA: One of my people took care of the pages on duty yesterday at the door during the council, or rather during a small meeting between the King, Alvar Gonçalves, and Egas Coelho. Two of the pages knew nothing, or wouldn't say anything. The third, the youngest, had listened, and listened well.

INES: The youngest! The one who's so handsome!

THE INFANTA: A young demon is always handsome.

INES: And he talked? But—from thoughtlessness, I suppose?

THE INFANTA: No, from passion.

INES: How horrible!

THE INFANTA: You mean: what blessed good fortune! So, Egas Coelho and Alvar Gonçalves demanded your death. The King could have cut them short, with an energetic no. But they argued interminably. "Like lawyers," the page said. At the end the King said: "I will think it over." Afterwards he remained alone with Egas Coelho, but the page had gone to look for you.

INES: "I will think it over." . . . That is not a sentence of death. . . . The King, in all this business, has treated me with such openness—

THE INFANTA: My father says of King Ferrante that he plays with his perfidy as a baby plays with its foot.

INES: "I will think it over." . . . Perhaps he wanted to give himself elbow-room.

THE INFANTA: Doña Ines, Doña Ines, I know the world and its ways.

INES: Oh, yes, you know them. To think that in three days you, a foreigner, and so young, find out such secrets. I could have lived for years in the palace without knowing what was being said about me.

THE INFANTA: I was brought up to rule.

INES: And Don Pedro—did the King speak of him?

THE INFANTA: According to the page, Ferrante did not speak

about his son. And now, Doña Ines, I must tell you: I leave tomorrow, profiting by the fact that the winds are favorable. Look: a cloud in the shape of a wing! It's flying toward Navarre. And fleecy clouds: they are seeking pasture toward my Navarre, which is always a-stir with flocks. Yes, tomorrow at this time, God willing, I shall be cleaving the shadowy sea: with what vehemence the waves will rebel before my ship's bow, only to abase themselves amazed, as if they knew who I am! My Navarre! I desire so much to see it again that I am almost afraid of what I shall see when I get there. Well, I invite you to come with me. You will be a member of my house. You will not be in safety as long as you are in Portugal. But from the moment I take you under my mantle, the King will not dare to touch you: offend me a second time, never! Only, you must decide at once, and leave your Mondego just as it is. I know, people prefer dying to dropping their affairs, or to taking the trouble to put them in order promptly. But you must see what is important to you, whether it's the Mondego or to be alive. So follow me to Navarre and wait. Either the King will die, and you will return and reign. Or the King will destroy his son—

Ines: Oh!

The Infanta: Forgive me!

Ines: But who can have made you believe—

The Infanta: I do not believe that Ferrante has any such thought today. But today and tomorrow are no sons of the same mother, and less than ever so in the shadow of the King. He is by nature uncertain, and his art consists in making his uncertainty pass for policy. He plays a situation as if he were playing a fish; he does it out of hesitation and inconsistency, but manages to disguise this dallying play as profound calculation. He affirms both of two contradictory things, at once spontaneously, because he is irresolute, and systematically, to cover up his trail. He makes dangerous mixtures of irreconcilable elements; and so nobody knows what he thinks, but it's because he thinks nothing definite, except, sometimes, about his immediate interest. How long will he believe it is in his immediate interest to spare Don Pedro and you?

INES: I am overwhelmed. But do at least realize that I am grateful. . . . That it should be you!

THE INFANTA: There are two forms of glory: divine glory, which consists in God's being satisfied with you, and human glory, which consists in being satisfied with yourself. By saving you I win both glories. And especially the second, for nature would, if anything, command me to hate you. But I attach little importance to nature.

INES: True, madame, for in your place—

THE INFANTA: You forget yourself, Doña Ines. Nobody can put herself in my place.

INES: Forgive me, Infanta. It is true, your rank—

THE INFANTA: Where I am, there is no rank. Doña Ines, I let you off your politenesses: you are not very happy at them. But what of that? You are charming as you are. Let me tell you that I have never been jealous of you. I was not even curious to know you, so indifferent is Don Pedro to me. People kept telling me: "She is beautiful," but I thought: "I am great. And the beautiful can never equal the great." Then they told me: "She is full of gentleness for everyone," and those words pleased me. I translated them into my language as: she is the friend of all the gentle things of the earth. They gave me this instance: that, for years, you let your hair be done in the worst possible way by your hairdresser in order not to give him pain by dismissing him. [*Ines puts her hand up to her hair.*] No, no, your hair is not so bad. You have your hair done by the hands of Charity; it is marvelous.

INES: It's because my hair sometimes needs to be given a

rest. So for a whole day I wear it in a chignon. Only afterwards it won't come straight. . . .

THE INFANTA: Your hair is very nice, I assure you; stop worrying about it. Finally, I heard that for twenty-four years you had lived in Spain: after that I was no longer astonished at your merit. Also that you were a natural child: and that pleased me. And so I wanted to see you, and I gave orders to one of my ladies-in-waiting, the Marchioness of Tordesillas, to place herself near you at Mass, at Santa Clara, and not to leave you, so that I might recognize you. But as those ladies got up and changed places on the slightest occasion, the better to exchange their gossip, that and the uniformity of their clothes and the darkness of the church made me in the end lose sight of you. So I had the Marchioness recalled, and instructed her to tear your cloak a little—

INES: What, Your Highness, it was you!

THE INFANTA: It was. The opening the tear made was at your neck. I followed you by that little pale patch moving in the half-light. I looked at you for a long while, Doña Ines. And I saw that Don Pedro was right to love you.

INES: If you knew him better, you would know that I am a thousand times more right to love him.

THE INFANTA: I believe you, to please you. And do you know whom I shall find, at my return, on her knees? The Marchioness of Tordesillas, I'm sure, praying that our meeting may have turned out to your good. Come, Doña Ines, grant the good Marchioness's prayers. Tell me that you'll accompany me into Navarre.

INES: No, Princess, I cannot.

THE INFANTA: Why?

INES: When the bird of noble breed is captured, it doesn't resist. You spoke of a cloud in the shape of a wing. If I had a wing, it would not be for flying away, but for protecting.

THE INFANTA: I know, being noble is dearly paid for. But

you are not "captured." You may have only one night before you: at least you have it.

INES: No! No! I cannot any longer exist anywhere but at his side! In whatever state, however wretched, provided I don't leave him. And, if necessary, to die with him or for him.

THE INFANTA: There is no human being worth dying for.

INES: A man one loves!

THE INFANTA: I have not yet come to understand how one can love a man. Those whom I have come near I have seen, almost all, coarse, and all cowardly. Cowardice: that's the word that's brought into my mind irresistibly by men.

INES: Have you never, then, been in love, Infanta?

THE INFANTA: Never, by the grace of God.

INES: But you must have been loved?

THE INFANTA: If a man had been so ridiculous as to love me, I should have paid so little attention to it that I should have no recollection of it. [*With bluntness and candor*] You hear the sparrows? They are singing my praises. Oh, don't think me proud: I have no pride, not an ounce. But to love being praised, one doesn't need to think oneself worthy of it. Now, Ines, come with me! I offer you your life. The breath of kings is fiery. It will consume you.

INES: It consumes what will be consumed anyway. I was not made to struggle, but to love. As a little child, when the formation of my breasts was not yet visible, I was already full of love for my dolls; and there was always one of them I called the Lover, and the other the Beloved. And already, if my bosom had been opened up, love would have flowed from it, like that sort of milk which flows from certain plants when you break their stems. To love—I don't know how to do anything else. Look at that waterfall: it doesn't struggle, it follows its course. One must let the waters fall.

THE INFANTA: The cascade does not fall: it hurls itself headlong. It also works mills. Water is guided in channels.

The oar beats it, the prow cuts it. Everywhere I see it suffer violence. Oh, how soft you are!

INES: It's when the fruit is rather soft that it receives right into its heart all the rays of Creation.

THE INFANTA: Please don't sing me the praises of softness: you wound me personally. Come to Spain instead: there you will recover vigor. Don't try to deny it: I know that Spain is not much liked here. Portugal is a woman stretched out by the side of Spain; but Spain, which stays none the less apart and burns alone and is mad, prevents Portugal from sleeping. If I had married Don Pedro, I should have been the man: I should have prevented him from sleeping.

INES: Highness, since the King, you say, cannot but do what you ask, I beg of you, before you go, obtain pardon for Don Pedro!

THE INFANTA: It is not Don Pedro, it's you I want to save. Come to Pampeluna. Pampeluna is like the inner courtyard of a citadel, shut in between high mountains; and around it there is my soul, going from height to height, watching, and not allowing. . . . The King's hand will be powerless to reach you, over those mountains. Come to Pampeluna, even if my court has no attractions for you. The sensation of being in security would give some charm to any place, and you will recover your soul with your security.

INES: He is my soul.

THE INFANTA: You are soft, and at the same time too courageous.

INES: Don't tell me I have courage: I should lose it at once.

THE INFANTA: There, where your breasts rise, in the down between your breasts, one of your eyelashes has fallen. It lies there like the feather of a swallow wounded in flight; it moves a little, one would think it was alive. The swallow is wounded, Doña Ines. How many times more will it fly if it does not find shelter? One day it will no longer be there to announce the spring, one day there will be no more spring for it on earth. Give me ground for believing I can still find the words to convince you. To think that you will have eluded me! And I, to be the Infanta of Navarre and fail to convince! And fail to convince the person to whom one wishes so much good! How is it that the good you wish a person does not shine out on your face and does not pass into the tone of your voice, so that there could be no mistaking it? But no, on the contrary, it's perhaps my face that frightens you. Perhaps new faces frighten you? Or is it perhaps that mine is covered with sweat? Or have I perhaps said too much? When one wants to convince, and when one has passed the point where it was still possible, all that one says in addition merely makes one suspect and hardens the person one wants to convince. You must be thinking: "Why is she so keen on it? Mustn't there be a trap? . . ." O door, door! What word is there to open you? I'll stop, for my mouth is dried up. [*Pause.*] I see, you are looking at the foam at the corners of my mouth. It comes from my mouth's dryness, and from the burning glare of that road, which was pale like a lion. All the inside of me is dried up as if I had had driven down my throat, to the hilt, the fiery sword of the nocturnal angel; you know, when the voices from the wall cried yet again: "Sennacherib!" Ah, the senselessness of it, that a violent desire should not suffice to shake down from the tree the thing one desires. For the last time, Ines: are you coming with me?

INES: Princess, do not blame me: I can't.

THE INFANTA: Very well, so be it! You have let pass the moment when I loved you. Now you annoy me. Why should your life matter to me, when it does not matter to you?

INES: I, madame, I annoy you?

THE INFANTA: You disappoint me. Well, go and die, Doña

Ines. Go and die quickly, as quickly as possible now. Let your face not have the time to imprint itself in me. Let it be washed away, and may I be able to forget it—washed away like a stain of blood on the flagstones, which is washed away with water. I should have liked the whole of my stay in Portugal to vanish like a bad dream, but that is no longer possible, because of you. You alone are poisoning the sweet honey of my forgetfulness, as it is written of the fly in the ointment in our Holy Scriptures. Go, Doña Ines, God be with you. Is it not fine that, whatever happens, and even if one has sinned, one can always say to oneself: "God be with me"? Look up at the heavens, where He is who will protect you.

INES: God will protect me if I am worthy of it. But why look up at the heavens? Looking up at the heavens always brings me back to the earth, for it is on earth that I have experienced those divine things that I know. Our passions are the Lord's angels.

THE INFANTA: Then, my dear, if you will not look up at the heavens, turn right away in the direction of hell. Try to win the page, who belongs to hell, and to find out through him the King's intentions. His name is Dino del Moro. He is Andalusian. The Andalusians are not reliable. He will betray anything one wishes.

INES: I think I should never have the heart to tempt a child into betraying.

THE INFANTA: Even if your life and the life of Don Pedro are at stake?

INES: Pedro! . . . But, all the same, a child! A child—like what, one day, a son of mine might be. . . .

THE INFANTA: Very well, Doña Ines, be sublime, then, since that is decidedly what attracts you. Sublime by refusing to leave. Sublime by refusing to tempt into betrayal. All right, take your fill of being sublime, and die of it. Good-by.

[*Ines bows, takes the Infanta's hand, and is about to kiss it. The Infanta's jeweled bracelet comes undone and falls to the ground. Ines picks it up and holds it out to her.*]

THE INFANTA: Keep it, Ines. In our country a princess of the royal blood may accept nothing that is not offered to her by someone of her house. This bracelet which clasps so badly will remain to you as a symbol of our own failure to clasp.

INES: If it is a symbol, there are things so much purer than the diamond—

THE INFANTA: That's true. [*She throws the bracelet to the ground and crushes it with her heel. A pause.*] Embrace me. [*They embrace.*] God keep you! [*Left alone, gazing at the waterfall in the distance*] One must let the waters fall. . . .

CURTAIN

ACT III

A hall in the royal palace. It is almost in darkness. Only the part near the hearth, on which a fire is burning, is lit by a few clusters of candles.

SCENE I

FERRANTE, INES, *later* A PAGE

FERRANTE: The smells that rise from the sea have a savor less bitter than the smell breathed out by the heart of a man of sixty. I don't know why men of that age pretend that they're going to live forever. I don't deceive myself. Soon death will be pressing his black helmet well down over my head. Indeed, I've been dying for a long time; it's simply a question of finishing it off.

INES: Always, my lord, always that somber presentiment!

FERRANTE: I have my visitations. At night above all: night is mother of all things, and even of appalling gleams. At the deepest hour of night, deep as the deepest place in the hollow of a wave, as I lie there in the dust of pride. My hands are paralyzed and cold as if in death; a long moment is needed, when I wake, before the blood comes back to them and they unstiffen. I lie there in the position of those recumbent stone figures on tombs, but without having, like them, to warm me, my feet on a greyhound or on a little page-boy. At those moments, often, my heart stops beating. . . . When it starts again, I am quite surprised to find myself alive—and a little bit put out.

INES: But your doctors—

FERRANTE: I speak of my illness to nobody, and the world

believes I'm going to live a thousand years. Besides, doctors— It is a sin to want to change the time that God has chosen. All the same, you are perhaps right, and one can lay it down as a general axiom that it is better to be assassinated by one's doctor than by one's son. [*Pause.*] Last night—perhaps because of an extreme sadness that came upon me yesterday—I dreamed that I was in the death agony. No physical suffering, and absolute lucidity. There was surely someone present, for I was pointing out to him that I was getting weaker moment by moment. And, moment by moment, reddish marblings kept appearing on my skin. I kept writing on my skin, and it was so rotted that in places the pen burst it.

INES: And what did you write?

FERRANTE: I kept writing: "Much better and much worse. . . ." For I have been better and worse than the world can know. Then dawn showed through the curtains and the casements of my room, and those long lines of whiteness seemed to be great funeral candles surrounding me. Every night, or nearly, abysses like that open for me. Then, at those hours, I see. . . . I see all that I have done and undone, I, King of Portugal, conqueror of the Moors, victor of the Indies, terror of rebels, Ferrante the Magnanimous, miserable sinner. And I see that of all I have done and undone, during more than a quarter of a century, nothing will remain, for it will all be overturned, and perhaps very quickly, by the hazarding hands of time; nothing will remain but a portrait, among a dozen others, in the Armeria at Coimbra, the portrait of a man of whom the people who will come after will be unable to cite a single act, and about whom all they will think, as they look at that portrait, will be: "That one has a longer nose than the others."

INES: My lord, the glory of great men is like shadows: it lengthens as they set.

FERRANTE: Ah, don't talk of my glory. If you knew how far

away from myself I am. And the foetid breath of admiration. . . . And besides, I am not a king of glory, I am a king of sorrow. On the standard of Portugal I have increased the number of the signs that represent the wounds of Christ. It is a king of sorrow that brings you that great belling of a stag in the forest. But I don't have to withdraw, before dying, into forests or onto a mountain, for I am my own forest and my own mountain. My network of souls is the undergrowth of the forest, and I have had, being king, to make of my own thinking a high place and a mountain.

A PAGE [*entering*]: Sire, Don Alvar Gonçalves insists that Your Majesty deign to receive him at once.

FERRANTE: I have to see him tomorrow morning. . . .

THE PAGE: He says his message is extremely urgent.

FERRANTE: Tell him that I'll see him tomorrow. [*The page goes out. To Ines*] But perhaps you would have liked to make the acquaintance of a man who is asking me to have you assassinated.

INES: Sire!

FERRANTE: To see your faces, the two of you, would, one must admit, have been diverting. [*To the page, who has just come back*] Again!

THE PAGE: A note from Don Alvar.

FERRANTE: [*having read it, with changed face*]: Terrible! Terrible! Terrible! Have Don Alvar brought to my private room. I'll join him there. [*To Ines*] Doña Ines, wait for me here for a moment. [*To the page*] After that you will make up the fire. It's going out. [*He goes, in the direction of his private room.*]

SCENE II

INES, DINO DEL MORO

INES [*aside*]: So the page told the truth: they want my death. [*The page comes in again, accompanied by Dino del Moro. They set about poking the fire.*] God! It's he! If I could get him alone! Speak to him—win him—know, from now on, through him— [*Dumb show. The first page goes out for a moment. Ines draws near to Dino. The first page comes back. At last he goes.*]

INES [*embarrassed*]: I know your name is Dino del Moro.

DINO DEL MORO: At your service, my lady. Although—that's only a nickname. My father is Fernando de Calla Fuente, Marquis of Duero. He is Governor of the Genil province. But they call him Fernando del Moro because, when he found out that his steward, a Moor who had abjured, was going on with the pagan practices, he stabbed him with his own hand. My father has the strength of two horses.

INES: Bravo! Was it long ago that you left Andalusia?

DINO DEL MORO: A year. You don't know the Genil? It's the biggest river in Europe. They say its source is in paradise.

INES: Like the rivers of Navarre, I suppose. And—doesn't it depress you, living separated from your parents?

DINO DEL MORO: Oh no!

INES: What a cry from the heart! Someone's been speaking to me about you, Dino del Moro.

DINO DEL MORO: Ah, the Infanta!

INES: So—you listen at the King's keyhole?

DINO DEL MORO: I wasn't listening, my lady. A few words I caught in passing—

INES: No, no, you were listening. Your whole face proclaims it. Oh, if you could only see it! You're just as physically incapable of hiding the confession in your face as you are of lifting up a chest in your arms. [*Aside*] How can I ask him? I don't know what to say to him. . . . [*Aloud*] So you are aware that there are men here who wish me evil, great evil. It is very important for me—

[*Loud voices are heard, coming from the King's private room.*]

Dino del Moro: Sh! The King! Say something to me, anything.

Ines [*in a loud, affected voice, and pointing at a sprig of jasmine the page is wearing in a buttonhole of his doublet*]: That jasmine, page— The other day, too, you were wearing a carnation. So you like flowers so much?

Dino del Moro: When I was small, my mother liked me always to wear a flower.

Ines: When you were small! . . . And those gold and silver threads twined in your hair—

Dino del Moro: That too was my mother—she used to twine them like this for me when I was small. She used to say it was to bring me luck.

Ines: But now, so far away from your mother—

Dino del Moro: Now I put them there myself.

Ines [*aside*]: How strange he is! [*To Dino*] Your mother— [*Aside*] This conspiracy with this child— And his mother. . . . No, it's impossible! I can't! [*To Dino*] Dino del Moro, why do you listen at your King's keyhole? That's work for valets, not for the son of Fernando del Moro.

Dino del Moro: The King isn't fond of me. Why should I be fond of him?

Ines: He isn't fond of you?

Dino del Moro: He never stops laughing at me. Yes, all the time! About my hair, about my accent. He can't say a word to me without laughing at me.

Ines: If he makes fun of you, it is because he is fond of you, don't you see? The cat always leaves his mark on his friend.

Dino del Moro: At night—because I'm the best dancer of

all the pages—I'm the one who leaps up and catches the fireflies and I bring them to him in the hollow of my hand. Well, he isn't a bit grateful.

INES: That's certainly a most important charge you've got against him. But is the King, then, so fond of fireflies?

DINO DEL MORO: He says they are like him: by turns dark and luminous, luminous and dark. I—when he told me they were like him, I told him they were nasty creatures.

INES: If you say disagreeable things to the King, don't be surprised if perhaps he's a little annoyed with you. But even if he were annoyed with you, that would be no reason for cheating him.

DINO DEL MORO: Everybody cheats him here.

INES: That's just why *you* mustn't do so. If you don't like serving him, ask your parents to call you home, on some pretext or other. Don't stay with someone who puts trust in you, only to betray him. You who are so small! How old are you?

DINO DEL MORO: Thirteen.

INES: Thirteen, you say. Then you must be twelve, for you have to pretend to be big. Twelve! You're a little man, already with your full power of doing evil. No, don't go on like that. I tell you as your mother would. [*Tidying his hair*] The gold threads in your hair mustn't be there simply to bring you luck, they should also remind you that you must be pure like them.

DINO DEL MORO: But, my lady, wasn't I very useful to you when I repeated to the Infanta's messenger—

INES: That's true! That's true! And yet—don't go on!

DINO DEL MORO: The King! [*He rushes out.*]

SCENE III

FERRANTE, ALVAR GONÇALVES, INES

FERRANTE: Putting up with things! Always putting up with things! Oh, that wears one out. To be without cease in the hands of other men! To have reigned nearly thirty-five years, and still bound hand and foot.—Doña Ines, Don Alvar Gonçalves, who often enlightens me with his counsels. But perhaps you know him already?

ALVAR GONÇALVES: If I had met Doña Ines, I could not have forgotten it.

INES: And I, Don Alvar, if I have met you, I have forgotten it. But rest assured that I shall not forget this meeting.

ALVAR GONÇALVES: I beg you, madame, to keep me in your good graces.

INES: For just as long as you keep me in yours.

FERRANTE [*to Alvar*]: Come back and see me tomorrow morning. But with no illusions. For there is nothing to be done, nothing, nothing!

SCENE IV

FERRANTE, INES

FERRANTE: If you have remained free, if Don Pedro has been allowed back to his apartments in the palace and only kept under house arrest, that was because I thought I held the Bishop of Guarda. And now he's escaping me. The Nuncio sends me word by Don Alvar that the Pope would take it as an outrage if I let myself go against the Bishop. According to him, the Bishop, in joining you to Don Pedro, was only obeying the Prince, as was his duty; above all, he is covered by ecclesiastical immunity. Not only must I spare the Bishop, but the Nuncio even desires that he be set at liberty. It is of little consequence to me now that Don Pedro, so you tell me, has again put off promising to marry the Infanta if the Pope were to grant the annulment. The Pope will not grant it: at present that is certain. I am like a lion that's fallen into a trap. I can bite, leap, roar—in vain. You are bound to Don Pedro, and this bond can be broken only by the Pope's dying and being succeeded by someone differently disposed toward me. Oh, I am tired of this situation. I wish it would take some other form. Normally I find that great affairs are settled easily and quickly, while the small ones are interminably drawn out with a thousand hitches. This one is great and full of hitches. And I am tired of you, of the fact that you exist. Tired of wishing you well, tired of wishing to save you. Ah, why do you exist? The infuriating obstacle that human beings are! A river, a mountain, one understands, one accepts. But a poor soft thing of flesh and nerves, that stands up one can't think how— Well, everything I have done is destroyed. I have been scooping with a sieve. And, true enough, why should what I've done go on existing, since I have long ceased to exist? The bow of my intelligence has come unstrung. I look at what I have written, and ask: "Who wrote that?" I think of what I had understood, and I've ceased to understand it. And what I have learned I have forgotten. I am dying and it seems to me that all remains to be done, that I am at the same point where I was at twenty. My hands are open, everything has fled me. I've been playing the flute for the love of God.

INES: Isn't that our common fate?

FERRANTE: Happy the man who has given little and has taken back what he has given. Happy the man whose children do not bear his name.

INES: Happy the man who heard those words and over whom they flow without affecting him!

FERRANTE: I have flowed away like the wind of the desert, which begins by chasing before it waves of sand like a cavalry charge and ends by being diluted and exhausted: nothing is left of it. Such are the deep thoughts that King Ferrante imparts to you, thoughts of which, deep as they are, he does not guarantee the originality. For I heard one day, as I was passing down a passage near a kitchen, a spoiler of sauces proclaiming with emphatic gestures: "The final somersault, they'll all have to come to it, yes, all! The King like the rest of them!" And I thought it right that at the end of my philosophy I should find a kitchen varlet. We were coming together even sooner than he said.

SCENE V

THE SAME, THE GRAND ADMIRAL AND PRINCE OF THE SEA, EGAS COELHO, TWO OTHERS, VARIOUS LORDS

THE PRINCE OF THE SEA: My lord, the gravity of the thing obliges me to force a way through your guards. An odious insult has been offered to Your Majesty, and its reparation requires immediate orders. A party of Moors has landed at Tavira, massacred some of the harbor people, and crucified the captain who hurled some men against them, by the side of a dog's crucified carcass. They have re-embarked almost without loss. The insolence of those wretches calls for exemplary punishment. They keep their enterprises for Your Majesty alone. Do you think they'd have dared attack a port belonging to Andalusia or Valencia? Never!

FERRANTE: There was nobody, then, guarding the sea along the south coast?

THE PRINCE: As the result of a most grave negligence, the fleet commanded by Don Lourenço Payva was at that moment all cruising north of Cape St. Vincent.

FERRANTE: Yes, that's the way, there are always certain hours during which a realm is without defense: a hole, you need only go in. And in the same way there are always certain hours when a man is so weak, morally and physically—quite astonished to be still standing—that a little push and you would make him fall over. Luckily, it is rare for the enemy to smell out those hours. Ah, if he knew!

THE PRINCE: It's above all at those hours that it's important to look determined. I request an implacable punishment for Lourenço Payva.

FERRANTE: What punishment?

THE PRINCE: In normal times I should have requested a heavy term of prison. At this moment I request death.

FERRANTE: Why be more severe at this moment?

THE PRINCE: Because at this moment we have need of guilty men.

FERRANTE: I have observed that putting to death is nearly always done too soon. A day or two later and the person put to death wasn't any longer so guilty. How many assassinations are misunderstandings!

EGAS COELHO: In that case, Sire, one would never again put anyone to death!

FERRANTE: Isn't Payva an old and faithful servant?

EGAS COELHO: Sire, I was expecting your royal anger, and I am dumbfounded—

FERRANTE: When one grows old, fits of anger turn into fits of sadness.

EGAS COELHO: Or of pity. And to arrive at pity one has only to let oneself slide, but to arrive at firmness one has to raise oneself up. Well, one should always be raising oneself up.

THE PRINCE: Is the King the man to forgive an insult?

FERRANTE: Yes, when forgiveness is to his advantage. No doubt that is not the case here. The fate of Don Lourenço shall be considered. Let it be brought up again.

THE PRINCE: So then that man has a chance of going scot-free! Sire, let's make an end: allow me to go and seek death in Africa, that death from which traitors are spared. Dead, I shall no longer witness their impunity.

FERRANTE: Don't flare up so.

EGAS COELHO [*under his breath, to the lords*]: Ines's face is calm. I don't like these conversations she has with the King. She comes out from them fortified. Let us stay in the shadows for a while and listen to what they say.

FERRANTE: Very well! Let Don Lourenço be brought before my privy justice. I shall not be lenient.

EGAS COELHO: O King, you are yourself again!

THE PRINCE: And shall we not set on foot, at once, something against the Moors?

FERRANTE: That I shall consider later. [*Heavily*] I have made enough decisions for today. [*Aside*] War. . . . Men who don't deserve to live. And ideas that don't deserve to be died for.

SCENE VI

FERRANTE, INES. *At the back in the shadows*, EGAS COELHO *and the* LORDS, *later* MORE PEOPLE

INES: Are you going to have him put to death?

FERRANTE: I am inclining that way. There are those who say that an old man should be severe, because he hasn't much time. And again, that cruelty is the only pleasure left to an old man, that for him it takes the place of love. In my view, that is going too far. But I could easily believe that one of the best guarantees of long life lies in being insensitive and implacable; there you have a buckler against death.

INES: If you were really so wicked, you wouldn't say so.

FERRANTE [*ironically*]: I see you have a profound knowledge of the human soul.

INES: But if Lourenço Payva were only half-guilty, what remorse you would be laying up for yourself!

FERRANTE: Remorse dies, like everything else. And in some cases the remembrance of it is balm. But perhaps the whole of this business will blow over like smoke. For do you know what I think? That it has been invented, lock, stock, and barrel, or at any rate appreciably magnified.

INES: Invented?

FERRANTE: The idea is to humiliate me, on top of the humiliation I had from the Nuncio—all too well founded, that one. "The Moors would never dare make a landing in Andalusia or in the kingdom of Valencia." It is reckoned that, being wounded, I shall want to wound; that, having played the mouse once, to avenge myself I shall play the tomcat next time. And tomcat against whom? Against Pedro and you. But their childish calculations have not come off. I can see too clearly through their machinations.

INES: You are generous toward us, my lord.—So if it's made up, Lourenço Payva will not be executed?

FERRANTE: Upon my soul, it might be a good opportunity.

INES: A good opportunity! But execute him? Why?

FERRANTE: The Grand Admiral said it: we have need of guilty men at this moment. Well, Lourenço Payva is certainly guilty of something. Everyone is guilty of something. All those who are at liberty owe me more than they realize. So do all those who are alive. But from time to time I must say no and let fly, more or less at a venture: simply to regain control. Yes, one must go on sacrificing the lives of human beings, even when one has stopped taking their guilt seriously, just like that empty suit of armor in the legend, which was drawn up against the wall and used to hit on the head anyone passing under its iron gauntlet. Or again I'm thinking of that story of our King Enrique IV of Castile, to whom a certain Sultan was bound to give up the city of Trujillo, which he was occupying, at the King's death. And so the King's men, fearing that the Sultan would decide to defend the city if he heard the news of the death, set up the King's corpse on a throne, lower the lights in the hall—heavens, yes, just as in this hall now—and the Sultan's envoys give up the keys of the city to the dead King. I too have withdrawn myself and my whole soul from my appearance of royalty; but this appearance still receives the honors like the corpse of King Enrique or even still deals death, and dealt death almost at a venture, like the empty suit of armor.

EGAS COELHO [*aside*]: The King's delirious. That sorceress is bewitching him. His awakening will be terrible. He'll drive into the silence from which there's no return those who have surprised his secret. He'll have the sorceress put to death. Me too, if he finds me here. [*He makes his escape.*]

INES: Can one put someone to death for a thing one doesn't believe?

FERRANTE: Of course, that is regular. And even die for a thing one doesn't believe. People die for causes in which they don't believe, just as they die for passions they don't feel, and for persons they don't love. The Moors I saw in Africa worshipped stones and springs. But let 'em be told that Islam was menaced, and they would arise and go and perish in battle for a religion that was not theirs. In our country, during the rebels' war, there were so many corpses heaped up all along the Mondego road that from here you couldn't see a horseman passing down the road. Well, the greater part of those men had been civilians, and the rebels had killed them simply because they lived on land where the loyal troops still held out; they were supposed to have loyalist convictions because they lived on one side of the river; if they had lived on the other side, it would have been my soldiers that would have fired on them, as rebels.

INES: How can the King have so deserted his own colors, the King who a few days ago led me to the window and said to me: "It's I who uphold all that. Behold the people with whom I have a treaty"?

FERRANTE: Ines, this night is full of prodigies. I feel that in it I am going beyond myself, that in it I am taking up my largest measure, the measure I shall have in my tomb, and that this night is made for me to say in it things that are frightening in their purity. When I said to you: "There is my people . . ." I wasn't lying, but I was saying words of habit, in which I had believed once, in which I no longer believed altogether at the moment when I was saying them. I was like an old hen laying empty eggshells.

INES: My lord!

FERRANTE: Do not be surprised. I like to confess to women. It's a taste I have.

THE PRINCE OF THE SEA: Let's not stay here! [*He makes his escape.*]

FERRANTE: I have also to try to make people believe that I still feel something, when in fact I no longer feel anything. The world no longer does more than brush against me. And that is just, for I perceive that all my life I have done no more than brush against the world.

INES: You no longer feel anything!

FERRANTE: There are the words one says and the acts one performs, without believing in them. There are the errors one commits, knowing they are errors. And there is even the obsession with what one doesn't desire.

ONE OF THE LORDS: It's the drunkenness of Noah! [*He makes his escape.*]

[*During the following dialogue, up to the departure of the shade of the Infanta, shades appear in the darkness at the back of the room, listen for a moment, then disappear with horrified gestures.*]

FERRANTE: Just now I lamented in front of you like a beast; I cried out like the wind. Do you think that that can possibly fit in with faith in the kingly function? To play the king, one needs faith, courage, and strength. Courage I have. Strength God gives me. But faith neither God nor I can give me. I'm prisoner of what I have been. One of the Infanta's ladies-in-waiting was saying in my presence that the Infanta was always crucified upon herself. I too, in a different sense, am crucified upon myself, upon duties that for me no longer have reality. I'm no longer inside my armor of iron. But where am I?

INES: Certainly, I understand you, Sire, for duties of State they're beyond me! So is the future of Christendom! Christendom is within us. But why, then, do you hold against Don Pedro an indifference that is your own also?

FERRANTE: I have reached the age of indifference. Pedro has not. What's one to do with one's life if one doesn't busy oneself with those sorts of things?

INES: Love. I should like to bury myself in the deepest retreat of mutual and lawful love, as in a tomb, and then let all cease, let all cease.—But if you no longer believe in the affairs of the kingdom, there are the acts that a king can do for his people and that are simply from man to man. There is in your kingdom that great poverty, that disease of hunger which is continually in need of healing. At Lisbon, on the quay where one lands, I've seen the captains of your army, my lord. They were standing up, their backs to the wall, they had their hands joined as if in prayer, and they were following with their eyes those who were landing, without moving and without saying anything. And their hands were in fact joined for a prayer, for they were asking for alms. These were your war leaders, Sire, and they had not had their pay. And I, if I'd been the King, I should have wanted to go and unknot their hands myself and say to them; "Never more shall you feel hunger." And since that day it has seemed to me that, from now on, it is all very well for me to eat and to eat my fill, I shall always be hungry as long as they are not satisfied.

FERRANTE: People are glad enough to ask the heads of states for charity. People ought also to have a little charity for them. When one thinks of the temptations of absolute power, resistance to them calls for respect. As for your captains, if I were younger I should say that there was a disease to heal, far worse than their bodies' danger, and that is the disease of their immortal soul, which without cease hungers after sin. But at my age one has lost the taste for looking after other people. Nothing's left today but an immense: "What does it matter to me!" which for me covers the world. . . . I should like now to look after nobody but myself, at so few days' distance from appearing before God; to stop lying to others and lying to myself, and to deserve at last the respect that is given to me, after having for so long usurped it.

THE SHADE OF THE INFANTA [*at the back of the hall*]: Ines!

INES: Who is calling me?

THE SHADE: Someone who wishes you well. Leave this hall immediately. Stop listening to the King. He is throwing into you his despairing secrets, as into a tomb. Later he will slide back upon you the tombstone that you may never speak.

INES: I shall not leave the person who has said to me: "I am a king of sorrow." At that moment he was not lying. And I am not afraid of him.

THE SHADE: How you do woo your death! How you will have wooed it! Ines, Ines, remember: kings have lions in their hearts. . . . Remember: the mark of the necklace on your neck. . . .

INES: Oh, now I recognize you!

The Shade: You have never recognized me. Ines, Ines, as soon as I was out at sea, I found the words I ought to have used to convince you. Already all full of the open spaces, already my soul was beating back against the wind toward you. And a few moments from now, when it'll be too late, I shall find what I should have been saying to you now. Ah! it is frightful not to know how to convince.

Ines: She repeats forever the same cry, like the Malurus bird, at the fall of evening, above the melancholy of the lakes.

The Shade: Ines, for the last time, get away from here.—No? You will not? Very well! You too, in your turn, shall fail to convince. [*It disappears.*]

Ferrante [*his back turned to the shades*]: Do they imagine I don't hear them as they whisper and make their escape? They say that I'm delirious because I tell the truth. And they believe they are escaping out of fear of my reprisals, where they are escaping out of fear and horror of the truth. The noise of the truth alarms them like a leper's rattle.

Ines: O my King, I shall not desert you because you tell the truth, but on the contrary I too shall tell you at last the whole truth, which I have kept back a little till now. O my King, since this night is full of great things, let me at last confess it: a child of your blood is forming in me.

Ferrante: A child! Another child! So the thing will never have an end!

Ines: And what does it matter to you if he troubles your plans, since you have just cried aloud that you no longer believe in the kingly function! This is where we are going to see if you were really being truthful.

Ferrante: Another spring to begin all over again, and to begin again less well!

Ines: I, who so much love being loved, shall myself have created a human being, and it will depend entirely on me whether I can win his love! How I long to give him an idea of his mother that will keep him safe from everything all his life! One will have to be even stricter toward oneself, to guard oneself from every baseness, to live upright, firm, clear and pure, so that a human being may later retain of one the fairest possible image, tenderly and without any reproach. He is a revised version, or rather a second creation, of me; in making him I am making myself anew. I carry him in me and he carries me. I melt into him. I pour into his mold my wealth. I desire with passion that he may be like me in what is best of me.

FERRANTE: And the reproach he will bring against you is precisely that: that you wanted him to take after you. Come, I know all that.

INES: If he does not think as I do, he will be a stranger to me, he who is me. No, no. He is the dream of my blood. My blood cannot deceive me.

FERRANTE: The dream. . . . You say better than you know. You are simply dreaming.

INES: Is it mere dream, this flesh that I have created out of mine? Oh, it is heady and immense.

FERRANTE: Really one would think you were the first woman to give birth.

INES: I believe every woman who is having a child for the first time is in fact the first woman to give birth.

FERRANTE: I dislike naïveté. I hate vice and crime. But if I have to choose between them and naïveté, I believe I prefer vice and crime.

INES: It's as if I can see him, five or six years from now. Look, he's just passed us, running along the terrace. Running, but at the same time his head is turned toward us. My little boy.

FERRANTE: One day, as he passes, he will no longer turn his head. But who told you it was a boy? The astrologer?

INES: I want it too much to be so.

FERRANTE: I understand that a second Pedro must really be an intoxicating prospect.

INES: Yes, intoxicating. We shall call him Dionis. My little boy with the improbable eyelashes, handsome and coarse at the same time, as boys are. Asking to be fought with, to be danced with. Not letting himself be touched. An excess of pleasure makes him sigh. And if he isn't handsome, I'll love him even more, to console him and to ask his forgiveness for having wished him other than he is.

FERRANTE: I have known all that. How he used to kiss, that little one! We called him Pedrito (but sometimes, if he was asleep and someone whispered him his name, he would say in his sleep: "Pedrito? Who's that?") His incomprehensible affection! If I teased him, if I made fun of him, if I scolded him, he used to answer everything by throwing himself on me and embracing me. And he used to look at me long, close to, with an astonished expression. . . .

INES: Already!

FERRANTE: At first I was embarrassed. Later I accepted it. I accepted his knowing what I am like. He used to get on my nerves a little when he used to romp with me. But when he no longer did that— For he has become a man—that is to say, the caricature of what he was. You too will see the self-undoing of what was your child. To the point where no more of him is left in you than there is left of that sheet of paper on which for the first time, when five years old, mine wrote his Christian name, that sheet of paper which I preserved for years and finally tore up and threw to the wind.

INES: But one day, perhaps, if you had kept it, you would have wept on seeing it again.

FERRANTE: No, neither their delicate words nor their delicate ways save human beings at the hour of the great settlings of accounts.

INES: I consent to being obliged to despise the whole world, but not my son. I think I should be capable of killing him if he did not answer to what I expect of him.

FERRANTE: Then kill him as soon as he comes out of you.

Give him to the pigs to eat. For as surely as through him you are not rapt in dreams, you will through him be rapt in nightmare.

INES: Sire, it is sinful of you to curse this child, who is of your own blood.

FERRANTE: I like discouraging. And I do not like the future.

INES: The child who is going to be born has already his past.

FERRANTE: Nightmare for you. Nightmare for him too. One day people will tear him to pieces, people will speak ill of him. . . . Oh, I know all that.

INES: Is it possible for people to speak ill of my child?

FERRANTE: People will detest him—

INES: People will detest him, him who never asked to be born!

FERRANTE: He will suffer, he will weep—

INES: You have the art of finding the words that are made for destroying hope!—How hold back his tears, take them upon me, make them flow in me? I can bear everything; I can suffer in his place, weep in his place. But he! Oh, how I wish my love had the power to put into his life an everlasting smile! Already, though, they're attacking it, this love of mine. They disapprove of me, they give me advice, they claim to be better mothers than I am. And here are you, Sire —not content with that!—upon this love of mine you have just cast anathema. Whereas it seemed to me sometimes that if men knew how much I love my child, perhaps that would be enough to make hatred dry up forever in their hearts. For I, ever since I've been carrying him in me, I've felt in myself a wonderful power of tenderness toward mankind. And he is the defense of that deep region of my being from which there springs all that I can give to creation and to God's creatures. His purity defends mine. His candor safeguards mine against those who would destroy it. You know against whom, my lord.

FERRANTE: His purity is only a moment of him, it is not himself. Women are always saying: "Why bring up a child to be killed in war!" But there is something still worse: to bring up a child that he may live and degrade himself in living. And you, Ines, you seem to have staked a singular amount on his living. Have you looked at yourself in a mirror? You are indeed fresh, for someone menaced by great suffering. You too are part of all those things that want to go on, to go on. . . . You too, like me, are ill: your illness is hope. You deserve that God should send you a terrible trial, ruin, once for all, that mad candor of yours, so that once at least you might see things as they are.

INES: My lord, it's no good, believe me, reminding me of all the things that threaten me. Whatever may seem to be sometimes, I never forget them.

FERRANTE [*aside*]: I believe I love in her the pain I give her. [*Aloud*] I am not threatening you, but I get impatient at seeing you start out afresh, all sails set, upon the inexhaustible and infinite sea of hope. Other people's faith depresses me. It takes children to believe like you in the void, without being depressing. Hope! Lourenço Payva too, at this moment, is full of hopes. And yet he's going to die, a sacrifice to the good of the State.

INES: Die! Is it then decided?

FERRANTE: Yes, a moment ago it was decided.

INES: Die! And for the State! Your Majesty can still talk of the State!

FERRANTE: And why not? Ah! I see, you are thinking of how I said I did not believe in the State. I did say that, in fact. But I said also that I wished to act as if I did believe in it. Sometimes you forget, sometimes you remember too well, Doña Ines. I advise you not to remember too well the things I said during that sort of crisis of sincerity when those rascals were making their escape so as not to hear me.

INES: Perhaps I should have made my escape too.

FERRANTE: It's the fate of men who constrain themselves excessively that a day comes when nature snaps; they burst forth then and pour forth all at once what they have held back for years. From which it follows that, all in all, it's useless to be discreet.

INES: Sire, since Your Majesty from now on knows of the existence of my child—

FERRANTE: That's enough about that child. You've displayed your vitals before me, and you've gone looking for mine, which is tactless. You've made use of your future child to stir my past child. You've thought it clever to make your maternity known to me at this moment, and you have been the reverse of clever.

INES: So Your Majesty is reproaching me with not having been clever!

FERRANTE: Yes, I'm reproaching you with that.

INES: I have not "thought it clever." I have talked to you of your grandson at a moment when you were suffering, when you were weak, not to profit from that weakness, but because then you were telling the truth. I wanted also to tell you the truth, and to give you back trust for trust. I put trust in human nature in you, just as I have put trust in it all my life. Let me have trust in you, Sire. Would it not be a fine thing to be able to say to you: "O King like a hand upon my forehead—"? You never put trust in man, you?

FERRANTE: I sometimes put trust in his fear.

INES: I've never been able to believe that man, save some rare exceptions, could render misdeeds for generosity. You are perhaps astonished, Sire, that I am not afraid of you. But, at those times when one is doubtful of a person, when one is tempted to be afraid of him—at those times when people were putting me on my guard against you—I kept saying to myself: "No, the father of the man I love, to whom I've never wished or done anything but good, will not do anything against me." And besides, if one must be punished simply for having trusted too much, well, it can't be helped: one is punished by men, but one isn't before God. There,

Sire, that's why I am not and cannot be very much afraid of you, although I've long been vaguely afraid of *something*.

FERRANTE: I see that you are very conscious of your generosity, and that you expect a reward for it. But enough of that. Out of all you have said to me, I retain the fact that you believe you have surprised me at a moment of weakness. What a joy it doubtless is being able to tell yourself, as women do: "King though he is, he's just a poor man like the others!" What a triumph for you! But I am not weak, Doña Ines. It's a great mistake you are making, you and one or two others. Now I must ask you to withdraw. For a good hour you've been circling around me, like a butterfly around a flame. All women, I've noticed, are obstinate circlers around the thing that's destined to burn them.

INES: Are you going to burn me, Sire? Little as I am worth, there are two human beings who have need of me. It's for their sake that I must live.—And besides, for my sake too, oh yes, for my own sake!—But—your face has changed; you look ill at ease. . . .

FERRANTE: Excuse me, being alone with good people always makes me rather awkward. Come, let's break off there, and you go home to the Mondego reassured.

INES: Yes, you would never kill me before I'd embraced him once more.

FERRANTE: My only fear for you is of the bandits on the road, at this hour. Is your escort numerous?

INES: Four only.

FERRANTE: And armed?

INES: Barely. But the night is light and free of ambushes. Look. It will be fine tomorrow: the sky is full of stars.

FERRANTE: All those worlds which have not had the Redemption. . . . Do you see the ladder?

INES: The ladder?

FERRANTE: The ladder that goes right up into the heavens.

INES: Jacob's ladder, you mean?

FERRANTE: No, not at all: the ladder from hell to heaven. I, all my life I've done nothing but make that climb; all the time going up and coming down, between hell and heaven. For, with all my sins, I've none the less lived enveloped by the hand of God. Another strange thing.

INES: Oh! There's a star that has gone out.

FERRANTE: It will light up again elsewhere.

SCENE VII

FERRANTE, *then* A GUARD,
then CAPTAIN BATALHA

FERRANTE: Why am I killing her? There is doubtless a reason, but I cannot pick it out. Not only will Pedro not marry the Infanta, but I'm arming him against me, irredeemably. I'm adding yet another danger to this horrible mantle of dangers which I drag about on me and after me, always heavier, always more loaded, and I load myself at will, and under its weight one day— Ah! death, which puts at last out of reach— Why am I killing her? Useless action, fatal action. But my will is driving me before its wind, and I'm committing the error, knowing that it is one. Well, at least, let me get rid of this action straightaway. Remorse is better than prolonged hesitation. [*Calling*] Page!—Oh no! Not a page. Guard! [*Enter a guard.*] Call me Captain Batalha. [*Alone*] The more I measure the injustice and atrocity of what I'm doing, the more deeply I plunge into it, because it gives me the more pleasure. [*Enter the captain.*] Captain, Doña Ines de Castro is leaving here and making for the Mondego, with four men of her own, ill armed. Take some men, catch up with her, and strike. It's cruel, but it's necessary. And take care not to bungle your business. People have all sorts of tricks for not dying. And do the thing at one blow. There are people it's wrong to kill at one blow: it's too quick. Her at one blow. On my soul, I want her not to suffer.

THE CAPTAIN: I've just seen the lady go past. From the look of her, she was a long way from imagining—

FERRANTE: I had reassured her forever.

THE CAPTAIN: Should I take with me a confessor?

FERRANTE: No point. Her soul is as smooth as her face. [*The captain makes to go.*] Captain, take men who are reliable.

THE CAPTAIN [*pointing to his sword*]: This is reliable.

FERRANTE: Nothing can be too reliable when killing's to be done. Bring back the body and put it in the palace oratory. Painful as it may be, I shall have to see it myself. A person's never dead until one's seen the body dead with one's own eyes, and until one's touched it. Alas, I know all about that. [*Exit the captain.*] There would still be time for me to give a counter-order. But could I? What invisible gag is it stopping me from giving the shout that would save her? [*He goes and looks out of the window.*] It will be fine tomorrow: the sky is full of stars. . . . There would still be time.—Still. Multitudes of acts, for year after year, are born of a single act, of a single instant. Why?—Still. When she was looking out at the stars, her eyes were like calm lakes. . . . And to think people believe I'm weak! [*With sudden tenseness*] Oh!—Now it is too late. I have given her eternal life, and I—I shall be able to breathe.—Guards! Bring lights! Tell everyone you can find in the palace to come in. Here, what are you waiting for? Lights! Lights! Nothing here has happened in the dark. Come in, gentlemen, come in!

SCENE VIII

FERRANTE, PALACE PEOPLE, *of every condition,* EGAS COELHO *among them*

FERRANTE: Gentlemen, Doña Ines de Castro is no more. She informed me of the approaching birth of a bastard of the Prince. I have had her executed to preserve the purity of the succession to the throne and to end the trouble and the scandal she was causing in my realm. That is my final and weighty justice. Such a decision is not taken without pain. Beyond this unfortunate woman I have my kingdom, I have my people, I have my souls; I have the burden God has entrusted to me, and I have the contract I made with my peoples, when I consented to be king. A king is like a huge tree which must cast shade. . . . [*He passes his hand over his forehead and staggers.*] Oh! I think the saber of God has passed above my head. . . .

[*A seat is brought, and he is made to sit.*]

EGAS COELHO: My King!—Quick, get a doctor!

FERRANTE: I've finished lying.

EGAS COELHO: Don't die, for heaven's sake! [*Aside*] If Pedro's King, I'm lost.

FERRANTE: Now I'm no longer asking you for your secret. Mine is enough for me. I'm leaving you in peace.

EGAS COELHO: You're leaving me in hell. But no, you're not going to die, are you?

FERRANTE: In a moment I shall be dead, and my son's paw will have come down on you.

EGAS COELHO: Ines is perhaps not dead. A note, scribble a note. . . . I'll try and catch up with them on the road.

FERRANTE: She is dead. God has told me. And you, you're dead too.

Egas Coelho: No! No! It's not possible!

Ferrante: They'll tear your heart out of your breast and show it to you.

Egas Coelho: No! No! No!

Ferrante: Before breathing your last you shall see your own heart.

Egas Coelho [*haggard*]: Who has told you?

Ferrante: God has told me.

Egas Coelho: Don't push me to despair.

Ferrante: Other people's despair can no longer frighten me.

Egas Coelho: Live, my King, live, I beseech you!

Ferrante: You don't know yet that at a pinch I can give way to someone who doesn't beseech me; never to one who beseeches me.

Egas Coelho. Live! You must live!

Ferrante: Draw away from me, Egas. Your breath's in my face. And I don't like it.

Egas Coelho: Then let me escape. Live a little while! Only a little while! Long enough for me to escape. . . . [*To all present*] Living flesh and blood, my companions, you who will go on living, isn't there one of you that wants me to remain alive? [*Silence.*] So there's no one who wants me to live? [*Silence.*]

Ferrante [*taking him by the wrist*]: Gentlemen, I do not know how the future will judge the execution of Doña Ines. Perhaps as a good thing, perhaps as a bad. However that may be, here is the man who, before everyone else, inspired it. See that he answers for it before the King my son. [*Some of those present surround Egas Coelho.*] O my God! In this respite which is left me, before the saber passes again and strikes me down, make it cut this appalling knot of contradictions within me, so that, at least for one instant before ceasing to be, I may at last know what I am. [*He pulls Dino del Moro to him and holds him clasped against him.*] May the innocence of this child serve me for safeguard when I am about to appear before my Judge.—Have no fear, and stay close to me, whatever happens—even if I die. . . . God shall requite you for it, God shall requite you for it, my little brother.—Much better and much worse.—When I revive—Oh, the saber! The saber!—My God, have mercy on me! [*He falls in a heap.*]

[*Extreme confusion. Various voices:*] The King is dead!—Let's go and set Don Pedro free!—Long live King Pedro! [*Scuffles. Some of the grandees are stopped from going out.*] No, you shan't go out!—Shut the door of the King's private room!—Find the key to the desk!—Someone arrest Alvar Gonçalves!—[*In the midst of this tumult Ines, dead, is brought in on a litter. The tumult at once dies down. In silence all leave on one side the corpse of the King where it sprawls on the ground and mass together on the other side of the stage around the litter, kneeling on one knee, with the exception of Dino del Moro, who, after a gesture of hesitation, has knelt down near the King. At this moment there appears Don Pedro; he throws himself upon the litter, sobbing. At the extreme right the corpse of King Ferrante sprawls, with nobody near it except the Andalusian page-boy kneeling by its side. The page-boy steals a look, several times, in the direction of the group of people in prayer. At last he rises and goes over, he too, to kneel among them. The dead body of the King lies there alone.*]

CURTAIN

MALATESTA

⚜

A Play in Four Acts

CHARACTERS

SIGISMONDO PANDOLFO MALATESTA, *Lord of Rimini, aged 51*

PORCELLIO PANDONE, *man of letters at the court of Malatesta, aged 39*

POPE PAUL II, *aged 60*

BASINIO PARMENSE, *man of letters at the court of Malatesta*

PLATINA, *man of letters, member of the Roman Academy, aged 63*

VENIERI VARRANO, *Lord of Camerino, Malatesta's son-in-law, aged 21*

GASPARE BROGLIO, *captain in the household of Malatesta*

FEDERIGO DA MELDOLA, *captain in the household of Malatesta*

SACRAMORO, *fencing-master in the household of Malatesta*

CARDINAL RODRIGO BORGIA (*later Pope Alexander VI*), *aged 37*

MONSIGNOR PERUGIA, *Papal Secretary*

BENEDETTO DE NARNI

CLAUDIO SCARAMPA

THE CARDINAL OF PAVIA

CARDINAL MARCANOVA

FIRST PAPAL CHAMBERLAIN

SECOND PAPAL CHAMBERLAIN

CINQUEDENTI, *servant in Malatesta's household*

A SERGEANT

ISOTTA DA RIMINI, *Malatesta's wife, aged 45*

VANNELLA, *aged 13*
ALOYSIA, *a nurse, carrying the little* CONTESSINA *in her arms*

CARDINALS, OFFICERS, COURTIERS, ECCLESIASTICS, MEN-AT-ARMS, RUNNERS, *etc.*

At Rimini and in Rome, June to October 1468

ACT I

AT RIMINI, *in the Rocca Malatestiana, a fortified castle of the Malatestas, the room used by Sigismond Pandolfo Malatesta.*

A bed with curtains, two cassoni, *a dresser with bound manuscripts and two classical sculptures. A table and chairs. On the bare, rough walls, some pieces of gold brocade, some arms, armor, packsaddle panniers, and military harness. The impression given by the place is sober and rather feudal.*

Through the window one can see the top of a tower and a stretch of battlements, ocher-colored, and on the horizon the blue-tinged buttresses of the mountains of San Marino.

Doors right and left.

SCENE I

MALATESTA, SACRAMORO

[*As the curtain rises, the stage is empty, and it remains so for quite a long while. Then, just outside the garden door, are heard gasps for breath and broken and spluttered words. Through the door appears part of a man clinched in a wrestling-hold, then his whole body, then the bodies of two men in a clinch, with daggers in their hands. Thus struggling, they get onto the stage, foot by foot.*]

MALATESTA: Look, that's the pass with which I killed Malipiero! Look, and that's the one with which I would have burst his warts for Messer Federigo of Urbino, if he had accepted the single combat to which I challenged him, but he got out of it, the worm!

SACRAMORO: Twenty gods! My lord, I'm not letting you burst my warts! It's I who am telling you: "Parry that one!" —Hey! if I hadn't held my hand back?

MALATESTA: On guard! [*They attack.*] This time I'll chop up your genitals. I'll chop them up and eat them for my dinner!

SACRAMORO: A-y, mother!

MALATESTA: Better say: "A-y, wife!"—Stop! Let's break off and have a drink. I can see over there a little mug making signs at me. For a good while already it's been asking me why I don't do it the honor of emptying it.

[*He drinks, then offers the goblet to Sacramoro. As he is pouring himself out a drink, Malatesta hurls himself on him.*]

SACRAMORO: Ah, my lord, that's a bit of cheating worth putting in a book!

MALATESTA: I detest people who are trusting.

[*Onslaught.*]

SCENE II

THE SAME, PORCELLIO, BASINIO

[*Porcellio and Basinio are in dark clothes, with tortoise-shell-rimmed spectacles.*]

MALATESTA [*grasping Sacramoro by the neck and pressing the dagger under his armpit*]: Is that how you like it? Are you already seeing God the Father with all His angels?

SACRAMORO: Ah! ah! ah! Ah! ah! ah! My lord, stop!

MALATESTA: I don't know what's holding me back, really. . . . I don't know what's holding me back.

SACRAMORO: Enough, enough! For pity's sake!

PORCELLIO: My lord, I do think you're gripping him a bit tight, and he's suffering cruelly.

MALATESTA: You learned your fencing from a cooper. Bungler! Oh, what a temptation to kill you!

BASINIO: My lord, I swear to you, if you go on you'll finish him off for good.

[*Malatesta lets go Sacramoro, who staggers a few paces, then collapses on the ground.*]

MALATESTA: What, dead? The idiot! He never understood a joke.

PORCELLIO [*after feeling Sacramoro*]: He's breathing.

MALATESTA: You there on duty! Take away this muck.

SCENE III

MALATESTA, PORCELLIO, BASINIO

BASINIO: Watching you at that wonderful piece of gymnastics, I was saying to myself, my lord, that at forty-nine—

PORCELLIO [*under his breath*]: Fifty-one—

BASINIO: —you had the same vigor and the same suppleness as when, at twelve—twelve years old!—in front of Rimini you personally mustered a troop of men, you crossed the Foglia under cover of night, and you fell upon the enemy camp and broke it up!

MALATESTA: In those days my glory was young; it sang and burnished its wings in the first morning sunshine. And yet it seems to me that from then onwards I, whose destiny it was to be a man of war, thought as I do today that all the warlike exploits in the world are not worth a fine sonnet or a fine harangue or a fine moral maxim.

PORCELLIO: On the predominance of the spirit I have said all there is to be said in Book III of my *De excellentia hominus:* the subject is henceforth exhausted. [*Pause.*] Your lordship doesn't remember? One would really think your lordship has read nothing of what I have written!

MALATESTA: But I do remember, Porcellio. It's an unforgettable page.

PORCELLIO: There are several pages!

MALATESTA: I am going to the Four Winds Tower, to inspect our new mortar.

SCENE IV

PORCELLIO, BASINIO, *and, in a moment,* CINQUEDENTI

PORCELLIO: What a savage! And note that he had a sort of friendship for that Sacramoro. That gives an idea of what is waiting for us the day when the mood takes him to have a joke with us.

BASINIO: My dear colleague, we are hired literary men, let us never lose sight of that. We get board and lodgings, the run of a good library, the protection of a man who is powerful and on occasion generous. In exchange what is required of us? To praise the Prince in every circumstance, to write poems that are supposed to be the work of our mistress, Donna Isotta, who can scarcely sign her name—

PORCELLIO: And to compose—this is my portion—the monumental biography of the new Alexander, *Vita Magnifici et Clarissimi Sigismundi de Malatestis*, a work that is made perceptibly easier for me by the fact that the hero himself dictates the greater part of it. In the times in which we live, and perhaps in all times, since nothing is verified and everything is done lightly and without conscience, why the devil shouldn't one be a fraud? Facts wholly fabricated, false evidence, altered dates, imaginary quotations, forward! I guarantee you success and total impunity.

BASINIO: And in return, at the same time, we do risk getting ourselves hacked to pieces by the hero, in one of his moments of gaiety. On the other hand, he protects us from the other heroes. You know that, you who owe the Lord of Rimini your escape from the enterprise of certain excited persons who are decidedly dangerous. And when your compatriots asked him to extradite you, he made them a present, in your stead, of a hippopotamus; that was nice of him. In fact, my dear colleague, if you are alive, it is thanks to Sigismondo.

PORCELLIO: His good turns were done not for my sake but for my talent, which he wanted to have on his side; and so they don't count. I am, though, reasonably grateful to him for them. Not wildly grateful, reasonably grateful. All the same, it's well known that certain people can shower us with marks of their friendship without managing to win ours. It's galling for them, but I'm powerless against nature.

BASINIO: At one time you felt a real attachment to him; don't deny it. You used to speak of him with warmth and take up his defense against all comers.

PORCELLIO: It's true, but that has gone sour. I should have to explain you a lot of things. . . .

BASINIO: I've several times seen his hands tremble when he was touching very beautiful objects: because of that I sometimes feel a gust of sympathy for him.

PORCELLIO: Sacramoro too has found out by experience that Malatesta has nervous hands.

BASINIO: Sigismondo isn't merely, what nobody contests, a master when it comes to war: the little lord of a petty territory who only gave in before an alliance of most of the powers of Italy. He's a man of remarkable wit and real culture. Look here, I know nothing that could be more to his credit than that Latin letter he wrote me, in a style worthy of Cicero, just as he was striking camp in front of Cesano, in critical circumstances, when by a hair's breadth he missed falling into the hands of Messer Federigo. An epistle like that bears witness equally to his erudition and to his firmness of character.

PORCELLIO: I don't think much of the culture of a person who doesn't respect culture in others.

BASINIO: What do you mean?

PORCELLIO: Sigismondo has no respect for my work. He sends for me when I am in the full tide of inspiration, fixes me audiences at the sixteenth hour without caring whether such a time cuts up and disorders my whole working afternoon. Much worse— But no, my friend, these are things one is too ashamed—

BASINIO: What things?

PORCELLIO: He has even sometimes given me manuscripts to copy! No, he doesn't like my culture, he likes my services. He is not generous.

BASINIO: No more are you, my dear colleague, generosity is not your strong point.

PORCELLIO: When one has given to mankind what I have given through my work, one is quits.

BASINIO: You have started to write your chapter *On Revolutions*?

Porcellio: Started and finished. I am even going to read it to you. [*He pulls some sheets of paper out of his pocket.*]

Basinio: My dear man, tomorrow, do you mind? Just now my own work calls me.

Porcellio: The chapter is very short. [*At this moment the servant Cinquedenti comes in, but, seeing Porcellio preparing to read, stops on tiptoe. Porcellio reads.*] *On Revolutions.* "Revolutions waste a great deal of time."

[*A silence.*]

Basinio: Yes. And what then?

Porcellio: That's all. That's all the chapter.

Basinio: Better still: troubled times waste a great deal of time. Half one's life is spent on saving one's neck. So much the less for the things that matter.

Porcellio: And you, Cinquedenti, what do you think of revolutions?

Cinquedenti: They say revolutions give us the chance to put to death the people we don't like, or at least to take their place when it's a good one, or simply to give them a very bad time. They say, even, that that's the only use they have. But I—it's just my luck!—there aren't any people I wish ill, and revolutions are wasted on me.

Porcellio: Poor Cinquedenti! But tell me, what did you come about?

Cinquedenti: I came to tell my lord that Captain Sacramoro is all right and is going home. He wishes to say that he'll be there for the fencing-bout tomorrow at nine sharp. [*He goes out.*]

Porcellio: Sharp! Well, that's really what is called sticking one's neck out. The throttled man asking for more. Ah, to be free! Free!

Basinio: "It takes slaves to make such a fuss about freedom." One of our authors has coined that admirable phrase. You know whose it is?

Porcellio: Yours?

BASINIO: Of course. It's one of the most profound things I've written. But after all, my friend, if we are Sigismondo's employees, Sigismondo is only an employee of the princes who use him as condottiere. He receives a wage, haggles over contracts, asks for rises and advances, is beset by his lords and masters in the shape of liaison officers, supply officers, ambassadors, all of them there to spy on him, and is obliged, every time the tether jerks, to come back for orders, submit accounts, and give explanations; if they are not found satisfactory, he risks getting his neck chopped, as Venice did to its condottiere Carmagnola, and as Siena would have done to him if he had not fled in time. At this moment, with the campaign in the Morea finished, he is out of a job and is throwing out feelers toward Ferdinand of Naples, like a sponging juggler who wants to get invited to a castle. Not to mention his treasury, which is not very well filled.

PORCELLIO: I knew all that, but you have done me good by reminding me.

BASINIO: The reason for his flourish over Sacramoro? He felt he could still inspire fear: and that pleases him. From a certain point of view, Sigismondo is to be pitied.

PORCELLIO: Never mind, it would be better for us to be ruled by Donna Isotta alone. How well off we were when Sigismondo was in the Morea! Donna Isotta has as much wit as virtue, and a cool head too. With her, no need to fear the whims or the rushes of blood of her animal of a husband.

BASINIO: Donna Isotta took fifteen years to get married: that trains a lady. She had to develop modesty, and she has kept some of it, in spite of the idolatrous lucubrations with which Sigismondo, and we at his orders, have besieged her.

PORCELLIO: If our Sigismondo died, do you know what would happen? His eldest son is in the Morea, Roberto's a weakling, the others are too young. Either the Pope or Venice would have little trouble in getting their hands on Rimini, and something tells me that they would leave Donna Isotta as regent.

She is popular here; it would be the best way of keeping the town at peace.

BASINIO: Sigismondo will perhaps be assassinated in an hour's time. That men of this kind remain alive is a continual miracle.

PORCELLIO: You should add: a continual provocation. And he won't die just like that! His egoism gives him the solidity of a rock. His terrible assurance disarms evil destiny. Even when things are going badly for him, there's nothing but feasting within him. You heard what he said, yesterday evening: "If people knew all the things I have done, for which I haven't been punished and ought to have been, they would see then that it's self-evident that I am protected by the gods." "If people knew all the things I've done!" Ah, how he deserves that people should find out the horrible things he's done and they don't yet know of, and that he should be punished for them appallingly!

BASINIO: Ha! A mouse. At home I'm infested by them. I killed another of them just now.

PORCELLIO: When one's an intellectual, one kills what one can. When one's a man who's never had any blood on him except the blood of his fleas—

SCENE V

THE SAME, MALATESTA

BASINIO: My lord, Sacramoro sends word that he is alive, and that he will come tomorrow morning at nine sharp to let himself be throttled again.

MALATESTA: Good.—I have seen the engines and I have sent for my charming son-in-law, who didn't have time for a chat with me yesterday evening; he was dancing almost as soon as he'd dismounted after his ride from Rome. So we are going to have fresh news from Rome.—Gentlemen, till dinner. It is quite a long while since I read Thucydides. I was taking a look just now, and I found the fourth chapter so magnificent that I should like you to converse with me about it this evening with your usual knowledge and taste. I shall never become tired of learning something from you.

SCENE VI

MALATESTA, CAMERINO

MALATESTA: Well, young Venieri? I am pleased to see you. I was watching you dancing yesterday, when you'd hardly had time to wash off the dust and fatigue of the journey: you were still as fresh and charming as you used to be; you looked like Bacchus in India. Talk to me about Rome. Afterwards you shall talk to me about my daughter; you shall tell me if she is still my lovely daughter, and if she still gives you pleasure.

CAMERINO: Yes, let's talk first about Rome. My lord father, I've a piece of good news to announce to you.

MALATESTA: Good for whom? For you?

CAMERINO: For you.

MALATESTA: Ah, bravo! Does that mean you are bringing me money?

CAMERINO: Unfortunately, no.

MALATESTA: Then everything you are going to say to me is of no consequence.

CAMERINO: The Holy Father has made me his messenger and has charged me first to fold you in a most large embrace. He next said to me: "We have had a good thought for our dear son Sigismondo. We shall disclose it to you, as to one in whom we have entire confidence."

MALATESTA: To the point, please. You are throwing me into extreme anxiety.

CAMERINO: Here it is. The Holy Father has asked me to transmit to you a most advantageous proposition.—Advantageous for you.

MALATESTA: To the point! To the point!

CAMERINO: The Holy Father offers you Spoleto and Foligno!

MALATESTA: No less than that! Against what?

CAMERINO: Against nothing.

MALATESTA: Hmm. . . . Spoleto and Foligno, those pearls! Can it be that people are beginning to recognize my services? That is not credible.

CAMERINO: I should like also to put before you a desire of the Pope's.

MALATESTA: Ah. There is a desire. . . . I don't like people's desires.

CAMERINO: The Holy Father remains anxious about the presence here of the Venetian troops called in by Donna Isotta to guard Rimini while you were in the Morea. He is afraid that Venice, being already at Ravenna, may intervene in the affairs of Rimini.

MALATESTA: I don't understand. That matter is settled. On the request that the Pope made to me, I have pressed Venice to recall its troops. Venice has promised to do so. This recall is going to be carried out immediately. And the Pope knows all that.

CAMERINO: Venice is always eager to get a foothold in other people's territory; will it not seek to dig itself in?

MALATESTA: What are you leading up to?

CAMERINO: His Holiness would like to send you some Papal troops.

MALATESTA: But, the devil take me! I've no need of the Pope's troops.

CAMERINO: The Pope is convinced that you have great need of them.

[*A pause.*]

MALATESTA: Venieri, what is the meaning of that? Is it—is it that the Pope would claim to impose his troops on Rimini?

CAMERINO: I am imparting to you simply an offer. And Spoleto and Foligno are capital cities.

MALATESTA: Yes, Spoleto. . . . But what is your meaning? What is your meaning?

CAMERINO: The Pope considers that it is inevitable that one day you will have to cede Rimini to Venice if you are left alone to defend it.

MALATESTA: And therefore? And therefore?

CAMERINO: Therefore Spoleto and Foligno.

MALATESTA: Accept Spoleto and Foligno and give up Rimini to the Pope! That's it, isn't it? Well then, out with it, wretch! So that monstrosity is what the Pope wants? Rimini of my vitals! Rimini of my birth and of my youth, Rimini of my loves and of my spirit, Rimini of my eternal life! Give up Rimini, when I should like to place a crown upon her head! Rimini, which makes my heart contract when I think of her. . . . And that's the proposition you dare to make to me, with that same mouth with which you kiss my daughter. How much did you get for making it to me? Ah, would to heaven my daughter had died instead of marrying you! The best son-in-law is the tomb.

CAMERINO: Everyone is leagued against you. That is not enough for you; you must needs risk making one more enemy, of me, who wish you nothing but good. It's a vice in you, this seeking to make yourself odious, my lord father.

MALATESTA: Because everyone is against me, is that a reason why I should accept insults? Leave Rimini within the hour; if you stayed, the very stones would rise of their own accord to stone you. [*He pushes him out.*] Great God, to what purpose have I done all that I have done? If I have done all that I have done in the fifty-one years I have been on earth, and if they treat me like this, at the end of all that I have done I have lived and I have done in vain.

[*He throws himself on the bed and begins to tremble. He trembles convulsively; his jaws chatter. He can be heard saying:* "Oh, may he rot! . . ." *then:* "My soul hurts. . . ." *After a moment he goes to look for a cape and spreads it over his body. Suddenly he sits upright. His face is distorted, and he is no longer trembling. He rings a hand-bell. To the servant who appears:* "Go and look for Ser Porcellio."]

SCENE VII

MALATESTA, PORCELLIO

MALATESTA: Porcellio, your hour is come. [*Porcellio starts.*] I mean: the great hour of your life has come. A humiliation has just been inflicted on me that surpasses any infliction on me since I began to exist. Porcellio, there is in Rome a man who must disappear: if he survives, I shall die of his life. You will make your way to Rome, install yourself there under some pretext which we shall think out together, and use against the man in question that art of which you have written so well.

PORCELLIO: Which art? I've written well about a great many things?

MALATESTA: The art of giving people indigestion.

PORCELLIO: I, my lord, I'd kill willingly. If only in order to act like everyone else. Only here's the trouble: I'm scared of the consequences.

MALATESTA: The enterprise is of sublime greatness. The man to be killed is the Pope.

PORCELLIO: The Pope!

MALATESTA: I wish I could bite him. I wish I had poison in my teeth and could bite him. I wish I could see him go through the death agony while I held him in my teeth.

PORCELLIO: Lord Malatesta, you are offering me a task for which nature never made me.

MALATESTA: You have written about poisons, and about the art of using them.

PORCELLIO: I am made for describing things, not for executing them, like the illustrious Demosthenes, of whom Plutarch said that he was fitter for praising the virtues of ancestors than for imitating them. A murder! That is not the domain of the spirit.

MALATESTA: The spirit is not made for limiting, but for liberating.

PORCELLIO: It is madness to confine oneself to a half-vengeance when it's possible to kill without risk. But in this it would be more than a risk, it would be suicide.

MALATESTA: All right! You will die for me. Thousands of my soldiers have died for me, and were prepared to do so. But you, you are not willing!

PORCELLIO: If I die, the biography of the divine Malatesta will remain unfinished.

MALATESTA: I shall have it continued by Basinio.

PORCELLIO: Basinio! Your lordship! Are you saying that seriously? Ah, that would be to die twice over!—I should add that there's my brother-in-law, whom I'm expecting at Rimini, as you know, for that inheritance business.

MALATESTA: A brother-in-law! An inheritance! At the moment when you are being presented with the chance to perform an act whose stature antiquity could not parallel! But you must be without any ambition! And I, I couldn't shake hands with one who has no ambition, and inadvertently I've so many times shaken yours.—Besides, I want someone who advances when I advance, stops when I stop, never goes more than three paces away, and none the less never lets it appear that he has any fault to find with this state of life. Those are the men I need. Not men with brothers-in-law and inheritances.—Forgive me if I'm a bit abrupt with you. I must admit I am beside myself.

Porcellio: I have an idea. The Pope's young nephew, Riario, whom the Pope cherishes so tenderly, is dying in Rome of a mysterious illness. I will write in your biography that it was you who had him poisoned, to avenge yourself on the Pope. In that way you will have the honor of this death without having the risk. What matters is not what happened, it's what is believed to have happened. A moment comes when anything is true.

Malatesta: At other times I should relish the subtlety of your invention. At this one I need something solid. You are just like the others: you always offer me what doesn't give me pleasure. But as for what would give me pleasure— And all that from cowardice. What dominates in you, and I've certainly proved it, is ignoble cowardice.

Porcellio: Ah, my lord, you have put your finger on my intimate sin. But don't let's speak ill of cowardice. Cowardice pays, since we are alive.

Malatesta: We are alive above all because of the cowardice of others. What am I to do with you? I used to call you my friend, but what's the use of having friends if they draw back every time they are required to aid you in your misdeeds? What is a man who isn't an accomplice? A dead weight, a ghost, a void. . . .

Porcellio: There are accomplices and accomplices. In an enterprise like this, my clumsiness would cause you untold trouble. One of my fellow writers said of me that I had no power of decision except when the issue was flight. That's a great exaggeration. But the fact remains that presence of mind is not my strong point. You know it rarely goes along with high intelligence, which the best authors hold to be of its very nature irresolute. Besides, after all, my lord, to kill a pope! . . . Even professional assassins have never tackled that.

MALATESTA: Oh, please, Porcellio, don't drag in virtue and vice!

PORCELLIO: It's not a question of virtue and vice, it's a question of damnation.

MALATESTA: The man who acts toward me as the Pope is acting proves that he is the most perverted of men. He who kills him is only forestalling divine justice; he is in a way the instrument of Heaven. Besides, do you believe in God?

PORCELLIO: As a reasonable man, I do not believe in God. As a baptized Christian, I am bound to believe. Not to mention that, generally speaking, I always believe what is believed by the strongest.

MALATESTA: Ah, Ser Porcellio, you disappoint me.

PORCELLIO: And you also, my dear lord, you also, you— Leaving it to another man to take your vengeance is like putting your young wife into another man's arms on your wedding night. Neither Brutus, nor Harmodius and Aristogiton, nor Diocles of Megara yielded to anyone the glory of killing in their place. This glory must remain yours, you have no right to dispose of it. Nobody has stabbed a pope! Nogaro * only slapped the face of Boniface VIII, and merely for that his memory survives.

MALATESTA: Very difficult of execution.

PORCELLIO: The greater the difficulty, the greater the glory. Besides, what one reckons difficult often turns out easy, because one has thought it over maturely, whereas one doesn't give thought to what one takes to be easy, and so one stumbles.

MALATESTA: The risk is immense. You saw that all right when it was a question of your taking it. You don't see it any more now that it is a question of me.

PORCELLIO: Because you, you will always get away. Re-

* It was in fact a Frenchman, Guillaume de Nogaret.

member what the Venetian Ambassador used to say to me last year: "That fellow will always fall on his feet."

Malatesta: "That fellow!" What disrespect! Am I sixteen?

Porcellio: You are a magnificent demon, and demons are always sixteen.

Malatesta: Ah, Porcellio, what a temptation you are offering me! You are the demon.

Porcellio: That temptation, my dear lord, was already in yourself; my part has only been to reveal it to you.

Malatesta: No, Porcellio, no, my friend, I'll be frank with you; that idea hadn't come to me. Yes, incredible as it may seem, seeing that I hardly ever let the world forget me, there are moments when Malatesta forgets Malatesta. But you, you have been more Malatesta than I myself. Yes, you alone understand me. Basinio is an excellent man of letters, but he does not feel my greatness. I revere Anastagi as a Latinist, but he spreads around him an atmosphere of honesty that is unbreathable.—Yes, I am the man the Pope shall see in the instant when he renders up that dreadful soul of his: how could I have imagined anything else? I am the man who shall acquire that immortal glory. All that I have done till that day is effaced.

[*Enter Isotta. Porcellio retires.*]

SCENE VIII

Malatesta, Isotta

Isotta: Venieri has spoken to me.

Malatesta: The Pope will not survive. I shall leave tomorrow for Rome before dawn. I've thought already whom I shall take with me.

Isotta: To do what? To have the Pope killed?

MALATESTA: To stab him with my own hand. I liked that man, I had hopes of him. He is a disappointment to me, and disappointment is unforgiving. I have just begun to hate him. And if you are not ready to kill what you claim to hate, don't say that you hate: you are prostituting the word.

ISOTTA: The harm your hatreds will have done to you! More than to your enemies. Let's not talk of hate, let's talk of policy. The Pope dead, do you know who will succeed him? As things are, Paul II is well disposed toward you. He could not be expected to know your profound links with Rimini. He offers you two fine towns against one. It's a diplomat's proposition. Reply to it on the plane of diplomacy.

MALATESTA: If the Pope were laying siege to Rimini I should consider that fair war. But to come and bargain with me for my town, it's as if someone said to me: "Give me Donna Isotta to take to bed. I'll give you in exchange Carlotta, plus Ginevra, plus—oh, anyone."

ISOTTA: To have the Pope killed is a proposal that deserves examination. To stab him yourself is an extravagance born of a rush of delirium. You would be cut down there and then.

MALATESTA: The Pope receives me always in private audience. Before the fact is noticed, we shall be far away. Certainly the affair must be worked out. But I have seven days of travel in which to think it out with my companions.

ISOTTA: So you are bent on your death!

MALATESTA: In times like ours the risk is the same, crimes or no crimes. So best commit the crimes if they give us pleasure.—And besides, little do I care about dying if I've killed him first.

ISOTTA: My lord, when you were going out to battle, I never stopped you, never interfered. Nor on any of the innumerable occasions when you staked your life. But this time, in heaven's name, in the name of these thirty years through which I've cared for you, in the name of that strange taste which leads you to ask advice of me, come back to your senses.

You've a touch of fever. Decide nothing until your fever has abated.

MALATESTA: How do you know I have a touch of fever?

ISOTTA: I see it in your eyes.

MALATESTA: I've had a touch of fever, you're right, ever since Venieri spoke to me. You always see in me things nobody else sees.

ISOTTA [*smiling*]: That is natural.

MALATESTA: True, dear Isotta, that is natural.

ISOTTA: Promise me, then, to wait some days before leaving, and then you will see the folly of what you are doing.

MALATESTA: Let me keep my follies. A little flame of folly—if only people knew how life is lit up by it. And besides, if I did not watch myself living, what would be the point of my living?

ISOTTA: Sigismondo, don't get killed for nothing! Get killed if you must for something, but not for nothing, no, not for nothing!

MALATESTA: It's not mere living that matters, but living so as to be and to appear all that one is. For one is composing, and in composing one doesn't deceive or disarm anyone: all one gets is the exhaustion. And after all, even living a life like that is not enough: one must also live it with glory. [*Isotta weeps.*] Beware of shedding tears, Isotta. If I were still not decided on my action, your tears would decide me, simply and solely that I might not think it was they that had stopped me.

ISOTTA: I'm not weeping, I'm not weeping. It isn't my time for weeping.

MALATESTA: When you weep because of me, you ought afterwards to ask my forgiveness on your knees.

ISOTTA: I'm not afraid of suffering, although I do prefer joy. I can even say that, at the moments when I feel you are suffering, I would like to drink up in one draught all the pain of the world, if at that price I could deliver you from yours. But

I hate the idea of suffering because of an act of madness, which the stars would condemn just as men condemn it. Consult Corcos and you'll see.

MALATESTA: My star is more powerful than all the stars. It will devour them as the vulture devours the other birds.

ISOTTA: You will be killed, and there's no object in being killed; the object is to live, so as to be able to kill without risk. Killed, you will be just as much defeated as the Pope whom you have killed.

MALATESTA: Are you, then, my worst enemy, that you want to take away from me my vengeance?

ISOTTA: Too prompt a vengeance is no longer a vengeance; it's only a riposte. A vengeance worthy of you must be long and boundless.

MALATESTA: Boundless!—when already these seven days that separate me from his death fill me with anxiety. Ah, if he should escape its being me that kills him!

ISOTTA: He'll live as long as is needed. He takes baths and cossets himself, he's coated in unguents and stuffed with medicines. He's too fond of himself to die off like that. Your vengeance can be slow. It must also be indirect. You must kill him from up above, my lord, otherwise people will think you don't know how to make use of others, which is the prince's great art. And you must kill without exposing yourself, otherwise people will think your wisdom has begun to fail.

MALATESTA: But, supposing I were to act so, how make sure he knows it's I who am killing him? When I had Rosaspina killed, he muttered with his last breath: "Piccinino—the carrion!" My trouble was for nothing.

ISOTTA: Either he will know the man for a man of yours, and will understand; or the man will mutter your name to him in the act of striking.

MALATESTA: My first thought was poison and Porcellio. Porcellio declined the honor: one should never put a man of brains under the obligation of acting as one. Who could take on this business if I decided to give it to someone? Micheli? Boccanegra? No, no, I've confidence in nobody, in nobody! Follow someone in the street to spy on him, and let your eyes off him for an instant: it's enough, he's disappeared. In the same way, if I take my eyes for a single instant off those who are in my service, that settles it, they've betrayed me. I walk in the midst of traitors as one walks in the midst of trees in a forest.

Isotta: They betray one another first of all. That is why you are alive.

Malatesta: Long live my enemies! They at least cannot betray me.

SCENE IX

Malatesta, Isotta, Porcellio, *and, for a moment,* a Sergeant

Porcellio: My lord, two pieces of news, one good and one bad. The bad one: Sacramoro has just passed away. Here is the sergeant who's been sent to report it to you.

The Sergeant: My lord, Captain Sacramoro had scarcely reached his lodgings—

Malatesta: Enough. There's an individual who sends me word that he's living and then, ten minutes later, sends word that he's dead. Is he making game of me? And is it my fault if, into the bargain, the idiot had a chicken's neck? You may withdraw. [*To Porcellio*] And there's a piece of good news?

Porcellio: They're bringing the statue that was found in the earth in Carlo Buonfalcone's garden.

Isotta: No, not at this moment.

Malatesta: Nonsense, let them.—How lovely the matter of

it is! It seems as if filled with sunshine, as if one could make sunshine come out of it by pressing it between one's hands! [*He kisses the statue.*] If the success of a siege I was making depended on a little lime and if I could only get some by pounding up a bit of ancient marble, I believe I'd raise the siege.

PORCELLIO: *D. M. Diis Manibus.* It's a sepulchral statue.

ISOTTA: A sepulchral statue!

MALATESTA: My reading is not *D. M.;* it is *F. M.*, and *F. M.*, Porcellio, you understand what that means?

PORCELLIO: No matter, since it is *D. M.*

MALATESTA: *F. M. Fortuna Malatestensis.* The fortune of Malatesta. And here is the ear of corn that the statues of Fortune have.

PORCELLIO: An ear of corn? What I see is a wheel.

MALATESTA: It's an ear of corn, and that's my Fortune coming up out of the earth to be a marvelous sign for me in this solemn hour.

ISOTTA: Ah, away he goes again playing with his dreams.

PORCELLIO: Perhaps you are right, my lord. Oh yes, you are certainly right. . . . How could I have got it wrong? God be praised! To horse for Rome!

MALATESTA: What need have I of the stars and of the learned Corcos and of salaried murderers! I am the one who'll be the instrument of my destiny, not somebody else. At least myself in my own company and with all the security that comes from me to help me! [*To the statue*] Oh, the lovely thing, oh, the lovely being, created by the living, and purer than the person who created it! One more look at what perhaps we shall never see again. One more moment of beauty before the things of terror. Fortune of Malatesta, you who have cast me into the most profound abysses and from there exalted me to the highest star, be propitious to me! I, I will bestow upon you a whole year without sin; yes, a whole year of virtuous living, and of grandiose offerings to the poor, and of a sincere repentance for my faults, if you allow me to kill the Pope and not to be killed in doing so.

PORCELLIO: Ah, my dear lord, you who reproached me with being one moment a good Christian, next moment an idolater—

MALATESTA: Well?

PORCELLIO: Well, you have just uttered rather a strange prayer.

MALATESTA: Killing him shall be my prayer.

CURTAIN

ACT II

At the Vatican. A room in the Pope's apartments.

SCENE I

TWO CHAMBERLAINS

[*The scene takes place before the curtains.*]

FIRST CHAMBERLAIN: They're there?

SECOND CHAMBERLAIN: They're arriving. But, after all, what is there to fear?

FIRST CHAMBERLAIN: It's God that makes men's faces eloquent and so prevents some crimes. If the Lord of Rimini had composed his face better when he presented himself yesterday morning at the Vatican, the Pope would have granted him an immediate and private audience, as he always used to do for a former servant of the Holy See. But his disordered bearing aroused suspicion. The Pope was told, and put off the audience to today, and posted guards.

SECOND CHAMBERLAIN: Was the Pope disturbed?

FIRST CHAMBERLAIN: At first very disturbed. Later he found a small paper-knife which he had mislaid several days before, and that cheered him up again.

SECOND CHAMBERLAIN: The way Malatesta arrives before the appointed time! One would think he'd not had the strength to wait any longer.

FIRST CHAMBERLAIN: Yesterday I brushed against his hand. It was icy! Never shall I forget that touch.

SCENE II

THE SAME [*for a moment*], MALATESTA [*in black doublet*], GASPARE BROGLIO, FEDERIGO DA MELDOLA

FIRST CHAMBERLAIN: Gentlemen, please wait here a moment. His Holiness will receive you without delay.

[*They go out, leaving guards at the opening of the curtain. The three accomplices talk in low voices, at one end of the stage.*]

MALATESTA: It's killing me, it's killing me.

BROGLIO: My lord, in heaven's name, calm yourself, adopt another expression. A child would realize that you are contemplating some violence.

MELDOLA: Your face keeps contracting with a nervous twitch.

MALATESTA: People may think I am upset, without getting from that any inkling of what I am going to do.

MELDOLA: You're trembling?

MALATESTA: I don't know if I am trembling, but I'm cold.

MELDOLA: Your eyes have gone pale, just as the sea becomes livid before the storm.

MALATESTA: The devil take you! Can I stop my eyes from going pale?

BROGLIO: It's madness to carry out an action of this kind without self-control. You didn't sleep an hour last night.

MALATESTA: It's better to spend the night with anger than with repentance.

BROGLIO: And during a week's traveling you hardly took any food.

MALATESTA: My food has been the ill I wish him.

[*A noise.*]

BROGLIO: I think there's company arriving, in the next room. Is that usual? Is this the place where they normally make you wait when you have an audience?

MALATESTA: No.

BROGLIO: No? Ah! I fear the worst. Please, my lord, don't finger your dagger like that. Can't you see that the guards have their eyes on us?

MELDOLA: My lord, kiss your medallion of Victory. Kiss your medallion of the Virgin too—Holy Virgin, Mother of Jesus, watch over us, protect us!

MALATESTA: Ah! I ought to have made an offering of fruits to the statue of my Fortune.

BROGLIO: That you have thought of doing so will gain you at least a half-protection.

MALATESTA: May Victory inspire me and may the Virgin protect me! And may the genius of Malatesta plate my heart with steel and guide my arm.

SCENE III

THE SAME, FIRST CHAMBERLAIN

FIRST CHAMBERLAIN: My lord, His Holiness will receive you in an instant. [*To the other two*] Gentlemen, have the goodness to follow me and to wait in the pontifical antechamber.

MALATESTA: Messer Federigo da Meldola and Captain Broglio are here to speak with His Holiness for the same reason as I.

FIRST CHAMBERLAIN: The audience which His Holiness is granting to your lordship is a strictly private audience.

MALATESTA: The presence of my companions is indispensable to our interview.

FIRST CHAMBERLAIN: I am sorry, my lord, but I have explicit orders.

[*The chamberlain goes out, with Broglio and Meldola.*

When they have gone, the guards draw aside the curtain. It reveals the Pope, seven cardinals, some officers, some men-at-arms: an impressive company. When they catch sight of Malatesta, the cardinals begin to gather in front of the Pope, forming a bulwark for him.]

SCENE IV

THE POPE, MALATESTA, CARDINALS, OFFICERS, MEN-AT-ARMS

[*During this scene and the one that follows it Malatesta keeps on wiping his lips—because of their dryness—with a handkerchief.*]

THE POPE: You desired to speak with me. I am listening.

MALATESTA: I can only speak to Your Holiness if we are alone.

THE POPE: There is nothing that these my brothers cannot and must not hear of what you have to say at this moment.

MALATESTA: Then I have nothing to say. [*Bursting out*] Or rather I've to say that I'm choking at the thing you've done to me. To take from me Rimini! From me! From me! From me! But the sea that beats the shores of Rimini repeats, as it breaks on them, the name of Malatesta. Sacred sea of Rimini, sacred Adriatic, sooner would you engulf my city than let it be taken by anybody! Fifty years ago Gregory XII found asylum in Rimini. Is this today the recompense? Is this the thanks? That Pius II should have sent troops against Rimini, granted: that was in his character. But you! Pius II detested me; for six years he held me in his grasp and ground me down. And then in the Morea, when I heard of your elevation, I let myself dream of a pope who would get me out of the night of Pius II, of a pope who, though surrounded by my implacable enemies, would have in him a sort of freshness or a sort of honesty or a sort of pride which would make him dare to remain the only one among them who would not hate me. I came back, and my imaginings were faded by the sunshine of the real you. You welcomed me as the defender of the Church, who had just fought for two years against the infidels. I rode through Rome in great pomp, like the victorious Cæsars, escorted by all the cardinals with the most ancient titles, and one of them held the bridle of my horse. That day, the whole of glory, in my hand, like a bird—

A CARDINAL: You forget that the cardinals, on another occasion, accused you—and our memory is good—"of carnage, rape, adultery, incest, parricide, felony, and heresy," and condemned you to death.

CARDINAL MARCANOVA: And in this very city you were burned in effigy as "prince of traitors and perjurers, enemy of God and of mankind."

MALATESTA: We live in a time when, thank God, a death sentence no longer dishonors anybody.

CARDINAL MARCANOVA: Insolent fellow! How dare you!

MALATESTA: And you, how dare you be familiar with me! Who are you to do that? Oh, but I recognize you! You were on it, on that tribunal. Tribunal of justice? Tribunal of injustice, like the rest!

A CARDINAL: He insults the holy tribunal!

MALATESTA: Tribunal of Fickleness, of Vengeance, and of Hate. Yes, I recognize you, Satan, all red with the flames of your hell. And to begin with, whoever consents to judge his fellow men condemns himself. For he knows quite well that he is always as guilty as the man he is judging.

A CARDINAL: Enough! Enough! Won't anyone silence him? [*Several cardinals make to draw their swords.*]

MALATESTA: In any tribunal the world over, it's enough to

see the expressions of the judges to know that the accused is innocent.

CARDINAL MARCANOVA: Most Holy Father, in the name of the Sacred College I demand an immediate punishment for these blasphemies.

MALATESTA: Hide yourself, judge of your fellow men. You make my gorge rise.

CARDINAL MARCANOVA: Are you hoping to burn me up at ten paces with those fiery glances of yours? Do you imagine I'm a bunch of straw and you're the sun? I can remember the day you came before us to do penance. You mumbled in an unsteady voice your little speech, and the sweat was running down your ears.

A CARDINAL: Most Holy Father, have this man arrested!

MALATESTA: Most Holy Father, protect me against these men!

THE POPE: Your Eminences, Malatesta is a hotheaded son who forgets himself, but he has also been a zealous son.

A CARDINAL [*dyspeptic*]: A blackguard, yes, that's what he is! A blackguard!

MALATESTA: A blackguard so zealous that you bestowed on him the Golden Rose, that supreme honor which the Holy See only grants to its outstanding sons. At that moment I thought I had found once more the Holy See as I had known it under your uncle Eugenius IV, whose condottiere I was at the age of nineteen; to whom for years I brought only victories; the passage of Pius II was no longer anything but a horrible dream. I thought that, in spite of everything, because *you* were a true Christian. . . .

THE POPE: There you are. A man leads a life of crime, the Church condemns him, he has suffered cruelly from the priests, but, when everyone else fails him, it's to the priest he turns as a last resort, it's to a priest he throws his last confidence: "You who are a true Christian—" Such is the strength of a single ray of Jesus Christ.

MALATESTA: Yes, is it not? It's enough to make one tremble with pride.

THE POPE: With pride? With pride! . . . Poor Malatesta, you are indeed astray in the night.

MALATESTA: Why "the night"? Was it the night when all I asked was to serve you and to be a devoted son, I who have our Holy Church in my veins? I loved you, and it took a deadly insult from you to turn me against you. To feel a liking for someone who hates you is horrible. Ah, if you had been willing! But no, you too are like the others. . . .

[*His eyes fill with tears. He hides his face in his hands. The Pope signs to those present to withdraw. They withdraw, not without hesitation.*]

SCENE V

THE POPE, MALATESTA

THE POPE: You have a weapon on you: throw it away. [*Malatesta, after hesitation, fumbles for his dagger and throws it down.*] You haven't another? [*Malatesta indicates that he has not.*] Lift up your head. [*Malatesta raises his head and takes a step towards him.*] Don't come any nearer—not a single step—or I call back my guards. [*Pause.*] I had no intention of dispossessing you of Rimini. I have proposed to you an exchange, of which the initiative, incidentally, came from my brothers of the Sacred College. You were free to reject that exchange. We will try to find some other means of preserving you from our dear Venetians.—You make a great parade of your love for the Church. Let us say that sometimes you have served and sometimes attacked her. You change very often, Malatesta.

MALATESTA: The times change, not I.

The Pope: It is rumored that even now, in spite of all your recantings and promises, you laugh a great deal at those who find their strength in Christ.

Malatesta: How could I laugh at those who find strength in Christ when they believe in him, since I find strength, for instance, in the myth of Adonis, in which I must admit I don't really believe?

The Pope: What is this myth of Adonis? I'm out of patience with all this paganism which people parade everywhere nowadays. Drop Adonis and let us talk seriously. You tell me you have our Holy Church in your veins. That's in the style of your defense before the ecclesiastical tribunal: not with me, please. Can I forget that you were fifteen the first time you fought and even beat the troops of the Holy See? Can I forget that one day, when hard pressed on all sides, you had the diabolical idea of offering your alliance to the Grand Turk to help him invade Italy, and that at the very moment when Pius II was preaching the crusade against him—which is certainly the most characteristic and odious form of treason? Can I forget that you boast of having built in Rimini a scandalous church that is really a temple to the false gods, since all the decoration, all the inscriptions, all the symbols in it evoke the pagan legends, and since not one sign, not a single one, is there to recall Him who created you? Can I forget that not six years have gone by since Pius II held in the Vatican that special tribunal which pronounced your deposition from your sovereign rights, the confiscation of your property, and finally condemned you to the heretic's penalty—that is to say, to be burnt to death?

Malatesta: Your Holiness is reproaching me with nothing but stale deeds, for which I no doubt was condemned, but of which I have been absolved later, since no part of that famous sentence has been carried out, and since in the end it was the Golden Rose that flowered from the stake where I was to have burned. In March 1462 Pius II had me condemned to be burned alive. In March 1464 Pius II was giving me his solemn benediction as I left for the Morea.—Those voltes-face are salutary food for thought, let us remark in passing.

THE POPE: When Pius II blessed Malatesta embarking for the Morea, what he was blessing in him was the fact of being rid of him. You have been absolved, you say. No, what you were, that you still are. We know you, Malatesta, and have known you for the half-century you have been on this earth. We know well all your tricks, they are always the same. You tire us.

MALATESTA: I tire myself sometimes.

THE POPE: And they run from the greatest things to the smallest, from assassination to the silly schoolboy's joke. Is the story of the ink true?

MALATESTA: The ink?

THE POPE: They say that, not long ago, passing by a church at dawn, you had ink poured into the holy-water stoup, so that the faithful, falling into the trap because of the darkness of the place, would blacken their faces and fingers. Aren't you ashamed? At your age!

MALATESTA: The day I did that I must have been under an evil star.

THE POPE: You desire our confidence. In what way do you deserve it? Apart from your fantasies and your passions, you don't serve and you never have served anything but your interests.

MALATESTA: I have tried to reconcile them with the interests of those who were employing me. And me, who has ever supported me, except from interest? Interest gone, gone the support.

THE POPE: You have outraged all laws: the divine, the natural, and the human; come, hell knows your name by heart! They say that at night, alone in your room, you talk. . . . To whom do you talk? They say it is the devil.

MALATESTA: I talk to myself. We have always a lot to say to each other. I hold dialogue with what I am, with what I have been, with what I dream of being, with what I mean to be.

THE POPE: And the specters of your crimes sit at table beside you.

MALATESTA: Perhaps, sometimes, the specters of my political mistakes. Alas, they are terrible Furies, my political mistakes, and they will pursue me till I die.

THE POPE: Your mistakes are according to the common measure, but your crimes pass all measure. You laugh at Christianity. You laugh at Italy. Your family, your friends? You betrayed and tried to poison Sforza, your father-in-law. You are supposed to have strangled your first two wives. You tortured and killed your old teacher Ugolino de Pili. Nature? You slept with your son-in-law Camerino when he was adolescent. You soiled with your desires the corpse of the beautiful German girl from Fano after having put her to death. . . .

MALATESTA: Well, women are made to be loved.

THE POPE: So you admit it?

MALATESTA: Admit what? A witness! Was there ever a witness?

THE POPE: Worse still—and I can't mention this crime without a shiver of horror: you tried to possess your son Roberto, and he had to seize a dagger to defend himself against you. . . .

MALATESTA: May not even family life have its moments of fantasy? Besides, what you are now raking up was only a joke, which people have delighted in distorting.

THE POPE: Yes, yes, struggle to escape. There is in you an innate love of evil. You are a monster.

MALATESTA: I am not at all a monster, Most Holy Father; on the contrary, I feel I am the most benign of men when people give way before me. And I could say like Colleone on his deathbed: "Never give to another the power you have given to me. I could have used it so much worse than I did." For all you accuse me of is pure invention and calumny. I am accused of what I've done, of what I haven't done, and also of acts for which others are not blamed when it is they who have done them, and for which sometimes they are even praised. I am accused of what I am thought capable of, and I am thought capable of anything, because it is my enemies who have got the upper hand in the manufacture of my legend; to justify oneself by public opinion, when one has oneself created that opinion by repeated lying, is too easy. I am surrounded by hatred, by a hatred that for thirty-five years has not disarmed. To the north I have the hatred of Venice, to the west the hatred of Sforza, to the south the hatred of Alfonso and Urbino, here the hatred of the Pope. I have made acquisitions, for my own benefit, by violence or by finesse? What does it matter, since it has all been taken away again? I have had six cities, all I have now is Rimini; I am at the point where I was when I was twelve. Everything I have touched has been like those rusty sabers which are found sometimes on my seashore and which, when you seize hold of them, crumble to a little dust in the hollow of your hand. And my crimes? Why not forget them, since people forget the good I have done? I have given fourteen children to Italy, eight of them boys; I have seen five of my boys on horseback in front of me in a line of battle: their waists had the sway of the victory standard. And victory itself, this too I have given, many times, to those who for its sake entrusted to me their whole fate, I have given it to them in spite of them, against them, duped by them, betrayed by them, betrayed by my masters, betrayed by my brother, betrayed by my sons. Hatred! Always hatred! Ah, what a sum of beastliness I shall have had to bear!

THE POPE: Malatesta, is this you? Is it Malatesta complaining so dolefully? You dry up the justice one would like to render you, when you crave for it in a tone so unworthy of you.

MALATESTA: I'm thirsty.

THE POPE: Keep your thirst. You shall have a drink presently.

MALATESTA: When my tone is heroic, I am reproached for it. When my tone is human, I am reproached for it. Why should I not cry out for once? I've had enough of being always made of iron. All right, yes, you'll be able to tell everyone: "Malatesta is a weakling, a cry-baby. He's a façade of a man, a pasteboard braggadocio like the ones at a carnival, fit to give children a fright." What do I care, since, true or false, people will always say it to discredit me? Why should I give myself the trouble of holding myself erect since it will be asserted anyway that I stoop? Why should I do any good, since it will not be recognized by anyone? This is how people have corrupted and withered all that was good and flowering in me!

THE POPE: Come, Lord Sigismondo, you talk, you talk. . . . You remind me of what the Duke of Urbino used to say, that your eloquence was the mask you put on over your silent thoughts. And Sforza—

MALATESTA: Urbino, Sforza, Alfonso, always the same names that will have been buzzing around my head all the length of my life. If only there could be some others! If only I could have a slight change of contemporaries! And now it's going to be Ferdinand of Naples—

THE POPE: Ferdinand of Naples?

MALATESTA: He is pressing me to engage in his service.

THE POPE: Ah! [*Pause.*] Well, Malatesta, you said that you would have liked another chance of serving the Holy Church. You must also redeem the crime you were preparing to commit upon my person. I offer you the means of accomplishing these two tasks. Once more, you can be the pontifical condottiere. That is better than the service of Naples.

MALATESTA: Your condottiere?

THE POPE: Yes.

MALATESTA: O Pope after my heart! O true Jupiter! I come here to—and you—[*He moves to kiss his hand. The Pope withdraws it sharply.*] But what will you ask of me in exchange? You'll not ask of me my poor Rimini?

THE POPE: All I ask of you is your skill and your loyalty.

MALATESTA: I stand before you like Allutius before my ancestor Scipio Africanus. . . .

THE POPE: What I am doing, I am not doing for your sake. You are this and that, but you are one of Italy's greatest men of war. I am attaching that man to me; that is all. And I am giving him my confidence.

MALATESTA: You give him your confidence, or you have confidence in him?

THE POPE: I am giving him my confidence [*Pointing at the dagger*] Pick up your knife.

[*Malatesta makes a sign of refusal.*]

MALATESTA: And I desire to give you a similar mark of confidence, and beseech you to consent that I confess to you. You wanted to know how far I was a sinner. You shall know.

THE POPE [*with some embarrassment*]: Lord Sigismondo—

MALATESTA [*kneeling on the ground at the feet of the Pope, his hands joined*]: Why cannot I hold in my hands your Golden Rose and press it to my breast like a sword!

THE POPE: O Sigismondo! What a fine thing it would have been had you been a good man!

MALATESTA: What?

THE POPE: A good man. Upright. Spotless. Like that pure silver armor you wore the day of your triumph in Rome. And not that doublet of darkness you put on for my death.

MALATESTA: For mine.

THE POPE: O Sigismondo! Sigismondo! You who one day were the falcon of Christianity—

Malatesta [*crossing himself*]: *In nomine Patris, et Filii, et Spiritus Sancti—*

The Pope [*rising suddenly*]: After all, no, get up. Why should you confess to me? There is no lack of priests in Rome; go to them.

Malatesta [*rising*]: Most Holy Father—

The Pope [*ringing a bell*]: Let us not place confession between us, my lord. It might render one or the other of us less free. It is a delicate sacrament; it must be used with prudence. Do not persist.

SCENE VI

The Same, A Chamberlain, Guards

The Pope [*to the chamberlain*]: Lead our good son Lord Malatesta to the Pater Noster apartments, where he will lodge till further order. [*To Malatesta*] Tomorrow you will see Monsignor Civitale; you will examine together a draft contract.

Malatesta: May my companions remain with me? They are brave captains.

The Pope: Your men of all work will return as soon as possible to Rimini.

Malatesta: But, Most Holy Father, when will you be able to talk over with me the work that is to be entrusted to me? When, where, how am I going to start using my powers in Your Holiness's service?

The Pope: Monsignor Civitale will inform you.

Malatesta: Is Monsignor Civitale really the right man with whom to raise matters of war and, if necessary, to go into them? Are you yourself—

The Pope: Do not worry. Everything will come at its time.

MALATESTA: Your Holiness is leaving me in an extreme ignorance and uncertainty. Could I not, even now, be told a little—

THE POPE: I repeat that you will know in good time. Now go to your apartments. One of the officers of my personal guard will always keep watch, with his men, over your safety. They will also keep watch, wherever you are, over the safety of others. [*To the chamberlain*] You will give my lord something to drink. He is thirsty.

[*Malatesta, somewhat confounded, remains for a moment motionless. Then, after the customary bowings, goes out with the newcomers.*]

THE POPE [*alone*]: O Father!

CURTAIN

ACT III

At Rome, in the Palazzo Venezia, residence of the Pope, the great hall known nowadays as the Hall of the Globe. On the left, two steps rise to a bay giving on a balcony that overhangs the street. On the right and left, access to other rooms.

SCENE I

BENEDETTO DE NARNI, CLAUDIO SCARAMPA, OTHER COURTIERS, ECCLESIASTICS, LADIES, *etc.* . . .

[*Part of the assembly is massed on the balcony and on the steps leading to it. The other part fills the front of the stage.*]

BENEDETTO DE NARNI [*on the balcony*]: Look, all the young people in red are joining up. Side by side, they are going to form a letter, then those in green will form another letter, then those in yellow another, and so on; and all together they will trace a word.

A COURTIER: What word?

NARNI: Guess.

A COURTIER: Here's an *A*.

ANOTHER COURTIER: *M*.

ANOTHER COURTIER: *O*.

FIRST COURTIER: *R*. Bravo!

NARNI: The *R* doesn't move, and all the others are coming round in front in a graceful maneuver. . . .

FIRST COURTIER: *O*.

ANOTHER COURTIER: *M*.

FIRST COURTIER: *AMOR. ROMA*. It's charming!

NARNI: Now they're clearing the street for the arrival of the runners.

FIRST COURTIER: What sort of race is it? Women, old men, donkeys, or buffaloes?

NARNI: Of young men, quite simply. The finish is opposite. The first three are to come up here to receive a special benediction from His Holiness.

SCENE II

THE SAME, MALATESTA

[*Malatesta comes forward. The courtiers draw away from him, turning away their heads. Nobody speaks to him. They cast furtive glances at him.*]

CLAUDIO SCARAMPA: Look at that filthy Sigismondo. Embarrassment, humiliation, and rage are disputing the mastery of that drawn face of his. Since his segregation and his illness, you'd think he was always ready to bite. And he has got much older.

NARNI: Having, under his orders, the hundred and thirty Vatican guards, and that in name only, after having commanded—really commanded—seven thousand men facing the enemy in the Morea, what bitterness!

SCARAMPA: Wait, I've a noble task for him. There are two drunkards squabbling on the other side of the road. We might send him to separate them.

NARNI: Unless one were to give him the job of throwing small change to the populace in the Pope's path when the Pope leaves the palace.

SCARAMPA: One has to admit in the degradation of the great there is something exquisite.

NARNI: Pass by him once more, to show him that we are not greeting him. I'm afraid he may not have noticed it.

SCARAMPA: What I have noticed is that his eyes never meet other eyes. He looks above people's faces.

NARNI: Agreeable it must be, being out of favor. People no longer ask you to do them services.

A CHAMBERLAIN: Gentlemen, His Holiness is approaching.

NARNI: You know that Donna Isotta has arrived in Rome. It is thought she is coming to intercede on his behalf.

SCARAMPA: But why should he be so amazed at his fall from favor? The snubs you get at Rome, he knows that. Six years ago, when he was excommunicated, they burned on the steps of St. Peter's a dummy made to look like him, a striking likeness, dressed up in the clothes he usually wore. And similar dummies were burned in all the cities of the Papal States, while the Papal troops were marching on Rimini, while his own subjects were fleeing at his approach, as if he were the invader, and while his brother Novello, yielding to terror, was deserting him to go over to the Pope's camp. . . .

NARNI: And nevertheless he got his pardon!

SCARAMPA: At what a price! By coming to Rome to eat dirt before the Sacred College, to protest that he was a minor saint . . . and to renounce his rights over all his states except Rimini.

A CHAMBERLAIN: Gentlemen, His Holiness.

SCENE III

THE SAME, THE POPE, CARDINAL BORGIA, THE CARDINAL OF PAVIA, MONSIGNOR PERRUGIA, ECCLESIASTICS, OFFICERS OF THE PONTIFICAL SUITE, MORE COURTIERS, *among them* PLATINA

[*The Pope comes in and, after blessing the company, which kneels, moves toward the balcony. Cries from the crowd:* "Holy Father, the benediction!" *The Pope from the balcony blesses the crowd.*]

THE CROWD: Long live the Pope! Long life to the Pope!

THE POPE [*under his breath*]: The shouts that the Son of Man heard on the cross were different.

THE CROWD: Long live the Pope! Long live Paul II!

A VOICE: Long live divine Paul!

A VOICE: Long live Cæsar!

THE POPE [*under his breath*]: Do not give me glory, O Lord! Do not give me glory!

[*The Pope sits down, having retired from the balcony, and chats with the cardinals and courtiers; the assembly is massed in that corner, waiting for the runners to arrive. Two thirds of the stage on the opposite side are left empty, and it is there that Malatesta and Platina converse apart.*]

MALATESTA: Ah, Messer Platina, I didn't expect to see you here! [*Examining him from top to toe*] And—what is this extraordinary fancy dress?

PLATINA: You see me robed as a member of the Academy.

MALATESTA: I'm sorry I didn't receive in time my grand uniform as Prince of Traitors.

PLATINA: Don't joke about these things, my lord. One shouldn't joke about dangers: it arouses them.—I am pleased to see you. I was rather surprised that you stayed so long without paying me a visit in my library. I imagined you thought such a visit would now be compromising.

MALATESTA: Have you become so compromising?

PLATINA: What the Pope hates in the Academy is not only the men of letters, a race he cannot stand, but a spirit of liberty that inevitably turns against the Church. I am expecting to be arrested from one moment to another. Arrested or worse. Every time I go home at nightfall and see two or three men confabulating not far from my door, I think: "Ha, there are my murderers!" I commend myself to my genii, and I go forward saying to myself that in this business I shall at least have learned that dying is not so difficult as all that.

MALATESTA: Engage some bravoes.

PLATINA: My house isn't large. They would make a din and prevent me from working.

A VOICE [*in the bay*]: Here they come! Here they come!

ANOTHER VOICE [*in the bay*]: No, no, those are only urchins, probably to announce that they're coming.

MALATESTA: Why don't you speak to the Pope? Sometimes a frank explanation—

PLATINA: I shall not take the trouble. Besides, when one sees what men are like, how good it is to be vanquished!

MALATESTA: I'm sorry, I don't feel I'm made of the stuff from which martyrs are cut. Also, I'm a general, I can't be a philosopher; it's essential that getting beaten should rather annoy me.—But you, if that's what you have come to, what are you waiting for? What are you hoping for?

PLATINA: Events wear themselves out. I'm waiting for the time when the present period will appear ridiculous.

MALATESTA: And if you've been killed first? Why don't you flee while you still can?

PLATINA: And you?

MALATESTA: Me?

PLATINA: Yes, you, why haven't you fled? Come, you understood my question perfectly. It's curious this point of honor threatened men make of trying to make believe they're not in such danger as all that. Why don't I flee? Out of disdain of defending myself. I'm sixty-three. I don't want to give these marionettes the pleasure of seeing me trot at my age. The more so since, all my life long, I've hated forcing myself and hurrying.

MALATESTA: You prefer to give them the pleasure of assassinating you.

PLATINA: My God, yes. At least it shan't be said that they have put me out excessively. In Rome I have my manuscripts, my intaglios, my antiquities. I shall live in the midst of all that till the end. I'd rather not live than not live the life I like.

MALATESTA: Why do you treat them as marionettes? They are pretty formidable.

PLATINA: It isn't because a man toys with a dagger or a crossbow that he'll stop me from considering him a poor ape. Have you noticed that at a certain point infamy becomes almost comic? Meanness, too. Someone who two months ago used to call me "my dear friend" and now calls me "messer," without there having been the slightest ill feeling between us, without my having done anything wrong, simply because I'm no longer in favor with the Pope, what do you expect me to think of that, except to find it comic?

MALATESTA: I too found my excommunication rather comic. And I confess I feel a certain pleasure at the thought that they will doubtless desecrate my ashes. . . .

[*Murmurs from the crowd.*]

CARDINAL BORGIA [*looking through the bay*]: All those men I could grasp easily in my hand. . . .

MONSIGNOR PERUGIA: Instead of watching for the runners, those fools are going to have a fight.

CARDINAL BORGIA: How well placed one would be here to bombard that scum and clear the space at one blow! Ever since I have known the people of Rome I have seen the assassin in every one of their faces.

MONSIGNOR PERUGIA: And I—assassins or not—all enthusiasm freezes me. I have never seen enthusiasm except for stupid causes. If a crowd acclaimed me, I should give a jump and say out loud: "Someone make them shut up!" Enthusiasm is one of the dragons that devour a community.

THE POPE: Yes, but the people have to have holidays to keep them quiet.

MALATESTA: Since we last met, have you any fresh reasons for being uneasy?

PLATINA: One would be enough. What happened two days ago.

MALATESTA: What did happen?

PLATINA: Buonaccorsi—

MALATESTA: Well?

PLATINA: You didn't know that Buonaccorsi had been arrested? That just shows how low you have fallen: you are not told anything. I heard the news at the seventeenth hour. I swear to you that at that moment I was convinced I was going to be arrested that very night. All the rest of the day I lived, acted, like a phantom: I was in another life. And then, in the end, I found repose.

MALATESTA: I should like to know in what book the greatest humanist in Italy found repose, on the point of being thrown into prison.

PLATINA: The greatest humanist in Italy found repose by going to the brothel. Besides, as you see, I'm free and I'm here. They're arresting the other academicians. I'm being kept for the final titbit. The flood wants to make me savor to the end the way in which it rises around me.—But you yourself, my lord?

MALATESTA: I, I'm kept on one side, ignored, unemployed, nobody. . . .

PLATINA: A man of your powers, what folly!

MALATESTA: And supervised, spied on, my letters opened. In a cage, really: when I wanted to go and spend a Sunday at Francesco Mondavio's vineyard, I was refused the safe-conduct to leave Rome. The maneuver is obvious: in negotiating with me the Pope meant to paralyze me. And especially to prevent me from engaging in the service of Naples, which for him was the unknown factor. If I'd been innocent, it would be horrible. But I've at least the satisfaction of telling myself that I was guilty. How well I did to be so! Long life to me! I console myself also by looking up in the ancient authors all the passages dealing with illustrious men who fell on evil days. It happened to nearly all of them, thank God; and I've finished up by feeling happy in the midst of that great family of condemned men.

PLATINA: I know all that, and suffer from it no more than

you. There comes an age when even our disappointments are no more to us than a spectacle.

[*Cries from the crowd.*]

A COURTIER [*in the bay*]: They're bringing the apparatus for this evening's fireworks.

ANOTHER COURTIER: As usual, the fireworks won't be worth much. But they'll make the devil's own noise, and that's always the thing.

MONSIGNOR PERUGIA: To think that we are quietly on this balcony, when only a fortnight ago access to it was forbidden on pain of the dungeons, for fear suspicious signals might be given from it! Has the situation cleared up so much?

THE CARDINAL OF PAVIA: Look, they're carrying a streamer with the inscription: *Sanctus Petrus, Sanctus Paulus, dii tutelares Romæ*. Our holy Apostles, the tutelary deities of Rome! Really, they are going a bit too far!

PLATINA: That you, the man of victory, and I, the man of study, that you and I, who by good and by evil are henceforward through the centuries part of the patrimony of Italy, should be treated as enemies of our country, and more or less as common bandits, isn't a thing to lament, but to smile at. Misfortune adds to our glory exactly as success does; and the two even taste exactly the same. Does the seashore complain when the tide withdraws from it? It knows that the tide will come back. These comings and goings, these ups and downs, are the common currency of lives like ours. And, indeed, of all life: this rhythm is everywhere in nature, this rhythm is the very rhythm of nature, and if such a test had not come our way, we should have had to challenge it. There is no great destiny without a touch of melancholy.

MALATESTA: What you are thinking is precisely what I think. And when all's said and done, I don't believe that, in the immediate future, either my life or my liberty is in peril.

PLATINA: Ah, that! . . . Why are people so hard on fear? What we are afraid of always happens in the end.

MALATESTA: You are encouraging! But if you're applying that to yourself, and if you won't defend yourself, others could do it for you: Lazzari, Bontempi, who are friends of yours and have the Pope's ear. . . .

PLATINA: I know, there must be many steps one could take. But the time all that would take up! And my work, in that case, abandoned? I'm at this moment busy on Aulus Gellius—

MALATESTA: You've got an Aulus Gellius! Oh, Messer Platina, lend it to me; it's such a long time I've wanted to read Aulus Gellius. And couldn't I have it copied here?

PLATINA: Certainly, when I've done with it—that's to say, soon. And even if the Pope has me arrested I shall beg him to leave me at liberty for nine or ten days more; that's just the time I need to finish my study on that author's extremely interesting style.—But, my Lord Malatesta, I am going to confess to you something that will surprise you, after what I've just said to you. Well, look: at bottom, at the rock bottom of myself, I don't believe I shall be arrested. There are on my shelves nine hundred volumes that protect me: the flower of the thought and action of men for twenty centuries. When I am with Livy, with Marcus Aurelius, with Demosthenes, with Pericles, they are so much more real to me than my contemporaries that, if ever there turns up a myrmidon who dares lay his hand on my shoulder, I believe the only phrase that will come to my lips will be: "What is it?" My preoccupations are so impenetrable and incommensurable for those who will arrest me that it seems to me that at one moment or another the self-evidence of this is bound to flash out in the minds of my accusers themselves: in a single revelation they will see how deeply innocent I may be. And no doubt it was this same reason that drove the famous Arabic author Hariri of Basra to exclaim, in one of his *Conversations:* "O God, do not allow men of letters to be put in prison!" You don't answer?

MALATESTA: I don't answer because you don't exactly convince me.

PLATINA [*with a mysterious expression*]: Listen, there's another thing. It's that I've had luck on my side all my life. I don't place much hope in the destinies of Italy, but I continue to place hope in myself. . . .

[*Growing murmur of the crowd, and suddenly a loud burst of shouting: the runners are coming in sight.*]

A COURTIER: The violet!

ANOTHER: No, the blue!

THE CARDINAL OF PAVIA: By Hercules, thanks to the divine Paul, Rome might believe herself back in the time of Augustus.

VARIOUS PEOPLE: Violet, which quarter's that?
The Campo Fiore. And red, the Trastevere.
And blue, the Bianchi.
Violet's winning!
Blue's drawing up!

THE CROWD: Go on, Trastevere! Up the Bianchi!—Campo Fiore! Campo Fiore!

[*The shouting dies down; the race is finished. The company leaves the balcony and the space near it and comes down again to fill the whole stage. Malatesta has disappeared. Platina remains on one side.*]

SCENE IV

THE SAME *minus* MALATESTA, THE THREE WINNING RUNNERS

THE POPE [*to the winner of the race*]: What is your name, my son?

FIRST RUNNER: Romeo Manetti, Most Holy Father. Of the Campo Fiore.

THE POPE: Romeo, may God the Father give you one day a different crown from this which I am giving you today!—And yours?

SECOND RUNNER: Piere Giovanni Benzi, of the Trastevere.

THE POPE: The Trastevere is a tough spot, and perhaps for that all the more dear to me. . . .—And yours?

THIRD RUNNER: Andrea Alpago, of the Trastevere.

THE POPE: My children, to win this race you trained thoroughly. You must also train, and more thoroughly still, for the grand race whose finish is in paradise.

THE SECOND RUNNER: Ah, that, Most Holy Father, that's a different job!

THE POPE [*laughing*]: A different job, certainly! But rather of the same kind. My able patron, St. Paul, has said some excellent things about that.

[*He blesses them. The runners withdraw, and with them the company begins to melt away. Cardinal Borgia draws Platina to one side.*]

CARDINAL BORGIA: So, Messer Platina, out of favor has been consoling out of favor?

PLATINA: Your Eminence, there is no need for me to console Malatesta, who can certainly find in his situation grounds for consoling himself unaided. Is he so much to be pitied? A long time ago the Pope could have rendered him harmless.

BORGIA: Doubtless our Malatesta is too fond of novelty to be ever altogether reliable.

PLATINA: You don't know what he is capable of.

BORGIA: I see you are his friend.

PLATINA: I wish him no ill, but is not the sacred function of a writer impartiality? An impartiality obliges me to say that the fact that he is still at liberty surprises me.

BORGIA: Do you know why he has come to this? Of our four great condottieri, he is without question the most intelligent. And none the less his policy has never ceased to be stupid. It has been, all his life, a policy of moods, and a petty day-today policy, empirical and limited. That childish bad faith, those betrayals for the fun of them, those atrocities, those vengeances, all that's not serious. That fits in neither with continuity of conduct nor with lucidity. Nine times out of ten it turns against him; he knows it, and persists; it's mania. Malatesta for a moment held the destiny of Italy in his hands, but he didn't realize it. Perhaps even today he doesn't yet know it. . . .

PLATINA: Yes, he has to'd and fro'd for nothing, like the squirrel that turns its cage. He has succeeded in nothing, and nothing will remain of him.

BORGIA: My weakness is to love efficiency. That means I cannot stand that sort of person.

PLATINA: And what is most curious is that Malatesta loves to repeat that everything is easy!

BORGIA: He believes that everything is easy because he is incapable of conceiving anything great. He's the caricature of a great man; one side of the face is a grimace.

PLATINA: Perfectly true! So let's keep our pity for others, not Malatesta. For poor Tiburzio, for instance. Does Your Eminence know that he has just been found dead in front of his house?

BORGIA: God receive his soul. Let's go and dine.

[*They go out along with the last of the guests.*]

SCENE V

THE POPE,—ISOTTA, *and for a moment* A CHAMBERLAIN

THE CHAMBERLAIN: Most Holy Father, the magnificent Lady Isotta da Rimini waits in the Hall of the Round Gate.

THE POPE: Let her come in.

[*Isotta enters, makes three genuflections, kisses the Pope's slipper, and remains on her knees on the step of the Pope's chair. The Pope by a sign invites her to rise and be seated.*]

THE POPE: Well, Donna Isotta, you arrive just as the festival is over. . . . There was a time when I liked these festivals, when I liked them too much. Nowadays they depress me. I am tired of the riffraff—ah, so tired of the riffraff, if you only knew! Tired even of the roughs. And yet a festival coming to its end leaves you rather high and dry, as if it had been a good thing.—A good thing, that coarseness? You saw the naked men? I am persecuted by these naked men. It's as if I could still smell the stink of their armpits. . . . But one has to be in the fashion! One has to be Homeric, Virgilian! I am surrounded by a whole surf of literary men, who claim to think for themselves, pretentious and dangerous people. You, Donna Isotta, have the reputation of being one of the most educated women of Italy; but also of being prudent, wary, virile. Your renown is great, and you are respected by all, you whom they call "the mother of Rimini."

ISOTTA: It's not as an educated woman, supposing that I am one, that I have come to entreat Your Holiness, it's as the wife of Lord Sigismondo Malatesta da Rimini. It is for him that I come to ask for mercy.

THE POPE: Well, Donna Isotta, is it not customary that a person who is asking for something begins by talking for a long time about things that do not interest him? You are going mighty fast.

ISOTTA: I ask for mercy for Malatesta.

THE POPE: Mercy for Malatesta?

ISOTTA: Your Holiness is not ignorant of what I mean.

THE POPE: I am.

ISOTTA: I beseech Your Holiness to bring to an end the condition into which you have cast my most noble and most illustrious husband, a condition in which he encounters nothing but inaction, obscurity, discredit, insults, intrigue—and that opacity of isolation all around him. . . . He's eating out his heart with it, he's dying of it; if he gives up he is lost: you know how these things happen with men. Already the blow dealt him by your proposal concerning Rimini had so shaken him that it had made him ill. Your present severity is finishing him off.

THE POPE: When he fell ill, I had him looked after at the expense of the treasury, by a doctor who I took care should be a native of Rimini, in order to inspire in your lord every confidence. As for his present state, I will only say this: I have given to my assassin—to a man who had in his hand a weapon to assassinate me—a most honorable post, which many coveted, and which indeed he accepted without any constraint.

ISOTTA: Certainly, the promptitude of your change is one of the marvels of policy. But everyone knows that, for suppleness and boldness, the Holy See and Venice are in a class apart. And as you are, Most Holy Father, both the Pope and a Venetian—

THE POPE: I acted from policy, but also from generosity, and I have pushed this generosity to the limit. Apart from his pay, Sigismondo is receiving not only entertainment expenses for his service in the Vatican, but campaign expenses for a campaign in which he is not taking part. And I must say he accepts all this trifling rain of florins with no sign of embarrassment.

ISOTTA: Your Holiness would have shown still greater generosity by not making Sigismondo prisoner.

THE POPE: Prisoner!

ISOTTA: May Your Holiness spare me from describing to you a situation you know better than I.

THE POPE: Sigismondo has never complained. Yet his impatience is the devil's own.

ISOTTA: In three months Sigismondo has asked you for four audiences. At the first, he still had hope, and had no need to complain. At the second, as soon as he had begun to complain you broke off the audience. The other audiences were not granted.

THE POPE: He has approached me on many occasions.

ISOTTA: One day he had complained to you with utter distraction—and then you had given him this post. He knows what his complaints can do for him. That's why he has fallen silent, faithful to his motto: "A time for speech. A time for silence."

THE POPE: In short, you mean that on that day I laid him a trap.

ISOTTA: Yes, and all the more cruelly since it was done under the mask of magnanimity. With what innocence he let you dupe him, this alleged past master of perfidies! When I think that he thanked you for your magnanimity, and that you accepted his thanks! When I think that he wanted to confess to you!

THE POPE: But I did not accept his confession.

ISOTTA: When I think he had tears in his eyes before you: he wrote and told me! Me, who have never in my life seen him weep for me.

THE POPE: Donna Isotta, I see that you are a plain speaker: therefore I will speak plainly with you. Well, let us face it, one doesn't govern a state without any weapon but the rosary. A pope belongs to heaven and to earth; he is bound to be ceaselessly fluttering from one to the other. God is far, Donna Isotta, and men are near, terribly near, stuck onto us like incubi. I am within my part and within my duty as priest in sometimes inflicting penances on sinners. These last months do you think I did not perceive his suffering? I perceived it very well; I let him suffer: that has to be, sometimes. And I am within my part and within my duty as prince in not neglecting the precautions that need to be taken by a profound mind desirous of moving in safety. A man came to me with a dagger under his doublet to strike me down. It was my right to imprison him, to have him tortured, to kill him. All I did was to put him in a position where I hold him in check and prevent him from harming me. And it's that that you are asking me to bring to an end?

ISOTTA: I beseech Your Holiness to grant Sigismondo a leave of absence of three months, that he may go to Rimini to relax and get well in the company of his wife and children.

THE POPE: A folly! . . .

ISOTTA: By the sacraments that I received yesterday morning, I swear that he will perpetrate nothing against Your Holiness.

THE POPE: His unquiet and unbridled nature is one of those that must always be kept in hand. I fear the solitude of a man of his kind—and above all at Rimini!—a solitude in which he takes refuge in order to spring and in which, once at a distance, one no longer knows what his maleficence would do or can do. Let us be on our guard! Like the flame, he recoils before killing.

ISOTTA: His maleficence! You say one doesn't govern a state with no weapon but a rosary; has Sigismondo no right except to a rosary? You know him only in his conduct as a public man: in that he is what the others are. No one in Italy or in Europe expects Sigismondo, who is a condottiere and a prince, to follow a perpetually clear and loyal policy. And if he did so, no one would understand. But do you know his life as a private man? Do you know how he has been with me these thirty years? How he is with his children, even to the point of cherishing his legitimate children as much as his bastards? His kindliness, his ease, his gaiety? Don't touch him, Pope though you are, and don't speak ill of him, for you know nothing of him.

THE POPE [*smiling*]: All claws extended!

ISOTTA: The Turks, in the Morea, used to tell Sigismondo that when one starts a lion and a lioness together, one must always kill the lioness first. Because the lioness, if the lion is killed, attacks you, while the lion, if the lioness is killed, runs away.

The Pope: They say of your lord that he is more impious than ever. For instance, in the sacrilegious church he is building at Rimini, one of the reliefs, it seems, represents Apollo and Jupiter with, between them, Sigismondo. He himself has deified himself!

Isotta: That is a mere poetic imagination, no more to be taken seriously than, for example, when he pretends that he's descended in the direct line from Scipio Africanus. Those are things in which he doesn't believe, or believes only a little, but they exalt him at the moment when he has to accomplish great and difficult actions. A great many high personages of our time claim to be the issue of a hero of antiquity, or have themselves represented with divine attributes, but Sigismondo is the only one to be reproached for it.

The Pope: Because he does it with too much show. And at night, facing the enemy camp, one shoots at anything that shines.

Isotta: Say it's because, perhaps, he puts into it more candor than the others.

The Pope: Sigismondo's candor!

Isotta: Well, yes. He is, at moments, a man disarmed. Often he has woman's nerves and sometimes childlike ideas. He cannot persevere in dissimulation; his bitter and naïve vitality will always give him away.

The Pope: I see you know him well.

Isotta: A man gives his measure in one night.

The Pope: I remember his look the day he came to kill me, and when later on he lamented: his eyes crafty, with their columns of light. . . .

Isotta: You said, Most Holy Father, that all Italy respects me. Well, there is nothing he has done that I do not feel I am capable of doing. . . .

THE POPE: You would have strangled your previous husband if you had had one?

ISOTTA: More of these abominable calumnies! In all his life Sigismondo has had only one sure ally, the Marchese d'Este, and people would have us believe that the Marchese would have remained still friendly and faithful after Sigismondo had strangled his daughter! That such old wives' tales should go the rounds of the barbers' shops—let even that pass. But to hear them from the throne of St. Peter, that really takes the heart out of one. What disgusts me about hatred is its coarseness: it welcomes any old rumor, feeds on everything, without examination, without discrimination. How stupid it is and how stupid it makes people! A fine mind in hatred becomes as silly as a cowherd's. The infamy of Pius II consists in having made room in his *Life of Sigismondo* for all the idle talk that had currency against him, giving it by that the triple authority of talent, princedom, and religion.—But you, Most Holy Father, calumniated as you are, you are one of those who ought never to listen to calumny.

THE POPE: Am I more calumniated than another? Everyone is calumniated.

ISOTTA: More or less. The extra share of strength that the Holy See draws from its spiritual powers can only bring it an extra share of envy and hatred.

THE POPE: To the man of God it is too easy to despise calumny.

ISOTTA: Certainly, and I can understand that you worry very little about what is said of you by, for example, the burgesses of Rimini.

THE POPE: What do they say of me at Rimini?

ISOTTA: Things that deserve only a shrug of the shoulders, and that I could not dream of repeating to you. Although I was surprised to hear them repeated in this place, where I have only just arrived.

THE POPE: Tell me, please.

ISOTTA: I could not allow myself. . . .

THE POPE: But of course. A prince must be informed. You would be doing me a service.

ISOTTA: They say that the bull *Quemadmodum* was made by you without the approval of the Sacred College, and that the formula "By the advice of my brothers" that occurs in it has no right to be there.

THE POPE: That allegation is a pure lie, though it lingers everywhere, I know.

ISOTTA: You are also calumniated in small things; they are trying to diminish your majesty.

THE POPE: Let us see what they say.

ISOTTA: No. No. . . .

THE POPE: I insist.

ISOTTA: They say that at your accession you wanted to take the name Formosus, because of the good opinion you were supposed to have of your physical appearance. . . .

THE POPE: That idiocy is an old acquaintance. The truth is that Formosus was the name of my tutor, to whose memory I am very devoted.

ISOTTA: They are saying things that are sillier still. They say that every day you spend an hour making up your face. . . .

THE POPE: Making myself up! Have you heard that said? But, Donna Isotta, you didn't believe it, did you? What lunacy! So there I have been for four years, at the cost of infinite pain and at every instant defending the doctrine of the Church, and on that I have never weakened. For each of us has points on which he is willing to yield and others on which he means to hold fast. You, you stand firm on Sigismondo; I stand firm on Jesus Christ. And all that to the end that people may simply say that the Sovereign Pontiff paints his face. Isn't it rather horrible? Sometimes, by trying hard I manage to love my temporal enemies. But for those who spread these fooleries, no, no, and a thousand times no! Even if I tell myself that it's stupidity that is the great punishment of Adam's sin.

ISOTTA: This same stupidity and this same maleficence let fly against Sigismondo, and then you listen, Most Holy Father. Ah, we powerful ones ought to have an agreement between us, to spare each other and sustain each other, come what may, in order to make common front in all circumstances against our inferiors.

THE POPE: "We powerful ones"! Let us rather consider false power, which attracts hatred and has not the means to defend itself in proportion. The falsely powerful are of all men the most exposed. But, for them, no charity. Never any charity for those who have power. Ah, if there were not God!

ISOTTA: I have charity for Sigismondo.

THE POPE: Love is not charity. Besides, to have charity for the serpent is to have none for men.

ISOTTA: Most Holy Father, if some people treat him as a serpent, others treat you as a wolf. But destiny itself has pitied him, and has raised him up again many a time.

THE POPE: Pity for Malatesta! *Pity* and *Malatesta:* the two words swear. And on whom has *he* had pity? [*Pause.*] You see, you cannot answer.

ISOTTA: No, I cannot answer.

THE POPE: How you do love him!

ISOTTA: The nerves of my face relax when I see him happy.

THE POPE: The only one who loves him, I think.

ISOTTA: He has not sought to make himself loved. One can acquire certain things one covets by endearing oneself. But it is quicker to pay for them—or to take them.

THE POPE: Yes, yes, go on; love always finds excellent reasons. It's one of the strangest sentiments, this love of the creature for the creature. There's not much love in the palace of the Vatican. When our young people just now traced out that word *AMOR*, it was enough to set one dreaming.

Would to heaven the priests loved Jesus Christ as much as a woman can love her husband! And would to heaven these priests were also loved a little, including those who sit on the throne of St. Peter! Well, I am going to do unto others that which I should wish to have done unto me one day. I was not without an ulterior motive when I spared Sigismondo; this time I have no ulterior motive; I am acting in the sense of that prayer which I so often pronounce inaudibly and which I pronounced while you were speaking: "Make me feel Thy presence, O my God, that my conversation be with Thee in heaven while I am dealing with men on earth." My sister, I grant you what you ask of me. I do it for you, for myself—also for your Sigismondo, although that costs me something. I consider that it is a remarkable folly, but, as a Christian, I am authorized to commit from time to time a remarkable folly. Tomorrow Sigismondo will have brought to him, in good and due form, the leave of absence that is so dear to you. [*Pause.*] You do not seem to be satisfied.

Isotta: Most Holy Father, how can you think so! But words—I don't know how to express—

The Pope: It isn't words that fail you, it's feeling. My God, how difficult are relations with human beings! All our life passes in not satisfying people.

Isotta: Will you be seeing him before he leaves?

The Pope: No. Why?

Isotta: Because, if you had been going to see him, I should have said to you: "He must not know you are doing this from pity."

The Pope: I shall not see him. [*Quite a long silence. The Pope makes a sign that the audience is at an end. Isotta rises and kneels on the step, and there the Pope blesses her.*] We had more to say to each other when you were waiting for something from me that I did not mean to give you. Now that you have got what you wanted, let us become strangers again. All I ask you is not to turn against me what I have done for you. I have had through you a tiny instant of light. Do not make me regret it.

[*Isotta withdraws while Monsignor Perugia enters.*]

SCENE VI

THE POPE, MONSIGNOR PERUGIA

THE POPE: You will have Lord Malatesta given a three-month leave of absence, on full pay, to be passed at Rimini.

PERUGIA: At Rimini! . . .

THE POPE: Yes. [*He places his hand over his eyes, with weariness.*]

PERUGIA [*holding out a dossier*]: May I have Your Holiness's signature for one or two papers?

THE POPE: Later.

PERUGIA: Because—some of them are urgent.

THE POPE: Let that be, I do not feel very well just at present.

PERUGIA: Your Holiness is ill?

THE POPE: Yes, something is the matter with me. There is a sort of wave that has just washed over me and is plunging me into a deep—into a deep— An extraordinary sadness suddenly bearing me down and drowning me.

PERUGIA: Your Holiness— But I shall not have the audacity to ask—

THE POPE: Perugia, I have just done a good action. [*A pause, then to himself*] She will always believe that I acted from calculation, that it was a trap. . . . My hand was raised; I did not strike him down: where will that be counted to me? There ought, all the same, to be a reward when one does something good; if not a recompense from others, at least a reward from oneself. But nothing, my God! No, nothing, my God! No, nothing, my God, for goodness. Or rather, yes, a punishment. . . . [*Pause.*] Have Malatesta's leave of absence made out for two and a half months, and not three. And have it noted that he must leave behind as a pledge all that belongs to him, all that he brought to Rome, all that he has bought here, works of art, manuscripts, weapons—

PERUGIA: Can he keep his armor, as is the custom for prisoners of war?

THE POPE: Yes, of course. But—it will be necessary also for Donna Isotta to leave her jewels as a pledge. [*He takes the dossier, flicks through the papers, then gives them back roughly. A pause.*] I see there is nothing in this about the Academy. Perugia, you will give orders to the Governor of Rome to have Platina arrested immediately. I wish him to be in the dungeons of St. Angelo by tomorrow morning.

CURTAIN

ACT IV

At Rimini. Same scenery as in the first act.

SCENE I

MALATESTA, VANNELLA

MALATESTA: My little soul, now you must go. Holy child! For really it takes something holy to give such happiness.

VANNELLA: And if Donna Isotta—

MALATESTA: She'll find out and she'll bear it. She has been bearing it for such a long time! But half an hour of you is ten years of others' lives.

VANNELLA: I'm still afraid that—

MALATESTA: No! No! Don't be afraid, and listen to me: I have eternal things to say to you. I was in profound darkness. Rome had hit me as Rome does hit; to me Rimini itself had become a somber torpor. Then I came to know you, and all the words of your consent sank down into my soul like roses into the night, and my night was no longer anything but a single great rose. In Rome I touched despair. Because they no longer believed in me, I no longer believed in anything. One day I'll tell you all that, I'll tell you my whole life with all its secrets.

VANNELLA: You'll tell your life to a child like me—a man like you! But I'm not asking you about your life.

MALATESTA: You shall know it all. Because it's extravagant that you should. And because I love you.

VANNELLA: Lord Sigismondo, do you love me as much as you say?

MALATESTA: Yes, ever since you yielded.

VANNELLA: I too love you. I think of you every day.

MALATESTA: O my palm branch! O my grace! O weakness in my knees! Or rather strength of my knees. For this glory of mine, of which yesterday I no longer felt the need, once more I need it, to feed the love of this darling girl. There are some who would say: "He's fifty-one. It's too late." Too late? Is it so soon too late? No! No! It's not too late. I've forgotten all that has been said. I've forgotten all that has been written. I'm beginning again; your youth, which I hold in my arms, has given back to me youth with the fine wings; what intoxication, a life in which you and I will go on existing! O my breeze, O my lake, smooth out Malatesta's face! Take for an instant my face in your hands, and it will be healed.—But someone's coming. . . . Give me once more that paradise of a little head of yours. . . . Now go quickly. Tomorrow Ambrosio will come and fetch you at about the same time. And be very discreet with your mother!

VANNELLA [*with a little expression of complicity*]: Have no fear.

MALATESTA: Of all your many faces, including even your face in abandon, there's none I adore like the face-of-your-lie-to-your-parents.

[*Alone.*] Blessed be Providence, which has allowed this sin! Oh, happiness that shouts within her tresses! I believe happiness is making me mad. From now on, I swear it, by all the sap there is in my loins and in my thighs, from now on there opens a life so triumphal that it will frighten death itself. Let me merely hold in my hand the hem of her dress, and death will stop short in front of us, and we shall enter into an eternal impunity.

SCENE II

MALATESTA, PORCELLIO

[*A knocking.*]

MALATESTA: Come in. [*Roughly*] Ah! It's you!

PORCELLIO: Well, my lord, you asked us, Basinio and me, to be at your room at the nineteenth hour.

MALATESTA: Punctuality with you is an infernal mania.

PORCELLIO: It is a mania usually appreciated in subordinates, my lord.

MALATESTA: But you are not a subordinate, Porcellio! I wanted to talk to you about Poggio's coming; well, he announces that he's putting off his visit. He wants to present me with a copy of his new work, *De infelicitate humanæ conditionis*. I don't know why you men of letters always affect to find that life is evil. I, if I had a thousand years to live, what life would I ask to live? I'd ask to live, twenty times more, the same life as I have lived. I have loved swords, manuscripts, and women: this world of iron and blood which I love more every day, as one loves a little child that's sick. . . . I've had great enjoyment—and I've had great enjoyment also from myself. But here's Basinio.

PORCELLIO: Almost punctual, he too. Decidedly, what boors we are, we men of letters!

SCENE III

MALATESTA, PORCELLIO, BASINIO

MALATESTA: My dear Basinio, I wanted to discuss with you Poggio's coming, and to arrange with the two of you how we should do him honor. But his visit's put off: so we'll talk of it again another day. I'm going now to see Lunarda da Pallu.—Ah, Porcellio, I should like you to write to the Marchese d'Este. Tell him I've heard that he made one of his neighbors a present of a Barbary horse, that I know he possesses another in his stables, and that I am so bold as to say to him that if he would like to give it to me, I should get extraordinary pleasure from it.

PORCELLIO: Very well, my lord.

MALATESTA: Ask him also to send me some baskets of eels. I believe he's forgetting me.

PORCELLIO: Very well, my lord.

MALATESTA [*having started to go and coming back*]: Dear Porcellio, I must trespass still more on your kindness. The hedge of Donna Isotta's gardens is in such a state of ruin that it will soon be completely down. Would you mind telling Rambutino to attend to it?—Something else. The new dog's kennel is so placed that it gets the sun all day: he hangs out his tongue like a devil, poor beast. Rambutino should be told to move the kennel. Thanks. Au revoir, gentlemen.

SCENE IV

PORCELLIO, BASINIO

PORCELLIO: You heard? He humiliates me, and humiliates me in front of you, a fellow writer. After all, what am I here? Am I the bailiff? Am I the head gardener? Am I the kennelman? My dear colleague, I have my faults, I grant you. But I think no one has ever accused me of being vain. I can therefore remind you that at sixteen I pronounced a funeral oration in the pulpit of San Francesco of Genoa. That I wrote my first book at eighteen. That I am poet laureate of the court of Naples. That I have composed twelve works, three of them in two volumes—that is, a total of fifteen volumes: *tantæ molis!* That I am in correspondence with all the most distinguished and most illustrious minds of Italy. And all that to end up by being given charge of the dog's kennel. No indeed! No! No!

BASINIO [*quietly exulting*]: *De infelicitate conditionis litteratorum.*

PORCELLIO: Yes, he, he considers that mortals are happy and that one hasn't the right to complain! In Rome he showed a long face, or so it seems. Now, in the ten days he's been back, having no dealings except with groveling subjects, he has recovered his extravagant idea of himself. I find once more on his lips that triumphant smile which has exasperated me there so many times. Insolence smokes from him like the steam from a sweating horse. What folly to put back in the saddle people of that kind! One thinks one has brought them down; one finds them again more cocky than ever, and winking with a good-for-nothing air; there's only one stage from which they can't get up again, and that's the state of death: but that nobody understands. In short, Sigismondo is puffing himself up again, stuffing himself with plans, with dreams, with ideas, with threats, in a mood of malice and impudence all the livelier for having been bridled for some time.

BASINO: A sure road, indeed, toward "a state of death." For he would rather die than not excite envy, just as the mosquito prefers the light that will kill it. And they're all like that. They die for having puffed themselves up too much. They know, and puff themselves up for all they're worth: they have made their choice. And there are some of them surely who are a little disappointed at not having been judged important enough to be killed.

PORCELLIO: May God hear what you say! When I encouraged him to go to Rome to kill the Pope, I really thought I was sending him to his death. He has come back. But there is no joke so good that it doesn't have its end. I say "joke," for Sigismondo is also a comic personage. Sentimentality over a dog that hangs out its tongue, in a scoundrel covered with blood like him, is excellent fooling. He makes me laugh, does Sigismondo, at moments. Me, I tell you—he makes me laugh.

Basinio: Sigismondo wanted to kill the Pope. Therefore the Pope not only lets him live, but employs him. Sigismondo saves your life. And you have no dearer desire than to see him lose his. This game of life and death is a tricky thing to steer!

Porcellio: To think that nobody is willing to do us a service and to accept that it should be without any return: material return or sentimental return. To think that nobody is willing to do us a service and to forget he has done it. For that way of doing a service is the only way really worthy of a friend. Yes, Sigismondo saved my life, yes, he has been kind to me. But he has made me feel too much what I owed him. He has too often given me to understand that I had been a burden to him, and what would have become of me without him! Even to the point of reminding me how frightened I was when I took refuge in Rimini; frightened? My life was at stake, it was natural I should be frightened, it seems to me. What's more, even these days, every time he does me a kindness, he immediately insults me, to make sure I know the rights that his kindness gives him over me!

Basinio: There, my dear colleague, frankly, I think you are imagining things!

Porcellio: No! No! Besides, even if I were imagining them! Even if he had nothing but right on his side! Because he has saved my life once, must I waste my time and my trouble on humoring him, stroking him, waiting on him hand and foot, for the whole of this life? Must I *put myself out* for him during my whole life? Must I *pay* during my whole life? Ah, at that price it would have been better if he hadn't saved me! It's too dear! I tell you, it's too dear! Yes, I state here and now, it's better not to be alive than to live imprisoned and poisoned by the duties of gratitude. What is the good of receiving if one must give back? Next time someone wants to kill me, all right! I shall let myself be killed rather than enter afresh into the hell of gratitude. You see the gray hairs at my temples? That's the result of six years of gratitude. But there are some people who are going to expiate, one day, those graying temples!

BASINIO: Achilles says in the *Iliad* that hatred is sweet as honey. But most of the good authors profess that it is painful. Neither Homer nor the others see that hatred is sweet when it can slake itself, and painful when it can't. Your hatred can't slake itself. *Ergo* pain.

PORCELLIO: Too dear, yes, much too dear! And note that it isn't over. Even nowadays I ask him to do me services, though my tongue bleeds from repeating for six years the frightful word "thank you." But that is natural: he is at the source of everything. And at the same time it is torture to me to ask him.

BASINO: Aren't you also sometimes in the position to do services to him—how shall I put it?—as man to man, and apart from those implied by your situation? Do so, then, why not, and you'll be quits with him!

PORCELLIO: I do so all right on occasion, but what it costs me! It's so against my nature! My slope always runs back to myself. When I force myself to do something for someone else, it's agony. Look, take simply that little goblet I presented to him five years back; well, every time I see it again, I feel sick at the thought that I gave it to him. Ah, giving—what a Calvary! I believe I shall end by smashing it.—If only he could do me some grave wrong, which would at one stroke set me free! I ought to have the courage to provoke him myself to do me that grave wrong. But I haven't. Provoke that panther, no, thank you! And so one has to go on.

For six years I've been living in his shade. I suppose I might find that shade a comfort. But it's a shade that casts on me a chill of which I'm dying.

SCENE V

THE SAME, ISOTTA, ALOYSIA [*with the little girl* CONTESSINA]

ISOTTA: Lord Sigismondo is not here?

PORCELLIO: No, madam. He went out only a moment ago, to visit Lunarda da Pallu.

ISOTTA: Did he seem worried? Has he not mentioned to you any trouble?

PORCELLIO: He seemed extremely cheerful.

ALOYSIA: Smile, Contessina! No, she'll only smile at her father. Of all the men at La Rocca he's the only one at whom her face lights up. It's because he knows how to talk to children, just as he can talk to the ordinary people, just as he can talk to animals. . . .

BASINIO: I hear his step.

SCENE VI

MALATESTA, ISOTTA, ALOYSIA

ISOTTA: Ah! You are there!

MALATESTA: Well! That surprises you?

ISOTTA: No bad news?

MALATESTA: Not the slightest.

ISOTTA: All the time I was out I was in anguish about you. A sort of suffocation rising little by little in me. . . .

ALOYSIA: Donna Isotta always sees the Pope everywhere—the Pope or my lord Federigo. But I, although it's great presumption on my part to give advice to your lordship, the love I bear you leads me none the less to tell you you should above all mistrust Siena. I know the Sienese through my brother Gian' Antonio, who has set up as a carpenter at Siena. They are wicked people. Your lordship must never make an alliance with them!

MALATESTA: Well, Donna Aloysia, calm yourself! May the devil pluck out my guts if ever I ally myself again with the Sienese!

ISOTTA: Go, Aloysia, and wrap the child up well. Such heat in October is deceptive: the night will be cold. Oh, the sadness of this approaching winter!

MALATESTA: Winter is an unconscious spring. [*Kissing the child*] Contessina! Each time I kiss her, she smiles, and I see each time that starry mouth appear and disappear. The mystery of God dwells in a sweet-smelling mouth. Hers smells of orange blossom.

SCENE VII

MALATESTA, ISOTTA

[*Night falls during the first part of this scene.*]

ISOTTA: Just now, at the Signoria, the future placed on my hand its cold hand, and I could hardly suppress a cry. I learned that a merchant from Rome had put up at the hostelry here and was saying that Platina had been imprisoned, then put to the torture in the presence of the Pope himself. His property confiscated or pillaged, all his papers destroyed.

MALATESTA: Unlucky Platina! During my time at Rome he alone showed me any real sympathy. And now I remember his mad confidence: he believed he wouldn't be arrested. . . . The saying is certainly true, that Jupiter blinds those whom he means to destroy. I shall have that merchant sought out and summoned.

ISOTTA: I imagined you put to the torture. . . . I came back in a panic. . . . Ah, if only one could become another person, become Francesca d'Este or Beatrice Orsini, to whom nothing happens, who pass through everything, who take life so lightly! If only one could tear their soul out of them and put it into oneself in place of one's own!

MALATESTA: Come, Isotta, what's wrong with you? Can you have slept last night in the moonlight?

ISOTTA: Lastly, even here, on the wall of the staircase leading to your room, someone has traced this inscription: "Now we know that a man's worst enemy is his government."

MALATESTA: Too narrow a piece of thinking. He should have written: "A man's worst enemies are his compatriots."

ISOTTA: That inscription was not there yesterday.

MALATESTA: I feel more at my ease when people insult me than when they praise me.

ISOTTA: At each end of the inscription there is drawn an ivy leaf. Do you know what that means?

MALATESTA: I don't.

ISOTTA: We ought to ask Porcellio, who knows everything. Have him called back; he can't have gone far. That sign may give us a valuable clue.

MALATESTA: I'm not going to make Porcellio come back for a trifle. Look at that beautiful midsummer twilight, in October. And am I to rack my brains in such weather? Let it go, I promise you that tomorrow, if the sky's overcast, I'll be as harassed as you ask me to be.

ISOTTA: I will get Ventura to show you the state of the treasury. You'll see if you have food for laughter.

MALATESTA: Fine! The treasury now! You don't want me to have any peace.

ISOTTA: I can't bear your unconcern, when others are tormenting themselves because of you.—Call back Porcellio, I beg of you! An ivy leaf, that may be the sign of a group. [*She rings. To Cinquedenti, who appears*] Go and look for Messer Porcellio, who has just left here. Let him return. [*To Malatesta*] Something tells me that your life is in danger.

MALATESTA: My life is always in danger.

ISOTTA: More than usually. Your star is trembling as the stars tremble at dawn, at an ill dawn.

MALATESTA: It is fixed and motionless, like a nail set in the sky.

ISOTTA: People pretend you aren't threatened, in order not to have to offer you their help.

MALATESTA: It's true that, in the thirty-five years during which I have needed help from people—and God knows I've had enough of those moments when one appeals to all and sundry!—their initial devotion has had time to relax; they're tired of always coming to my assistance. But this fact has its counterpart: if their devotion wears away with time, my uneasiness also wears away with time. Since man finds it quite natural to entrust himself to a ship, protected from the appalling watery mass by a mere little partition of wood, and does so without apprehension, why should he not find it natural to live without apprehension in the midst of the most treacherous risks of civil or military life? "Without apprehension" is not altogether the word. One ought to say: calm even in the heart of his uneasiness.

ISOTTA: Escape from the death-trap of Rome to come and die at Rimini. . . .

MALATESTA: Die, I? Die, and leave Urbino alive? Ah! I could die if I knew he was dying with me. No, no, I shall still torment them for a long while. For years and years!

ISOTTA: I gnaw myself away wondering what trap the Pope set for you when he let you come back here.

MALATESTA: That's going far! He did grant you what you were asking!

ISOTTA: That's just what frightens me.

MALATESTA: Fear is a sickness, and anxious people of your sort are the sore on a community. As soon as I'm back in Rome—

ISOTTA: You're not going to return to the Pope!

MALATESTA: My contract—

ISOTTA: Ah, keeping one's word, what a habit!

MALATESTA: When I was at his knees, he said to me: "O Sigismondo! Sigismondo!"

ISOTTA: Your taste for the Pope is leading you astray. You are burning to serve him! Being the man you are, you ought to have abhorred his clemency, even in that first moment when you could believe it was sincere. To despise means to be readier to die than to accept the favor of the man one despises. But no, you accepted it and embraced it. Great God! I believe you still embrace it. But you are not going to return to Rome. For there is also that dream I had about you the other night. . . .

MALATESTA: All the women who have loved me have invariably dreamed sinister dreams about me: dreaming of my death is a necessary part of the way people love me. And yet here I am.—Besides, I, I never dream. My actions are in my life, not in my dreams.—Listen, Isotta, don't bore me with your forebodings. I find it very irritating that you should take my affairs more to heart than I take them myself.

ISOTTA: My only part on earth is to watch over you.

MALATESTA: I wasn't feeling any forebodings. Now perhaps I'm going to feel them: is that what you wanted? You are my anxiety, the anxiety I don't feel. When by good fortune my nature does not lead me to foreboding, must I come on foreboding through you? Is it worth while to be immune from certain weaknesses, to have them find their way back into me by stealth, brought in by you? Why tremble for me like this incessantly?

ISOTTA: What a question! Because I love you. A being whom one loves is always in danger. Those who reassure you do not love you.—And I admit that my anxiety is rather dear to me, for by it I can better measure how I love you.

MALATESTA [*laughing*]: Well, that's cheerful! Why not say you desire it? [*Serious*] Love me a little less, Isotta. As a certain strength is required for happiness, but not an enormous strength, so it is good to receive a certain quantity of love, but not too much. Your love makes me lose on one side what it gives me on the other. Your trembling spoils my steadiness. Your constant admiration entices me into a false view of things and leads me to believe that I'm surmounting great obstacles where the obstacles are middling. And your feverish tenderness has tired me many a time.

ISOTTA [*her head on Malatesta's breast*]: Well, if I am the source of all that's wrong, let me repose on your breast from being what I am, just as when I used to lay my cheek against your armor at your return from battle, and to feel your heart thumping against that armor of iron and gold, for all the world as if it were paper armor.

MALATESTA: Women, prudent mothers of human beings, you who at my age still carry me in your flanks! Ever since I was born, I've been surrounded, preserved, sustained, given life by women. It's in them that I get my strength and my venom. When something had to be done for me, in small things or in great, it was always women who did it, and you more than any, though the women who have wished me well are as numerous as the stars in an August night. Alas, taking from you has become a habit in me, and I blame myself for it. . . . By the side of yours, the devotion of all the others seems to me tepid; what injustice you have done them!

ISOTTA: The poor little services I sometimes do for you give me a joy so ardent that each time I'd like to thank you for the gift of it.

MALATESTA: Whatever the others may have been, I've never found except in you this giving which asks for nothing in exchange, this alliance which exacts no hostages, this advice in which you always forget yourself—this shelter solid and sure as death. And your evenness of temper and your lack of touchiness, what a treasure for one who knows to the full how much toil is added to the great toils of this earth by the exhausting obligation to humor people! . . . There's one thing in the world I cannot endure, it's horses with hard mouths. You have never had a hard mouth. That's why I've kept you.

ISOTTA: You said to me one day: "Perish Italy rather than our city!" And I say to you that I should consent that our city should perish, that there should remain of it not one stone, and that the whole of Italy should fall into the power of the French or of the Germans, if at that price you were saved.

MALATESTA: I shall be saved without any such cost. In tragic periods who dies, the brave man or the coward? He dies who believes he'll die. Well, there are people who, in the midst of the itch, don't catch the itch. There are people who, in the midst of risk of death, don't catch death. I don't catch death.

ISOTTA: You're smiling. What are you smiling at?

MALATESTA: At my memories and at my hopes. [*Looking out of the window*] Great night starred with signs and fires! Look at the lights of the city. Wouldn't one think they were the stern souls of the heroes, encamped around me to protect me? And look at the flaming signs of the heavens, those stars unsleeping as I. What an assembly! What a swarm of souls all alive with glory! It is the hour when one hears the constellations sing. What are they saying? They are telling of the mad adventure of lasting. And the sea, can you hear? Listen! Listen! It's the sea, the immortal sea, whose noise never changes. Men get tired of hearing the same words, of saying over and over again the same names. But the sea on my shores repeats eternally: "Malatesta"—on my shores full of sweet marble hands and divine sunken galleys. I told the Pope that; he didn't smile; he understood. Even if the shape of my coast were utterly altered, the sea, centuries of centuries from now, would be repeating upon it still: "Malatesta." Listen! Listen!

ISOTTA: It's all the time your heart I'm hearing.

MALATESTA: Go, Isotta, return to your room strengthened. The winds that run about the world leave on it only the lightest traces. Cares, like them, must touch only you with a gazelle's foot, and you must offer to this purest of nights a face, like it, at peace. It's nine o'clock. It's the hour when children yawn and ask to be hugged. Contessina is already asleep. She reposes between her little sheets like a flower between the leaves of a book. . . . Isotta *mia*, in an hour I shall be with you alone, and then you shall know fully what security is.

SCENE VIII

MALATESTA, ISSOTA, PORCELLIO

[*At the same time as Porcellio, enter servants. They light torches, then withdraw.*]

ISOTTA: Porcellio, it was I who had you called back. On one of the walls of La Rocca there's an inscription insulting to Lord Sigismondo. At each end it has two ivy leaves. Has the ivy leaf a symbolic meaning?

PORCELLIO: In antiquity it meant preservation. If it is alongside my lord's name, it means: "May we be preserved from him!"

MALATESTA: My faithful subjects are certainly right: may they be preserved from their Malatesta! There are days when I should like to have them under my feet, to trample them as one tramples the grape in the winepress.—Come, there's your ivy leaf and it's not very terrible. Dear Isotta, go in peace. Peace and security.

ISOTTA [*pressing her hands together*]: O God, give me unconcern!

SCENE IX

MALATESTA, PORCELLIO

MALATESTA: Men are like children, Porcellio; one frightens them and reassures them at will. That is sad. I—I can say I've lived reassured. During those three months in Rome, there wasn't an hour of the day or night when I didn't expect prison, if not death. That didn't prevent me either from eating well or from fornicating well, or from reading well, or from sleeping well. I've never slept so well as at that period, when I had the impression that my assassins were sleeping in my antechamber. I've never started as many women as I did six years ago, when I had just been declared liable to the stake. Their hatred was food and drink to me. It was to me what warmth is to a body that's cold. And if you were to ask me what one feels at the moment when one hears that one is condemned to death, I would answer: "One feels nothing."

PORCELLIO: Perhaps that is one of the symbols implied in the elephant on your escutcheon: it means that the Malatestas are thick-skinned.

MALATESTA: Well, it's enough for a woman to talk to you of her anguish on your behalf, with eyes wide as this, of her nightmares, of her presentiments, and what not, and in spite of yourself she makes you uncomfortable, as one wouldn't be in the face of a definite danger. Donna Isotta is the only person in the world who loves me or has ever loved me, which means that she has a mania for spoiling my pleasures and upsetting my balance.

PORCELLIO: Has Donna Isotta some serious reason for being uneasy?

MALATESTA: Not the slightest. Platina has been arrested. That inscription— She's had a bad dream about me. But there: by dint of playing with ancient history, we end by being caught by our own game. And Donna Isotta does trouble me a little in spite of me, because there have been Cassandra's trances and Calpurnia's dream.

PORCELLIO: Everyone believes in your star, my lord. If you alone don't believe in it, don't you think your star will be offended and take vengeance?

MALATESTA: There's no question of my not believing any more in my star. Only, sometimes, I'm a little tired of this horrible hand-to-hand struggle which for forty years I've been waging with destiny. These are mere spells of fatigue, but spells that are very dangerous. Do you know how I interpret the myth of Psyche? Love flies away, all's destroyed, because Psyche has looked upon Love while he was asleep. That means that one should never touch a soul when it is uncovered and without defense. How vulnerable one is at those moments! That's the moment when one catches cold—when a not quite fresh piece of food would poison you—when one would stammer if one were before a tribunal—when one's mind would go cloudy if one had a decision to make. In the Morea I saw men in an arena fighting with wild beasts. As soon as they showed fear, the wild beasts dominated them and hurled themselves upon them. In the same way destiny, which is always watching us, would hurl itself on us if it smelled these instants of lessened resistance.

PORCELLIO: So, my lord, you are conscious that you are affected and that a little thing would be enough at present to finish you? Very curious, very curious. . . .

MALATESTA: In moments like this, one feels the need of attaching oneself to some abiding thing. This evening, since you are there, we will speak a little about that book you are devoting to me—take up the manuscript on the *cassone*—and tomorrow morning I will give you the material to enable you to describe my triumph at Rome four years ago. Perhaps we ought to contrast it with the depths of my present abasement: there is a curve there which is the curve of heroes. You know that, in the *Vita*, I have always somewhat veiled my reverses. But I am wondering if, on the contrary, it would not be opportune to exaggerate my current misfortune: the Titan struck by the thunderbolt. . . .

PORCELLIO [*with impatience*]: Obviously it will be necessary to choose. . . .

MALATESTA: I seem to see that this plan only half commends itself to you.

PORCELLIO: It commends itself to me, my lord, it commends itself.

MALATESTA: Speak out the whole of your thought.

PORCELLIO: I was engaged in a work of my own. But it is only natural that I should give up—

MALATESTA [*with animation*]: The *Vita* too is a work of your own, it seems to me. It's not because I supply you with certain documents. . . . And that work will do much for your renown—after all, I mean, it is bound to have a greater circulation than those philosophic treatises of which, indeed, you are a past master.

PORCELLIO: Do you not fear that the publication of the *Vita* may arouse many hatreds and increase your dangers?

MALATESTA: Who cares? Who cares?—But what is this

work of your own that is keeping you so busy at this moment?

PORCELLIO: Much honored that Your Highness—for the first time in the ten days since your return—should ask me a question about my work. I am writing a complement to the *De beneficiis* of Seneca. I take up again Seneca's title and add to it a subtitle: *Benefits, or The Race to the Abyss.*

MALATESTA: What do you mean?

PORCELLIO: That benefits lead the benefactor inexorably to the abyss. I should like to show the hell of gratitude and how one day the man under an obligation is ready to do anything to get out of it.

MALATESTA: Has man so much blackness in him?

PORCELLIO: He has in him that much blackness when he believes he can have it without risk.

MALATESTA: It's true: the sole counterpoise to man's malice is doubtless his cowardice.

PORCELLIO: Yes, only—"Push not the coward to despair: you would render him courageous." That is precisely the motto of my treatise.

MALATESTA: Taken from whom?

PORCELLIO: From an unknown author.

MALATESTA: Ah, Porcellio, all that is hardly the stuff to chase away my gloomy ideas.

PORCELLIO: I am being converted little by little to the thought you expressed some months ago to Sacramoro: I abhor people who are trusting.

MALATESTA: Much more than your treatise, I should like you to read to me some fine ancient text capable of holding my head up well above this evil wave. Wait, take my Plutarch. Read aloud to me about Pompey in the fatal bark, when no one speaks to him, and he questions kindly that old centurion of his armies who is going to assassinate him in a moment, and the man answers him with a sign of the head, without saying a word. Or the hunted and haggard Cicero of the last days, leaving it to his servants to choose his place of refuge. Or Cato, a little before he kills himself, when he goes to sleep once more for a few moments, before dawn, "when the birds were beginning to sing." There are things there which, at my age, can still make my heart beat more strongly and my eyes moisten. Come, open at random and read.

Porcellio: That's what they do with the Gospel.

Malatesta: I do it with Plutarch. Besides, I'm going to amuse you. You are going to realize that I didn't waste my time in Rome, in spite of being under surveillance. In the binding of the volume you see that gray powder I've brought back? A pinch of it kills your man within the quarter-hour. Yes, but there are many problems which that doesn't solve. It needs also some force of character to use it, and you should know that, you who shirked so brilliantly when I wanted to send you to Rome to make the Pope take medicine. Ah, how you amused me; I mean, how you made my blood boil that day! "A murder, that is not the domain of the spirit!" Dear Porcellio, come now and, out of the book that contains death, extract for me resurrection.

Porcellio [*opening the book at random and reading*]: "He said: 'I commend my sons to the people, and I pray the gods that the injustice of my death fall not upon my country.' Xenias having then struck him the first blow, Septimius, taking his robe in his two hands, covered his face with it, and received with constancy all the blows that were dealt him, without saying anything or doing anything unworthy of the name of Roman."

[*While he reads, he tips a little of the poison into a piece of paper that he has taken from his pocket and puts back there.*]

Malatesta: Go on reading. The phantoms are dispersing. The sky is ready for the dawn.

Porcellio [*opening again at random and reading*]: "The body of Phocion remained a long time exposed in front of the gate. None of his friends dared so much as to touch it. Later, when it had been secretly burned, a woman of the country who was present by chance at these funeral rites, placing in her dress the bones, which she had gathered up, buried them under her hearth, saying: 'O my hearth, keep with care these remains of so great a man, that they may be rendered to the tomb of his ancestors, on the day when the Athenians shall have returned to reason.' "

MALATESTA: Isotta—

PORCELLIO: And yet even a fine text does not revive one so well as a goblet of wine, and its power, when all's said and done, is less mysterious than the power exercised over soul and action by a few drops of the juice of a fruit.

MALATESTA: That's true, it's one of the strangest mysteries.

[*He drinks. Porcellio drinks after him, then pours the poison into the jug.*]

PORCELLIO: One more draught, a libation to the shade of Plutarch.

MALATESTA: I drink to the noble texts that elevate the soul and make it believe that it will be, in face of death, what it has been in face of life. [*He drinks, and pours out for Porcellio, who stealthily throws the contents of the goblet out of the window.*] There are the texts. There is also this. [*He goes to look for medallions.*] The temple of Rimini is at the mercy of a bombard. At Rome they have already destroyed the inscriptions about my triumph. My fate will perhaps be like that of the Malatestas of Pesaro, driven out by the people, their palaces, their tombs ruined, their symbols everywhere effaced. But medallions are dispersed and can be buried. . . . Ah! the one by Pisanello, how lovely it is! [*He presses it to his heart.*] And the one by Montefiori, with the image of the rising sun. . . . [*He presses it to his forehead. He reads its legend.*] "*Jam illustrat omnia.*" Those are almost the same words that Philelphus dedicated to me, do you remember? [*He opens a volume.*] "Malatesta marks each object he touches with the seal of his intelligence." And Pius II, who hated me, even he wrote: "Malatesta excels in everything he undertakes." Do you really know everything that's been written about me? I'm sure there are things you have not collected. And yet that is important for the *Vita*. I must not be deprived of the praises that are due to me. I've been despoiled of everything; a sort of tribunal, a job-lot of nonentities, extorted from me my cities, my provinces, my subjects, my gold, which was so fine and so clear, alive as the cheek of a child. But there is my immortal portion, over which they have no power, inaccessible and intangible like the highest of the high mountains, which the foot of man has never trampled. That at least is safe, and I can lean on that. —What's this, you're trembling?

Porcellio: Am I trembling?

Malatesta: Yes, your hand is trembling.

Porcellio: Perhaps a slight chill from the open window. Besides, Your Highness is full of sad thoughts. How could I escape their malign influence?

Malatesta: There aren't any more sad thoughts when you are there, you and the *Vita*. Our witnesses for the defense always die before having borne witness. Or else they decamp. But you, you'll be faithful, Porcellio my friend, you'll be faithful? [*A pause.*] Won't you? It's on you now that I rely, for a book of which they'll make a great many copies has more chances than anything of surviving. Finish it as quickly as you can: I'm always in dread lest this one and only manuscript be destroyed by some squall of fortune. You alone can save me. And yet I'm not sure, not altogether sure of you. . . . I feel you are escaping me as at some moments I feel my life is escaping me, you who are now my real life. . . . "At the hour when silence shall be upon the things that I have done, as night falls upon the sleeping forests." Did I read that phrase somewhere? Or did I make it up? Or did someone say it to me? "At the hour when silence shall be upon the things that I have done." But here in my turn I'm not feeling very well. . . . I'm cold. . . .

PORCELLIO: I think really an evil draft has come in through the window.

MALATESTA: No, it's the soul has given its illness to the body. Ah, I feel ill. [*He tries to get up and falls back in the chair.*] My legs won't carry me. Come here, help me get up, I can't stand up alone now.—Well, come along! What are you waiting for?

PORCELLIO: You can't get up?

MALATESTA: No, my legs have gone dead. Porcellio, here! What is it? Why don't you come? What's happening?

PORCELLIO: You can't get up?

MALATESTA: No! No! I can't any more!

[*Porcellio goes and takes Malatesta's weapons and places them on the table, at his side of it, well away from Malatesta. Then he goes and takes the* Vita, *and, his eyes on Sigismondo, tears from it a leaf, lights it at the torch, and throws its ashes into a metal basin, and so on with the other leaves.*]

MALATESTA: Porcellio! What are you doing? The Vita! Traitor! Serpent! Ah, I understand, the wine, the poison. . . . Villain! My dagger! My sword! [*He tries to rise and falls back.*] The pain's depriving me of my reason. My hands are full of sweat. My mouth's drying up. [*He twists. He bellows. He bites his fingers. He tears open the doublet on his breast.*]

PORCELLIO: Come, my lord, a little dignity. History has its eyes fixed on you.

MALATESTA: Isotta! Isotta *mia!* I'm dying, and I was only beginning! I was at the foundations. . . . Isotta! Isotta *mia!*

PORCELLIO: And did not Your Magnificence write once to Duke Sforza that "a fine death ennobles a whole life"? At least I've read that in the *Vita*.

MALATESTA: All that is mortal about me is deserting me. My immortality, come to my help! Shades of the illustrious, my models, my idols, make me a sign, give me to understand that you accept me among you. Pompey, Cæsar, to me! To me! [*Apparition of the specter of Pompey, in a toga, bareheaded. Porcellio, terrified, crouches in a corner of the stage.*] Great Pompey, for whom his enemy wept. . . . [*Specter of Julius Cæsar, in armor, the laurel wreath on his head.*] And you, Cæsar, who harangued your troops in this very place, at Rimini, after crossing the Rubicon. . . . [*Specters of the Gracchi, wearing the tunic, bareheaded, holding each other by the hand.*] And you, the Gracchi, betrayed by all as I have been. . . . [*Specter of Scipio Africanus, in dazzling armor, with an immense and high plumed helmet.*] Scipio, savior of Rome, your glory three times dragged before the judges, condemned, exiled, O my ancestor! Say something to me, open your arms to me, say to me that my name will go on pulsing by the side of yours! Say to me that I am not going to cease to exist, that would be horrible.—No, nothing; not a gesture, not a sign. . . . Ah, they are fading!—Then let me, too, fade.

[*He collapses.*

Porcellio, after a moment, comes out of his shadowy corner and begins again burning, one by one, the leaves of the Vita Magnifici et Clarissimi Sigismondi de Malatestis.]

CURTAIN

Paris, winter 1943–4

NO MAN'S SON

or

MORE THAN BLOOD

⚜

A Play in Four Acts

CHARACTERS

GEORGES CARRION, *aged 43, a lawyer*
GILLES SANDOVAL ("GILLOU"), *aged 14 years and one month, his illegitimate son (unrecognized)*
A PORTER
MARIE SANDOVAL, *aged 45*
PAULETTE, *Marie's maid*

At Cannes, in the winter of 1940–1.

ACT I

A studio in the furnished villa occupied by Marie Sandoval. The end of October. After dinner. Lamps lit.

SCENE I

MARIE, GEORGES

[*As the curtain rises, Marie is reading an illustrated weekly. After a moment the doorbell rings several times, in a way that suggests a member of the family who is expected. Marie goes to open the door, and returns with Georges, who is carrying a briefcase.*]

MARIE: My dear, forgive me for not having been at the station to meet you. I've such a headache! This Cannes climate doesn't suit me at all.

GEORGES: You complain in this marvelous weather! One would think it was the dog-days, and in a week it'll be All Saints' Day.

MARIE: The Côte d'Azur is treacherous. Those streets that concentrate the wind from the sea—and the sunsets—

GEORGES: I see I did very wrong in making you come to Cannes. And that at Angoulême, this summer, lying on a mattress on the floor in the schoolhouse, among the hordes of the exodus,* you were better off than here.

* In May 1940, when the German army advanced on Paris, vast numbers of people took to the roads and made for the south. In France this is still currently called "the exodus." Readers will remember that the Germans did not then occupy the whole of France, but signed an armistice under which the country was divided into an occupied zone, ruled by the Germans directly, and an unoccupied zone, ruled from Vichy by Marshall Pétain's government. This division into two zones lasted until November 1942. Although the Vichy

MARIE: Don't be stupid. But I do realize that the Côte d'Azur frightens me. You found Gillou all right at the station? Why isn't he with you?

GEORGES: There was some movie star or other arriving by my train, and he stayed there open-mouthed, drinking him in with his eyes. Provided one has a suit of the latest cut, or merely a pale-pink silk scarf, one is a god to Gillou. Damn it, he got on my nerves and I left him. I think he'll be here in a moment.

MARIE: Nothing fresh at Marseille?

GEORGES: More and more work. Not that my fellow lawyers in Marseille are much pleased, I think, to see a well-known lawyer from the Paris bar come and settle among them. But the way I've been forced into this sort of exile for the duration of the war, and the fact that I'm an escaped prisoner, create a certain sympathy toward me here. Anyhow, sympathy or no sympathy! It weighs on one, the sympathy one gets. And it takes up time. More than hatred.

MARIE [*malicious*]: Mademoiselle Janine is well?

GEORGES: Mademoiselle Janine will be in the seventh heaven when she knows what an interest you take in her health. She is quite well.

MARIE: It wasn't by any chance for her, rather than for the attorney, that you stayed in Marseille this afternoon? To think that you reserve for your son—don't let's mention me, I don't count—a day and a half a week, and that you manage to whittle down that miserable day and a half! Getting here at nearly ten o'clock in the evening!

GEORGES: My dear, must I remind you that the basis of our relationship doesn't allow you to inflict on me scenes of jealousy?

MARIE: It's not for myself I'm arguing, it's for your son.

---

government was subservient to the Germans in many important ways, life in the unoccupied zone was easier and more free than in the other. (Translator's note.)

Georges: That's going a bit far! I set you both up in Marseille, where I'm obliged to live, because of my practice. Thereupon you declare after eight days that you can't bear that town. Then I set you up here, where I can only spend the week-end. And *you* reproach me with deserting my son!

Marie: It is a fact: I can't live at Marseille. That noise, that dust, and then that mistral. Oh, that mistral! If I had stayed at Marseille—I'm not joking or exaggerating—after six weeks I'd have had to go into a hospital for nervous diseases. And here's another fact: with you living at Marseille, and us two elsewhere, you can hardly see the boy any more. And that makes me wonder if the whole of our present arrangement, whose aim was to bring him near you, hasn't lost its point.

Georges: What are you getting at?

Marie: Sometimes I wonder if—if it wouldn't be just as well for Gillou and me—

Georges: To go back to Paris: that's it, isn't it? Parting. Gillou in Paris and me here, for years perhaps, because, being an escaped prisoner, it's impossible for me to go back to the occupied zone before the end of the war. And it would come to that, all that I've done, said, suffered, dreamed, hoped, contrived in the last four months. Or rather in the last two years. So that's all I mean to him, to you, after these two years of my affection and solicitude without reproach. Listen, Marie, you stupefy me. And you appall me. Is this a plan, or just a whim?

Marie: Let's say a wish. But a reasonable one, I think.

Georges: And the boy, you've told him of this wish?

Marie: Yes, more or less. . . .

Georges: And what did he say?

Marie: You know what kids are like. Sometimes he says one thing, sometimes another. Really, he doesn't mind. [*Noise of a latchkey, and of the apartment door opening.*] Here he is.

SCENE II

GEORGES, MARIE, GILLOU

MARIE: You did kiss your father, at the station?

GILLOU: Yes, twice.

GEORGES: It's true, now I come to think of it, I did find you rather cold and embarrassed-looking. The same sort of thing as your mother's headache! The little conspiracies during my absence. So, it seems you want to return to Paris.

GILLOU: Me!—I do what I'm told to do.

MARIE: Yesterday you had a more definite opinion. "This filthy place, Cannes!" and so on.

GILLOU: Yesterday I was in a bad temper because it rained all day. Rain at Cannes! Today it's different.

GEORGES: With your permission, I'd like to talk with him a moment alone.

MARIE [*sharply*]: With my "permission"! What is all this?

GEORGES: You have five and a half days each week to talk with Gillou alone. Grant me the same right for the day that's left.

MARIE: Granted! Granted! Besides, it hardly makes a change for me. Even when we're all three together, it's with him you chat, with him you laugh. I sometimes wonder what part I am playing between you.

GEORGES: You play the part of the mother.

MARIE: It's a poor part. Now, Gillou, be perfectly frank with your father. Above all, don't tell him anything to please me. I don't count.

SCENE III

GEORGES, GILLOU

GEORGES: I can't talk with you seriously when your mother is there. And I want to talk with you seriously.

GILLOU: All right, but don't be too long, because I've got school tomorrow at eight. I must go to bed early.

GEORGES: School on Sunday?

GILLOU: Oh, yes, it's Sunday.

GEORGES: So it's true, you want to go back to Paris?

GILLOU: No, no, I don't! It's Mother who said that!

GEORGES: In short, you tell her that you want to go back to Paris and me that you don't. I recognize your little game and your innocent dodges: accomplice with me against your mother, your mother's accomplice against me.

GILLOU: Paris or Cannes, I don't care two hoots. In Paris I have my pals, but here there's the sun. So, one or the other—

GEORGES: It's a long time since your mother got this idea of a return to Paris into her head?

GILLOU: She began talking to me about it three or four days ago.

GEORGES: To go back to the Paris of the armistice, at the beginning of winter, to the Paris of cold and no heating, of restrictions, of occupation, perhaps of bombardments, when one can live so peacefully at Cannes! But you, sincerely, what do you want?

GILLOU: I—you know very well I should like to stay with you. Only, if Mamma—

GEORGES: And if your mother insisted on going back to Paris, wouldn't you like to come back and live at Marseille with me? Each time you remain for a while without seeing your mother, you improve.

GILLOU: What about my school work? I'm not going to change every month, that's a bit thick! June, at Janson's. October, eight days at the Marseille *lycée* and then Olivieri's school at Cannes. November, back to Marseille!

GEORGES: You seem, all the same, not to mind going back in November to Janson's.

GILLOU: That, I'll have to. I can't leave Mamma. It's my mother.

GEORGES: But me you can leave. Yes, I understand.

[*Silence.*]

GILLOU [*very much the little boy*]: I'm sleepy!

[*He links arms with his father. They are on a sofa.*]

GEORGES [*disengaging his arm*]: None of these affectionate gestures that your words give the lie to.

GILLOU: You're angry?

GEORGES: I had counted on you. I've lost. That too was a dream.

GILLOU: What a fuss you make!

GEORGES: It was a lot of good, loving!

GILLOU [*nodding with sleep, or pretending*]: Next installment of this conversation tomorrow.

GEORGES: What?

GILLOU: Next installment of this conversation tomorrow!

GEORGES: A charming way of dismissing me.

GILLOU: I'm sleepy!

[*He stretches out his arms toward Georges, to embrace him. Georges moves away abruptly, then leaves the sofa and goes and sits in an armchair some way off. He gazes a long while at his son, who has fallen asleep, then, after hesitating, rises and draws near him.*]

GEORGES: Gillou! Gillou! You've nothing else to say to me? Wake up for a moment. I can't spend the night on that. . . . You've nothing else? [*He moves away again, goes toward the staircase, and calls:*] Marie!

SCENE IV

GEORGES, MARIE, GILLOU, [*asleep*]

GEORGES: Your son desires to go back to Paris with you. You can therefore, if you so wish, take the first refugee train to leave. I shall maintain you in Paris in the same condition as at Cannes.—I thought I had suffered during the collapse all that a man can suffer. I was wrong, there remained this. I won't hide it from you, I'll confess it by using an expression that may seem to you rather literary, but that corresponds to the reality: it has broken my heart. Why is it always sad, in the end, loving someone? Oh, I know my conduct— To have abandoned one's mistress at the birth of the child one had got her with—with the saving check, of course; I mean the check of a man who saves his skin—and then to have stayed for twelve years ignoring them as completely as if they'd never existed doesn't give you any great rights over them. Twelve years! And then one day in the subway—at the Châtelet station—face to face with you, you and a great little person. I looked at him; I liked him: I said to myself: "Why not love him?"—I loved him already. I must say that at that moment I was tormented by a sort of homesickness for fatherhood. You, you weren't happy, you were up against a difficult situation. From that day on, I saw to it that material life should no longer be a worry to you. . . .

MARIE: There! Can't you feel that that's precisely what embarrasses me, being dependent on you like this? We have nothing here, as you well know: just the three suitcases of the exodus. To be obliged to ask you when I need to buy a dress— Always taking, and giving nothing in exchange. . . . In Paris I shall work.

GEORGES: Why is being dependent on me suddenly painful

to you? For two years you haven't complained of it. But let me talk; you shall talk afterwards.—When I came back into your life, you were very decent. You accepted a situation that perhaps few women would have accepted with such honesty. . . .

MARIE: I accepted being no more to you than the mother of your child.

GEORGES: You had your home, where the boy lived with you; I kept mine. We met almost every day; but my private life remained mine. The sort of pact between us, that our relations should be made definitely clean of any sentimental-sensual syrup [*Marie shudders*] had a great deal to do with the success of the arrangement. I'm shocking you? Excuse me.

MARIE: It's nothing. Or rather, if you like, it's your way of putting things. For a year, fourteen years ago, you didn't treat our relations as sentimental-sensual syrup.

GEORGES: Our liaison did not last a year. It lasted seven months.

MARIE: What a precise memory! Seven months and how many days? Really, my dear! But have I the right to call you "my dear"? Isn't it a familiarity that's out of place between people like us? Once when you were on leave and we went to the florist's in the avenue Mozart, where we used to go often in the old days, I did so want to whisper in your ear: "Take me by the arm for five minutes. I'm ashamed."

GEORGES: It's funny: that's what I was thinking at Marseille, last month, at the restaurant where I was lunching with Gillou, when he took it into his head to read the paper from the hors-d'œuvre to the dessert. I was all the time wanting to say to him: "Talk to me a little. Because of the waiter."

MARIE: Gillou! There we are again! All right, let's talk about Gillou, it's more to the point.

GEORGES: Yes, let me say the things my heart's full of just now. Well, I was reminding you of how, after we found each other again, a year went by, during which—how put it simply?—during which, for the two of you, I never ceased to put your interest before mine. Then the war came, and in nine months I saw Gillou only three times, when I was on leave. Meanwhile I was coming to love him more and more: the magic of absence. . . . Alas, under my deceptive tin hat, I had my head turned, not forwards, but backwards, and I kept saying to myself: "He is flowering far away from me. I shall have missed his flowering. When I get back to him, even his laugh will have changed shape. . . ." The last letter I received from you was dated May 20, from Paris. Then there was the occupation, I was made prisoner, I escaped, I settled after the armistice at Marseille, without knowing what had happened to you, or even if you were alive: my letters you no longer answered. I have never told you what that time was like for me.

Marie: Yes you did, my dear, when we saw each other again at Angoulême.

Georges: I told you then hurriedly and in an offhand way: I was ashamed, as one is, at being so moved. But today it's best you should know it; today when between the two of you you're making the whole thing so vain and ridiculous.

Marie: Vain! Ridiculous! Because you're angry, you use words that are—

Georges: At Marseille I set to work to rebuild my professional life. But the thought of you, the thought of him, were sucking me dry, sucking dry in me all other thoughts, just as a sponge sucks dry a pool of water. I had thought it was this or that that gave my life a sense: I now saw it was loving. Gillou had many times been pretty disappointing: ah, why hadn't he been more so! I could have freed myself from him. My affection was gnawing at me and poisoning me. One gets used to everything, to discomfort, to cold, to continence, to daily danger; but not to ignorance of the fate of the person one loves.

MARIE: Do you think we didn't feel it too?

GEORGES: I lived through that ignorance for two months and one week. I kept writing all over France, to find out where you were: no one knew. Each time the postman brought no letter—that's to say twice a day—I stood for twenty minutes in the line at the general-delivery window without finding anything from you there, and my eyelids were painful from so much waiting in vain. I took all sorts of steps: you know my character; I kept on climbing flights of stairs and waiting for people: they could make me walk just as much as they wished. And then, one day, your letter!

MARIE: And your answer, with its opening words: "I am trembling with joy."

GEORGES: You were at Angoulême, in the herd of refugees. I went there, I brought away Gillou; for the first time, at Marseille, I lived alone with him, for three weeks, while you were resting with your friends at Chantenay.

MARIE: And it was then, and then only—do you imagine that I didn't notice?—that you committed yourself fully over him.

GEORGES: I had measured my affection, and its obstacles, and I had accepted them. As for him, I had measured his failings and his gaps, and I had accepted them too. After that, I no longer thought of him except in terms of the future. Think, only eight days ago I swallowed several insults, from men with whom I didn't want to quarrel, because I said to myself they might be useful to him later on. If there had only been me, I'd have let them have it. And it's now you want to tear him from me, and for years—that is, forever. You want that, and he, when I ask him what he thinks, answers that he doesn't care two hoots.

MARIE: What has he said to you now? He's always saying what he shouldn't.

GEORGES: It's not a question of what he should and what he

shouldn't say. He's told me the truth; that is, that he didn't care two hoots.

Marie: No, no, it's not true that he didn't care, and besides—

Georges: He doesn't care. Not a sign of regret, not a sign of emotion, whereas I—my cup is full. When a child is heavy-hearted, one can see it, and I didn't see it in him. When a man, too, is heavy-hearted, one can see it. . . . [*Overcome, his eyes full of tears*] Excuse me, I'm ridiculous. If he saw me, no doubt he'd find me a perfect scream. But when one has lived through what a Frenchman has lived through this summer, one's a sick man, at the mercy of his nerves. Often, talking of this or that, you've heard me answer: "I haven't those weaknesses." At this moment, I confess, I'm weak. It's because, in the last four months, I haven't managed to regain my balance. One day I'll regain it. One day Gillou'll no longer have the power to hurt me. One day there'll be a Monsieur Gilles Sandoval at whom I shall look and say to myself, with stupefaction: "To think I cried because of that individual."

Marie: Georges, will you let me, finally, get a word in! All that you've said is pointless, for I shan't leave Cannes, since you take it so hardly.

Georges: What's the good? The harm is done. It's been proved that this child's not attached to me. Better, then, that he should go and that this long misunderstanding should come to an end.

Marie: He is attached to you, he's always showing it: haven't you told me a hundred times of your surprise at his affectionate character?

Georges: He does often embrace me with great emotion, for no reason, as if he had some feeling of all the trouble I take over him. But the number of times also he's affectionate at the wrong moment! His absurd "I love you!" if I make him a present of a forty-sou stamp for his collection. And besides, when there's a serious question—

MARIE: He saw I wanted to go to Paris, and he pretended that he wanted to go there, to please me. He wants quite as much to stay at Cannes. You'll see how happy he'll be when I announce it to him. Gillou! Wake up! We're staying at Cannes!

GEORGES: Don't wake him up, really! Especially as now I want you to go. I tell you once more that the harm is done.

MARIE: Whether the harm's done or not, your heart is burning for me to stay. So don't tell me to go, and above all in a voice so lacking assurance. If the sacrifice I—

GEORGES: Already your sacrifice! The only sacrifices that matter are the ones one says nothing about. What's more, I'm extremely apprehensive of the sacrifices women make for me.

MARIE: All men are apprehensive of the sacrifices women make for them. That doesn't prevent them from accepting them. You accepted mine, didn't you? All right, let's drop it: it belongs to the past. And look at your little boy. Look how handsome he becomes when he's asleep. . . . I do so love his sleep. I love it because in it he recovers the look he had when he was five.

GEORGES: And I because sleep gives him the mystery he hasn't when he's awake. But why does he take on, when he sleeps, so poignant a look?

MARIE: Poignant? I don't see it.

GEORGES: A look—as if he were—

MARIE: Georges! Shut up! What a horrible idea!

GEORGES [*turning toward her*]: You won't make it into a weapon against me, that you've seen me weep because of him, me whom you've never seen weep because of you? And you won't despise me for it?

MARIE: Women do perhaps despise the men they see weep because of them. But not those they see weep because of their child. You have wept over your child: I should be really vile to turn that against you or to despise you for it. What's more, I'm going to reveal to you something that, I don't know why, I've not said anything about to you till now. When I told Gillou, a week after our famous meeting in the Châtelet subway, that you were his father, well, he wept too.

GEORGES: Wept? Why?

MARIE: How can one know? A thing for you to dream over. You won't, will you, tell him that I told you?

GEORGES: And you, you won't tell him that today I wept because of him?

MARIE: No. [*Looking at Gillou*] But—wouldn't one almost say he's weeping at this moment?

GEORGES: So you don't know, even now, that when he's asleep, the sweat comes out on his face, while his body remains dry? No, you didn't know! Any more than you had noticed, during twelve years, that he had a little stain, as of wine, on the bend of his left knee. It needed me to reveal that to you, the third day after I found you again.

MARIE: Having him under my eyes almost without a break, there are little things about him I no longer see: it's the opposite would be surprising. [*Trying to lift her son*] Gillou, go to bed, my darling. Oh, how heavy he is! Good-by to my hopes of putting him back into shorts next summer and being still able to take him on my knees! Come, Gillou, go to bed!

GEORGES [*watches her for a moment in her vain efforts, then*]: Come, let me do it. You see very well you can't.

[*He raises Gillou easily and carries him out. Marie follows him.*]

CURTAIN

ACT II

Same setting. A month later [end of November].

SCENE I

GILLOU, PAULETTE

[*As the curtain rises, Paulette is finishing "doing" the studio.*]

GILLOU: Paulette, would it be a bother for you to keep this lottery ticket for me? My father doesn't want me to buy them, and I don't know where to park it.

PAULETTE: Why not let your mother keep it for you? *She* buys lottery tickets! A pile that high!

GILLOU: I know Mamma too well. If it came out a winner, she'd give me twenty francs and use the rest to buy me useful things. And that's not good enough.

PAULETTE: I'd say she's better, your mamma, today.

GILLOU: I think the doctor's coming this evening.

PAULETTE: If he comes as he came last time!

GILLOU: Yes, that was rather thick. A doctor should come when he says. It's we who pay him! Anyhow, if he does come, I hope he'll let Mamma go out.

PAULETTE: She's pining away. That's what's making her ill. You've been at Cannes for six weeks now: she can't take to it.—But tell me, why does your father forbid you to buy tickets in the National Lottery?

GILLOU: He says it's stupid. He explained to me why, but I can't remember. Oh, yes, it's immoral. . . . He said that if anyone made him a present of a ticket in the National Lottery, he'd give it to a poor man rather than keep it: that it would dirty his hands.

PAULETTE: He's a strict man, your father, Master Gillou.

GILLOU: Oh, yes, Papa's a tough one!—Like me.

PAULETTE: All right, I'll keep your ticket for you. But what'll you give me for my trouble?

GILLOU: I'll teach you the trick of getting into the movie without paying.

PAULETTE: Done. And what'll you do with the dough if you win?

GILLOU: If I win a thousand francs, I'll buy a handbag for four hundred francs for Mamma; I'll give three hundred francs to my father, because with him one never knows what he wants, I don't think he wants anything; and I'll keep three hundred francs to chuck around.

PAULETTE: To chuck around on what?

GILLOU: Oh, silly things.

PAULETTE: And you'll give three hundred francs to your father, who's forbidden you to buy tickets? Then he'll know you've disobeyed him.

GILLOU: Yes, that's a nuisance. But it would be rotten not to give him anything. [*Casually, he wipes his shoes with the lining of one of the curtains.*]

PAULETTE: Oh, Master Gilles!

GILLOU: What's it matter, since it isn't ours! They rent it high enough, their precious villa. [*Looking out of the window*] Here's the postman. Don't bother. I'll go and open the door.

[*Paulette goes out. Sound of voices in the hall. Gillou comes back with the letters.*]

GILLOU: Oh! there's a postcard from Havre, from Grandpa. But he must be ill, like Mamma; he's made somebody else write it for him. [*He reads.*] *Dear Mariette*—Mariette, that's new—*At last your father has found me something at Havre. I left Paris on Wednesday. I think this unhoped-for situation*—Oh! but it isn't from Grandpa. It's signed: *Roger*. Roger?

SCENE II

MARIE, GILLOU

GILLOU: Look, the mail. There's even a card from Havre.

MARIE [*after reading it greedily, with emotion*]: They gave you this card like that?

GILLOU: Yes. You had it sent to you general delivery?

MARIE: Before your father had taken the villa, I gave several people my address: Cannes, general delivery. The other day, when I saw I wasn't getting better and couldn't go out, I wrote to the post office to send the general-delivery letters on to me here. Usually in such a case the post office sends the letters on in an envelope. One has to come to this region of savages to see them sent on like this.

GILLOU: What does it matter that the post office forwarded you this postcard open?

MARIE: Oh, it doesn't matter at all. It's from a cousin of ours, a distant cousin—on Mamma's side. . . .

GILLOU: I don't know him?

MARIE: If you had to know all the family! Cousins, we've plenty of them! [*Silence.*] All the same, your grandfather might write more often, or your grandmother. What a life, my God, what a life! Far from one's home, far from one's relations, alone, without friends, without anything to do, in a climate that's bad for you, in a town one detests, and without even being able to correspond openly with the people one's fond of! And for how long! And always so disappointed, in everything, while elsewhere— And all this in order that your father may see you for a few hours a week, which he spends finding fault with you.

GILLOU: You never stop complaining. Let's go home, to Paris, and get it over once for all.

MARIE: You know quite well that I can't raise that again with your father. [*Passing in front of the window, she puts her hand quickly over her eyes.*] That sunshine blinds me! I'm going to take to wearing dark glasses—dark glasses at the end of November, the world's upside down!

GILLOU: You're the only one who'd think of complaining of its being sunny at the end of November.

MARIE: And suppose the sun hurts me, after all! People never think of my health. Oh, for the subdued sky of the Ile-de-France or the Atlantic! At Havre, in your grandparents' house, the wind from the sea has never made me ill like the damp heat of this Mediterranean. If only we were at Havre. . . .

GILLOU: You're not going to want to go to Havre, just now! Under the bombs!

MARIE: The bombs?

GILLOU: Didn't Grandfather write to you that they'd been raided?

MARIE: He wrote once or twice that there'd been a warning.

GILLOU: He wrote: "Daily air-raid warnings."

MARIE: So, you read all the postcards sent to me? A warning isn't a raid.

GILLOU: And with the chance that the English may attack any day.

MARIE: That's just radio propaganda. And here too one's in danger of being bombed.

GILLOU: Really, Mamma, there are limits!

MARIE: Besides, even if one were bombed, what can it matter!

GILLOU: Oh, come, what next?

MARIE: Better to die near a person—I mean, surrounded by affection, like that of your grandparents, than to live abandoned and disdained.

GILLOU: I, I don't want to die. I, I've all my life before me. You—

MARIE: I—what? I'm old, is that it? So I may as well die.

GILLOU: I didn't say that. But, after all, you've had your life.

MARIE: I've had my life! So that I've no longer the right to live! Well, all the same, I want to go on living, a long time, and to be happy.

GILLOU: You said a second ago that you didn't care if you were bombed.

MARIE: Oh, shut up now, little love-bird. Look at him: trying to make me think I'm contradicting myself! And, in the first place, the point isn't affection, the point is health. You've no idea of what it's like to feel that you're wasting away, that your health's in danger. The damp atmosphere of this place—

GILLOU: There isn't any damp at Havre?

MARIE: Your grandparents' house is a couple of miles from the town. Two miles inland, it's no longer a sea climate. Havre is a very healthy town. You'd feel fine there. Not to speak of the cost of living. Take one example, out of twenty: here chicory costs ten francs a kilo; at Havre, your grandmother writes, one can get it for six francs fifty.

GILLOU: No, no! Havre's the end!

MARIE: And you may be sure that at Havre you'll get better teaching than here. No humbug about those people.

GILLOU: But then I should be lower down in composition.

MARIE: Perhaps, but at the end of the year you'd have learned more, and you wouldn't be in danger of failing in your exams later on. Besides, your grandfather could give you some lessons.

GILLOU: He's old!

MARIE: He's old, but he's got leisure, whereas your father is always busy. Your father makes a fuss if you go into his room when he's working.

GILLOU: He did say, all the same: "I forbid you to come into my room when I'm working. But, at bottom, I'm always more or less waiting for you to arrive. I even left my door ajar yesterday to give you the idea of coming in as you passed."

MARIE: He said that to you once. . . . And besides, your grandfather would teach you to ride.

GILLOU: He has a horse?

MARIE: A beautiful little horse that's quite round: one would think he was fed on butter.

GILLOU: It's true? And he'd let me get on him? What's the little horse called?

MARIE: He's called Frison.

GILLOU: Frison! And you'd buy me boots?

MARIE: Of course. But forget it, my poor Gillou, for it's out of the question. Better not stir up such dreams. Come, darling, come and love Mamma, console her. My little one, always my little one to me! How silly it is to want to do anything else in life but hug you! [*She kisses him.*] Ah, how good it is! Your neck as fresh as the crumb of a loaf. . . . And your good smell. . . . You love me? I, I love you a little more each day; I'm so lonely. . . . I think I've never loved you so much as today. And besides, I, at least, when you hug me, don't say to you, like your father, that you're a little mollycoddle.

GILLOU: He says it as a joke.

MARIE: Not as much as you think.

GILLOU: So you want me to ask him to let us go to Havre?

MARIE: No, it's no use. After the scene he made a month ago. Think of it, in this very place, while you were asleep, he had tears in his eyes.

GILLOU: Why?

MARIE: Because you were ready to leave him and go back to Paris. But you won't tell him I've told you, will you? Draw away from me, I hear him coming. If he sees you loving me, there'll be more remarks.

GILLOU: You're sure you don't want me to mention it to him?

MARIE: If you like—without seeming to: simply to see what

he'll answer. . . . Above all, don't let it appear to come from me.

SCENE III

GEORGES, MARIE, GILLOU

MARIE: Monsieur Mauduit telephoned to know whether or not you agreed to take on his case.

GEORGES: No.

MARIE: He seemed very keen on getting a yes.

GEORGES: I like refusing.

MARIE: If he rings up again while you're upstairs, should I let you know?

GEORGES: Please. When one refuses, one should give oneself the pleasure of doing it oneself. On second thoughts, no. I care too damn little. Answer him for me.

MARIE: What reason shall I give for your refusal?

GEORGES: None. I don't have to give reasons.

MARIE: And if he insists?

GEORGES: Ring off.

GILLOU: Why are you refusing?

GEORGES: I've already told you that I only plead the cases of people who appear to me to be in the right.

GILLOU: And he is not in the right?

GEORGES: Everyone's in the right. But I don't like his sort of right.

GILLOU: I find that stupid, your refusing. So you didn't become a lawyer to make money?

GEORGES: That remark is you all over. Already, the other day, you were saying that Mademoiselle Bastien's a mug. Mademoiselle Bastien spends her time on social work with a disinterested generosity that's rare: that's enough to make you consider her a mug. Just as in your eyes a man of intellect is a poor fish. And a man who puts some poetry into his life has a screw loose.

MARIE: Really, Gillou, one can think certain things and not say them.—You love to scold him. Except when it's I who scold him, of course; in those cases this little personage is always right! But don't be too hard on our child. I found in my room a bouquet of mimosa. It was a present from Gillou. A sarcastic smile? That's all that that inspires in you?

GEORGES: Every young boy who's just done something silly buys his mother a bouquet. That is classic.

MARIE: You ought to be ashamed of interpreting in that way, and in front of him, this child's action.

GEORGES: And every young boy who's done something silly links arms with his mother. That also is classic.

[*Gillou withdraws his arm, which he had linked with his mother's.*]

MARIE: You're right to withdraw your arm, my darling. You know quite well your father finds it ridiculous for a child to love his mother. [*With some tartness*] Never mind, what a profound psychologist you are!

GEORGES: I understand what I like, and I don't understand what I don't like. And since there's little I like, in the last resort I don't understand a great deal. The years go by, and yet, as regards people's souls, I'm always going from darkness to darkness. About them I manage to make astonishing and infantile mistakes.

MARIE: My father has a theory that the men who are supposed to be psychologists by profession, the lawyers, magistrates, confessors, novelists—in their private life fail to see what is staring them in the face.

GEORGES: There are also, in a celebrated phrase, mothers who think they know their son because they darn his shorts.

MARIE: Just as there are fathers who think they're looking after their son because they say to him, as they thump him on the back! "Stand up straight, my child!"

GEORGES: A hit!

MARIE: "I understand what I like, and I don't understand what I don't like."

[*Gillou hums.*]

GEORGES: I forbade you to sing that song when I'm there.

MARIE [*to Georges*]: What is it? Is it a dirty song?

GEORGES: Worse: it's an inane song. And I prefer, if I must choose, a nation of toughs to a nation of ninnies. Two years ago Gillou was buying off street singers sentimental ballads, written by illiterates, printed with ten mistakes in spelling. Today he brings home songs said to be "for the young," also written by illiterates, with the same number of spelling-mistakes, but even more provoking than the others because these have pretensions to be educational and uplifting. And don't tell me that that belongs to his age. When I was Gillou's age, that song would have disgusted me just as it disgusts me today.

[*Marie, going out, makes Gillou a sign of connivance. Meaning: "Don't get in a panic. You know your father has his whims."*]

SCENE IV

GEORGES, GILLOU

GILLOU: Here, here's a ticket for the National Lottery I'd bought. But since you forbid it, I'm giving it to you. You can slip it to some poor man.

GEORGES: Good for you, Gillou! You're a decent child after all, sometimes.

GILLOU: Well, then, give me a kiss. You never give us a kiss.

GEORGES: I gave the lad in question a kiss first thing in the morning.

GILLOU: First thing doesn't count. If you haven't given me a kiss before I've got to "twenty," you'll see! One, two, three . . . [*Georges kisses him.*] D'you love me? I love you more every day. I've never loved you so much as today.

GEORGES: The devil you do!

GILLOU [*giving him a great jab in the stomach with his elbow*]: Laughing at me as usual! Even if I had a little sister, I'd love you more than her.

GEORGES: Poor little sister! Not yet born, and already done away with.

GILLOU [*with another jab*]: Still won't take me seriously!

GEORGES: You kiss me so much that I wonder if I haven't given you a pack of cigarettes without noticing it! [*Another jab from Gillou.*] Or if you're not asking for one. [*Another jab.*] Look here, old boy, you're a bore with that elbow of yours. It hurts! Do you know what they really mean, those jabs? They mean: "I'm too stupid to know how to answer him, so I answer him this way." Butchers' boys give each other just that kind of jab.

GILLOU: So I'm stupid?

GEORGES: You've been known to be.

GILLOU: But—really stupid? Or do you tell me so because you're fond of me?

GEORGES: What do you mean?

GILLOU: Don't you remember? At Marseille you used to tell me I was stupid; I said I wasn't; and then you explained: "Don't you understand? I tell you you're stupid because I'm fond of you."

GEORGES: Yes, I remember, I did say that. . . . But there are times when you are stupid *really*. With your petty way of seeing things, your worship of false values, and your instinctive animosity against the true ones, that sort of poor quality which all too often comes through in you—

GILLOU: So, you notice everything I say!

GEORGES: I should love you precious little if I didn't notice everything you say. Still, you're nice all the same. [*He passes his hand through Gillou's hair.*]

GILLOU: Don't! You're ruffling my hair!

GEORGES: I like ruffling your hair.

GILLOU: All right, ruffle it a little. But not the part.

GEORGES: What a bore your mother is, always wanting you to plaster your hair down. You're much nicer with your hair tousled. I feel much more drawn to take trouble over your education when you haven't got a jugful of water on your hair, like a hotel elevator-boy! It's incredible how mothers, who know so well what suits them, manage to have no taste where their boys are concerned.

GILLOU: Mamma thinks tousled hair is bad style. A part makes you look serious.

GEORGES: Alas, seriousness is more than that. I should like you to have hair like a mad dog, and to be serious. But everything serious makes you yawn, as with certain men everything tender makes them laugh. When one explains something to a woman, even if she doesn't understand, she listens, she thinks of an answer. You, you turn your head away and you talk of something else. You have a way of volatilizing anything in the least profound I say to you, of making it nonexistent, either by not answering or by answering beside the point. And we fall again into silence, and to waiting for your yawn, or to your petty nonsense. And everything dies like that, for lack of any grip on you. And yet, and yet—I'd have liked to make of you a man.

GILLOU: I'd rather be a woman, so as to get out of military service.

GEORGES: You see, there you are! Always answering frivolously. And worse than frivolously. "To get out of something": that's your whole ambition, all you boys of 1940.

GILLOU: I *am* ambitious!

GEORGES: You said to me the other day: "I'm not ambitious."

GILLOU: Oh yes, so I did.—Well, do you want me to talk seriously?

GEORGES: Certainly!

GILLOU: You won't scold me?

GEORGES: You'll be scolded if you deserve it.

GILLOU: Hangman!

GEORGES: "Hangman!" Magnificent! Shades of Molière. Oh, beauties of an expensive education! No, I won't scold you, if only because of "hangman!"

GILLOU: Well— Well no, you will scold me.

GEORGES: Promise I won't. Go on.

GILLOU [*plunging*]: How stupid you are not to live with Mamma again! I'm sure she'd like it.

GEORGES: Old boy, there you've touched on a question you don't understand. There's an immense gain, in many of the things of life, in having these things divided up neatly and without smudges. My present relations with your mother were decided by both of us, two years ago, without difficulty. Supposing they are sometimes awkward, if they were different they would lead, not to awkwardnesses, but to clashes. It may seem strange that I am with her as I am. In fact I am acting with extreme wisdom.

GILLOU: You might at least be nicer to her. When you wrote to me from Marseille, the other day, explaining me about my Latin translation, you didn't put any message for her in the letter. She read it and was upset.

GEORGES: I don't see why your mother reads the letters I write you.

GILLOU: She always reads them.

GEORGES: And she gets upset for a trifle like that!

GILLOU: She was upset too because you hadn't written to her.

GEORGES: I was writing to you for a special purpose: your Latin homework. I had no particular reason for writing to her.

GILLOU: Yes, but just now she is ill. She needs little things that can give her pleasure.

GEORGES: Don't let's waste too much breath on your mother's illness. Mine once described to me how, when she was little, she sometimes bandaged up one of her legs, without being in the least hurt, in order to make herself interesting and to get sympathy. Your mother is bored at Cannes and dreams of Paris. That's her illness.

GILLOU: She says she's disappointed.

GEORGES: People who are disappointed always deserve to be so.

GILLOU: Don't you see she's unhappy?

GEORGES: I don't see she's unhappy because I don't want to. Being unhappy is believing oneself unhappy. These phantom griefs don't deserve respect. And besides, let her suffer a bit. Pain is more soothing than joy.

GILLOU: If she could hear you!

GEORGES: She and I are real good friends, and nothing serious separates us. At moments she has a grudge against me, for loving you. And because you return it. Sometimes when you give me a kiss in her presence, I seem to feel her tremble: one would think I hadn't the right to receive those kisses. And I, at moments, bear her a slight grudge, because you love her. But at bottom I'm grateful to her for having loved you and loved you well, just as she too is pleased, I'm sure, that there's a man who loves you, and who in fact happens to be your father.

GILLOU: If only you lived with us, but she's got no one to talk with. At Havre she would have my grandparents.

GEORGES: At Havre, under the bombs, and with the English always on the point of landing!

GILLOU: That's all stuff and nonsense.

GEORGES: It's not stuff and nonsense at all.

GILLOU: And besides, at Havre living is cheap. Think, a kilo of chicory—

GEORGES: Please don't talk to me about chicory.—Oh, but—that chicory betrays your mother. I'm beginning to understand. Confess that your mother has now set her heart on Havre and that you were sent by her to sound me out.

GILLOU: Not at all.

GEORGES: You're a bad liar; one is a bad liar when one's lying for the benefit of someone else. Well, I forbid you to play the go-between in this way. My word, if your mother wasn't a calm sort of person, I should end by thinking there was some romantic infatuation in her mania to be gone from here. But the question of Havre, if question there is, is going to be quickly solved.—Marie!

SCENE V

GEORGES, MARIE, GILLOU

GEORGES: It seems there's an idea of Havre floating in the air. But I shall be very firm about it. Paris, even, at a pinch. . . . But Havre! With the aircraft, the risks of a landing, the health situation, which is bad—I'm in constant touch with the Havas Agency at Marseille and I know there is talk of evacuating the children from the western ports. Granted, I've only been a father for two years, but now I am one: it's my duty and my right to protect my son against no matter whom, even against you. Even if he isn't altogether what I should like him to be. Even if, very often, he rubs me the wrong way and makes me sad. You will not go to Havre. You could only go there with help from me, for, now that the refugee trains have been stopped, you need a permit. That's difficult to get; you are incapable of getting it by yourself, and I alone can get it for you, through Havas and Maurice Routier.

MARIE: So you do what you like with us, because of your social position!

GEORGES: Yes, I do what I like with you, because of my social position. Because of my money, even: why don't you say it? It's what you think. You have given me powers over you. You have given them to me formally, since you signed a deed delegating to me paternal rights over Gillou. You have given me powers: I am using them. Don't return to this subject. If you are capable of talking about something else at this moment, let's chat calmly, as if nothing had happened. If not, go up to your room: that'll be the best thing. [*Marie looks at him for a moment, beside herself, then starts to go, then has a second thought.*]

MARIE: Here, I'd better give you back this cachet you gave Gillou this morning for his headache. He brought it to me because it has marked on the top of it: "Not to be given to children." [*She goes out.*]

SCENE VI

GEORGES, GILLOU

[*A pause, during which Georges follows Marie with his eyes. Then he turns round and perceives that Gillou, having dipped two fingers in the water of a vase of flowers, is wetting his hair.*]

GEORGES: You're putting water on your hair again, after all I've said to you.

GILLOU: I'm just putting some on the tuft at the back.

GEORGES: All right, go up and join your mother. I'm sure that's what you want.

CURTAIN

ACT III

Same scene. A month later [beginning of January].

SCENE I

GEORGES, GILLOU

GILLOU [*buried in a newspaper*]: I say, they're giving *Lend Me Your Wife* at the Rex.

GEORGES: *Lend Me Your Wife!*

GILLOU: I've seen it already, but I'm going again. Oh, it is good! It's so idiotic!

GEORGES: In my time people would have said: "It's idiotic, so it's bad." Nowadays they say: "It's idiotic, so it's good."

GILLOU [*picking up an illustrated weekly*]: Do you like Rita Leandri? You know she's married Wonder Clark, in Hollywood. [*With a knowing air*] She's a great artist.

GEORGES: A great artist? Always your respect! Your respect given without rhyme or reason. Ah, if only you could be a little rebellious! A great artist? You've seen her act?

GILLOU: No, but it says so out of the paper.

GEORGES: *In* the paper, not *out of* the paper. How many times have I got to repeat that?

GILLOU: But everyone says *out of*. Our prof says *out of*. And the prof knows what he's saying, I should think!

GEORGES: Everyone is wrong. To say "*out of* the paper" is as incorrect and as vulgar as to say "the fift," for example.

GILLOU: You're the only one who talks good French.

GEORGES: If I were a stranger in the house, you'd listen to me; I should be the unknown, the seductive, perhaps the dangerous. But I'm the father—that is to say, the person one doesn't take seriously. Oh, obviously, if tomorrow I plead some sensational case and my photo is in *Paris-Soir* accompanied by three flattering lines of print, from that very day everything would be changed, what I say would cease to seem laughable to you. That's where we stand: my relations with my child, and the possibility of his becoming somebody worth while, depend on the fact of my photo appearing or not in *Paris-Soir*. [*Gillou shrugs his shoulders.*] You whine: "I wish I could see you every day," or perhaps you whisper, with graceful malice: "I rather missed you this week." You ask me to go out with you, you stupefy me with imploring kisses to make me keep you company in the studio, and then, when I'm there, you read the paper. A day when you haven't read the paper in my presence is a victory. And when you do read the paper! Plunged in it like a pig in a dung-heap. One could prick you with a red-hot needle and you wouldn't wince. You wallow in things that I can't even imagine without feeling soiled. Do you hear? Drop that magazine. One would have to be a case of arrested development to take pleasure in that filth.

GILLOU: Well, what do you want me to do?

GEORGES: Is there nothing in life, then, but reading the papers?

GILLOU: You know very well I like browsing.

GEORGES: You call that browsing!

GILLOU: Everything is forbidden! A month ago you forbade us to go to Havre. Now one can't read the paper any more. One can't listen to the radio. One can't play cards any more. You made a scene with Mamma because I played belotte with her every evening.

GEORGES: A self-respecting boy has other things to do than play belotte.

GILLOU: What things to do? Yes, you'd like me to play games. Games are all right. But belotte is wrong. Why?

GEORGES: I'm tired of trying to make you feel things you

ought to feel on your own. Tired of taking trouble for someone who always lets me down.

GILLOU: I—I let you down! . . .

GEORGES: You let me down by being what you are. Two years ago, when I took you back, you were twelve; it was a little young for it to be possible to form an idea of you. Then I lost sight of you for the whole year when I was mobilized. When we were reunited five months ago, you didn't disappoint me; on the contrary: all freshness, all grace. But later I got to know you, and I had to pipe down. And the better I know you, the more I find that there is little in you that's worth knowing.

GILLOU: What do you expect—I am as I am!

GEORGES [*after shrugging his shoulders*]: I think of those little sheets of paper on which I had noted down remarks on your character, advice for you, rules of life. When I said to you: "Would you like me to read them to you?" you answered: "By and by." It was better, after all, than if you'd answered: "What a bore!" as I thought you would. But time passed. I saw that you'd forgotten about it, that it didn't interest you, that my words would have no importance and no effect: they would fall on you like rain on the sea. . . . And I didn't mention it again. For weeks I brought those sheets home every Saturday in my pocket, without ever finding the atmosphere favorable enough to pull them out, knowing well that, if you listened to me, you'd only do so from politeness. Sometimes I thought of giving them to you and saying: "It's not a bit necessary for you to talk to me about them. All I ask of you is not to destroy them." But even that seemed to me still too much. And every Monday I took them back to Marseille, a little more dog-eared, and I kept looking at them with melancholy, as if what was written there was the whole story of my failure with you. And one day I came to the conclusion that the trial was sufficient, and I threw them away.

GILLOU: And you, Dad, when I showed you my end-of-term notebooks, you hardly looked at them. One little glance, a few times "Very good! Very good!" without interest. . . .

GEORGES: Gillou, for once there's come out of you a remark that touches me. If I hurt you a little by seeming not to be interested in your notes, I ask your forgiveness. But there, too, I must explain. You know I don't attach very great importance to your studies. What is important for you doesn't lie there.

GILLOU: Then where does it? At school at least I'm not bored.

GEORGES: At home you're bored?

GILLOU: Oh yes, stiff! It's not so bad when you are there. . . . But the rest of the time!

GEORGES: You're bored! Like your mother! It's catching. *I*'ve never been bored, in the whole of my life. Not one hour, even when I was a child: There is always an intelligent way of not wasting one's time. "One is never bored when one is doing great things." Do you know who said that? Balzac.

GILLOU: Is Balzac good?

GEORGES: "Is Balzac good?" One would think you were talking of a Camembert. Sometimes, like that, you offer me temptations. You seem interested. "Is Balzac good?" "Is it true that Condorcet was a tough?" I answer, but I see at once that your eyes are wandering, that you don't care two hoots, and that you said that as you might have said anything else. In the woods, in Alsace, at night, the fellows in the regiment used to ask: "Anyone following?" to know if the others, behind them, hadn't lost contact. Well, you, you're never following. How hard it is, how painful, this hopeless effort to touch another creature with words! And yet that is life.

GILLOU: Well, anyhow, Balzac?

GEORGES: All right, yes, "Balzac is good."

GILLOU: But how do you know when a book is good or bad?

GEORGES: That, old boy, is too complicated.

GILLOU: I'm not worth the trouble of explaining it to me?

GEORGES: Er—

GILLOU: I'll get the prof to explain it to me.

GEORGES: Your prof's an ass.

GILLOU: You're jealous of my teachers.

GEORGES: Is that remark yours, or your mother's?

GILLOU: Why my mother's?

GEORGES: I recognize in you the passages that are your mother's as one recognizes the doe in the forest by her tracks. You are always echoing someone or something. You echo the paper. You echo the professor. You echo your mother. Never anything of your own.

GILLOU: If I echoed you, you'd be very pleased. [*He laughs.*]

GEORGES: Why are you laughing?

GILLOU: You claim to know everything better than everybody and you don't even know the telephone number of your office in Marseille!

GEORGES: That's memory; it has nothing to do with judgment. Memory—you can have it; it's the intelligence of fools. [*Gillou, furious, plunges into his weekly again. Georges snatches it away from him and tears it up.*]

GILLOU: Oh, really, that's the limit! You make us sick of you. I'm fed up, I am! I'm fed up!

SCENE II

GEORGES, GILLOU, MARIE

MARIE: What's this shouting?

GILLOU: Papa's torn up your paper.

MARIE [*in consternation*]: And I hadn't read it!

GILLOU: It seems that only people with arrested development can read that paper.

GEORGES: Go up to your room. You will be severely punished tomorrow for your rudeness.

GILLOU: What punishment?

GEORGES: You'll see tomorrow.

GILLOU [*worried*]: No, you might at least tell me at once—

GEORGES: Go up to your room.

SCENE III

GEORGES, MARIE

GEORGES: My son is a cruel trial to me. The best part of me and my deepest self are oppressed by him. All that, in my eyes, gives value to life not only doesn't count in his, but is the object of his derision. I, who so love childhood, find that childhood, through him, disgusts me. A child, and it's mine, is making me ashamed for mankind.

MARIE: Why not simply say that it gets on your nerves to have him take up your time and disturb you in your work?

GEORGES: You don't understand. I would love to sacrifice to him a much more considerable part of my work if I didn't know that all I do for him is pure loss. From this moment I have judged him.

MARIE: Judged! A lad who was only thirteen a few weeks ago. If he were twenty, even so—

GEORGES: The soil is bad. I can feel it. Everything shouts it aloud.

MARIE: "Everything": what? A child's reflections and reactions, which it's absurd to take seriously.

GEORGES: One little word can condemn a human being more certainly than if you'd seen him stealing from a shop window.

MARIE: No, no. A human being isn't a glass, which you've only to flick once with your finger to tell if it's made of glass or of crystal. And besides, which of us is crystal? You who spend your life trying to save guilty people are very severe with your child.

GEORGES: With whom would one be severe, if not with one's child?

MARIE: With whom would one be indulgent, if not with one's child?

GEORGES: When I open my window on the world, what makes me suffer most is the spectacle of indulgence. I find it everywhere, high and low. . . . Indulgence, that serpent whose head one ought to crush.

MARIE: A lawyer's speech!

GEORGES: A lawyer's speech! Your expression. Every time I say anything with emphasis and emotion, something that comes from my heart or my vitals, to you it's a lawyer's speech!

MARIE: It's from hatred of indulgence, I suppose, that you wouldn't tell him at once how he would be punished?

GEORGES: Yes. To make his dread of it last.

MARIE: I never knew you be so cruel to me.

GEORGES: When I was young I pleaded in the juvenile-delinquency courts. I was full of pity for those children. But I've no pity for him, because he is my son.

MARIE: It's monstrous!

GEORGES: The others, I'd not given them anything. And besides, what should I think of myself if, while being hard in public affairs, I relaxed in private affairs?

MARIE: In short, you find Gillou is an utter bore. . . .

GEORGES: It's curious, you are always a bit to one side of the truth. The evening when I wept in this chair, you told me I was "angry." I'm not reproaching Gillou with being a bore: I should be worried about a child who wasn't a bit of a bore. I'm reproaching him with being of poor quality.

MARIE: You talk to him in a way that's far beyond his age, in a really extraordinary way. No wonder if he doesn't seem to you to rise to your height when he answers.

GEORGES: I talk to him in a style that comes out of me like fire. I couldn't talk to him differently.

MARIE: The deception he causes you would be caused to you by any child. You know as well as I do that conversation between a kid and a grown-up can't be carried on too long without tiring both of them.

GEORGES: No. At the time of the juvenile-delinquency court, I met children, working-class children too, with whom one could converse for an hour without getting tired, and what is more, with pleasure and interest. They were acute, they had the right reactions, they were sometimes inspired in their sentiments or expressions, it was a kind of genius. . . . Not only is Gillou of poor metal, but he cruelly lacks any spark of genius.

MARIE: You were not so smitten with children when you deserted your son for twelve years, without so much as bothering about what Christian name he would have, as one leaves it to the cook to give names to the kittens. Poor little wretch, over whose head are whirling the frightful forces of misfortune and of death; and his father has just added contempt. Contempt has hold of you like a disease.

GEORGES: If only I could inoculate my country with that disease. I should like to serve it as a master of contempt.

MARIE: What a way of speaking!

GEORGES: I speak the way men speak who are men, not monkeys and mongrels. That's why there are so many people who don't understand me.

MARIE: I'm afraid for that child. For there's not the least possibility of gentleness where there's contempt.

GEORGES: Don't say anything against contempt. With power and contempt one could blow the earth sky-high.

MARIE: We're not talking of the earth, but of our son.

Everyone pays me compliments about him. Only you. . . . The other day Madame Beaufumé gave him a set of rare stamps. And when I said to her: "I'm overwhelmed. There's no reason—" she answered: "He's so charming that it's really a duty to give him pleasure."

GEORGES: His charm isn't in dispute. When he's not making me sick at heart, I find him enchanting.

MARIE: Besides, it's more than charm. You know very well how affectionate he is.

GEORGES: A nation isn't made out of affectionate men.

MARIE: He's punctual, tidy, obliging.

GEORGES: He always has been.

MARIE: "Always"? How do you know? You've only known him for two years.—He has shrewdness.

GEORGES: The dog that pretends to be lame so as not to be beaten.

MARIE: And intelligence. Of all the household, including the cook, he is the one who manages best with the food tickets.

GEORGES: I realize too that he is incomparable at untangling the telephone wire when it's got twisted up.

MARIE: Laugh if you like, one isn't a fool when one has the reports he has, and congratulations from the principal at the end of the year. 17 for science, 18 for Latin, 18 for history and geography.

GEORGES: 18 for civics plus 25 for singing plus 50 for cosmography plus 75 for hygiene; draw a line and add up: total, zero. Total, a mediocrity.

MARIE: Total, a child who's not perhaps a child prodigy, but is a perfectly healthy child.

GEORGES: Yes, yes, yes, we know that, he's a perfectly healthy child! If only he were not that! If he had some passion! Running away, stealing, living in a dream world. . . . But he's smooth, and on that smoothness I try in vain to get a hold: I slip and get no hold. Flat as his flattened hair and his dull flabby features. . . .

MARIE: The face you loved in me fifteen years ago.

GEORGES: . . . And those flabby hands of a little Parisian, those white hands of his, too slender, the hands of a child brought up by women. . . .

MARIE: You dare! Where were you, you, while he was being brought up by women?

GEORGES: The advantage of being a father is that you can always say of your children, if they don't turn out well, that they aren't yours.

MARIE: That caps everything!

GEORGES: I should never have allowed myself to conceive such a thought. But it comes from Euripides, who is a classical author. And everything written by an author who's a classic is *ipso facto* admirable and claims an absolute allegiance.

MARIE: Your banter makes me sick. Sick, too, your injustice toward this little boy, you who in your job are working for justice.

GEORGES: Children! People like me are always dreaming of one day bringing forth something great out of one of these little formless molecules. And when one of these children is our own! Well, look what happens: my experience, my culture, twenty-five years of thinking about the world and knocking up against men—there's a child marked out doubly by destiny for me to pass all that on to him, because he's of my blood, and because I love him, and it's to him precisely that I can't do it, because he's silly, and because he's shoddy. How avoid being bitter? How avoid becoming unjust? And why indeed should I spend time on him if he's a mediocrity? Things must have some reason for them, especially when they're burdensome; and this one hasn't. At present he still has the charm of his age. But at thirty what will he be? Wouldn't I do better to buy myself a Gobelin tapestry, which is beautiful once and for all and will give me pleasure all my life, than to engulf my strength, my time, my money in a sack with a hole in it, which will never hold anything?

MARIE: Oh, shut up! You're no father! And what about the voice of nature, doesn't that exist?

GEORGES: What is it—the voice of nature? There's something of everything in nature.

MARIE: You took your son as a man takes a mistress, just like that, for his nice looks, at a subway station. No, you're no father.

GEORGES: You're right: I am no father. I'm a man who chooses.

MARIE: Well then, since you admit it, take an interest in him materially, if you still love him enough to do that, but stop trying to mold that little soul to fit your eccentricities. Ah, why did you come back into his life, to trouble its calm and simple course? My son has no need to be exceptional.

GEORGES: The nation has need that its sons should be. Contrary to what one hears droned on all sides, there's nothing left in France today to save honor except individuals, and individuals verging on the exceptional. To think that tomorrow the dawn will come, and through sons who will not be mine!

MARIE: Instead of always insisting with fury on the impossible, why not take men as they are?

GEORGES: I reject them as they are.

MARIE: Gillou will do honor to his country by being, perhaps an average, but a capable and decent Frenchman.

GEORGES: It's no use keeping on repeating that it's his mediocrity you love in him; and what you are defending, in taking up his defense, is—at last I've got it clear. When he shouted at me: "You make us sick of you!" how clearly he linked the two of you together, you and him! How you abet each other! As for me, I tell you, I can now only bear people who are a bit above the common. I've arranged, all my life, to have no or almost no fools around me. I shall not begin having them with my son. And I shall not bequeath my name to a Frenchman who will only be average, even if "capable and decent."

MARIE: That's it! You're no longer thinking of "the nation." It's your pride, or rather your vanity, that is hurt by your child. I was asking myself: "Why this enraged persecution? What is he avenging on the boy with such bitterness? Whom is he trying to punish in him?" Now I know. You're trying to punish in your son something that you have created and that isn't you. Ah, you're glorying, aren't you, in not having recognized him two years ago? Even when you were busy attaching him to you, even when toward him you were all fire and flame, you were keeping prudent, calm; you were reserving the right to recognize him or not at his coming of age, according to whether or not you would judge him worthy of you. And now you've made your judgment; two years have been enough.

GEORGES: The man submerged in the woman—I've experienced that. But the man and the woman submerged in the child—that, really!

MARIE: And yet God knows, poor little thing, he tries to be like you!

GEORGES: He tries to be like me?

MARIE: He was saying to me only yesterday, so simply: "Don't you think so? Papa and I have exactly the same character."

GEORGES: He's not hard to satisfy!

MARIE: In everything it's Papa here, Papa there. Whatever my life may have been like during those twelve years you were away, no man during that time paid attention to Gillou; no man lived under the same roof with him. And it's important for a kid, that is. Do you know he has adopted, or tried to adopt, even your handwriting? You're displeased? But everything you tell him to do, to my knowledge, he does: brushing his teeth twice a day—his physical training—getting up quickly in the morning without imploring me, as he used to do: "Let me sleep five minutes more! Long enough for one little dream. . . ."

GEORGES: Listening to me over the little things and leaving me over the big.

MARIE: Look, last Saturday, at the movie, do you remember? He was blissful and hilarious at the film, which was, I admit, a particularly stupid one, and you turned toward him and looked at him for a moment. He guessed at once that his attitude was shocking you, and he let his head fall on your shoulder, half laughing, half crying, as if to ask your forgiveness for being rather silly, as if also to say to you: "Let me be my age!" And there was in that gesture and in that expression so much confidence in you and so much desire to satisfy you. . . . He loves you, are you forgetting that? You raise your eyebrows. You don't believe me?

GEORGES: The people who love me astonish me.

MARIE: He loves you. And that's everything!

GEORGES: Oh no! It isn't enough that someone loves you!

MARIE: Not once, even, has he shown any sign of reproaching you for having abandoned his mother and him for twelve years. He appears to find that quite natural.

GEORGES: A real little man of the world.

MARIE: Haven't you ever surprised in his eyes this question: "Why doesn't he love me so much?" Weren't you bowled over the other day by his saying: "During the whole of lunch you haven't given me a single affectionate look?"

GEORGES: You're right, he loves me. Alas!

MARIE: Have you reached the point of longing for a pretext for him not to love you, in order not to love him any more in your turn?

GEORGES: He loves me, it's true! He loves me! It's no good my being more and more harsh with him, he is always equally affectionate to me. That wandering tenderness, alighting on me at random, perhaps in search of something else— He kisses me, and I say to myself: where do they come from, these kisses he gives me? Ah, Marie, he hurts me. I love him, and I should like to esteem him as much as I love him, and I can't.

MARIE: One doesn't take back one's child after twelve years of desertion. However sincerely you may love him today, he remains for you a little stranger. An adopted child, let's say, who hasn't fulfilled what was expected of him. . . . You've started loving him too late. If you'd had a normal home, instead of being a virtuoso of irregularity— The family—one believes in it or not, but one doesn't toy with it.

GEORGES: You still don't understand me. I repeat that I'm caught between the affection I feel for him and a certain morality that is mine, a morality that he blurs and contradicts. By turns I draw him to me and I push him away: a creature who is ceaselessly running low and being replenished in you. I love him—and I don't love his presence. I would sacrifice myself for him, if it were necessary—and I've known myself cross to the opposite sidewalk when I saw him coming in the street. Sometimes I say to myself: "Let him either be what he should be or not exist." And at other times: "Let him be what he is, provided he talks, and is silent, and hums his tunes, and sleeps in the house I have given him. . . ."

SCENE IV

GEORGES, GILLOU, MARIE [*during the first seven speeches*]

[*At this moment Gillou appears on the threshold, stops, and asks timidly:*]

GILLOU: May I fetch my bomber?

GEORGES: Your bomber?

Gillou [*pointing from a distance to a tiny paper airplane on a chair*]: On the chair.

Georges: Is that your bomber? Well, it had better have a few good meals and grow a bit.

Gillou [*seeing that Georges has softened, and becoming bolder*]: Won't you tell me what my punishment is?

Georges: No punishment.

Gillou: Oh, nice! You're a good guy. Here, I'll give you my bomber.

[*Marie goes out.*]

Georges: Gillou, in the three months you've been at Cannes, frankly, you haven't made me happy. You're not as you should be; so that in my turn I'm not as I should be with you. I know, I ought to love you more. But how, when I see you so unworthy? To love you more, sometimes I think it's possible; there are a sort of false starts—and then I can't; then I avoid you, so as not to have to show you a coldness that might astonish you. And I'm sad; sad that you should be what you are; sad at no longer loving you as much as formerly; sad at feeling that I'm a little bit turning against you all I've done for you with so much useless fervor. I remember that Sunday last April during my last leave, that fine sunny Sunday when we went on the banks of the Seine to look for books for you. What lightness, what youth, what certainty of never dying! How glad I was that you should be mine! A lot of life has flowed away since then. You have passed from the marvelous domain of those in which I have complete confidence to the domain, so commonplace, of those whom I rather mistrust. It's hard to say that to you, but I'm saying it. One must set fire to the brush on the heath, burn it all, and perhaps later, on the bare earth—[*Gillou, who seems confounded, comes and sits at his father's feet, his gaze fixed vaguely on a stool in front of them, on which there happen to be some papers and magazines.*] Now I see things clearly. I see why you wept when you heard I was your father. I see why you had such a poignant expression when you fell asleep three months ago on this sofa. Because I see how it will be later. Because I see before me, later, as clear-cut as if it were in the past, all that I shall not do for you. What are you, really? You are a deserted child. That's your destiny. Indeed, most of the children in France are deserted children. Either people don't look after them; or people look after them so badly; or people look after them for a time, with intelligence, and later desert them. But you, well! . . . I deserted you for the first time at your birth, from selfishness. I shall desert you a second time from despair about you. Alas, I'm deserting you already: when you said of yourself yesterday evening that you would do your holiday work in August and would buy the crib afterwards—as much as to say you must not count on anyone to help you in your work—I felt you were so alone—your good intentions so alone—it went to my heart. Yes, when you begin to be grown up, I shall desert you again. I see so well how that will happen. . . . I shall put off from day to day doing anything about your future, I shall let you think anything, do anything, go about with anyone, consort with any woman: all left to chance, instead of directing you. And all the time joking with you, because when one hasn't anything to say to people, joking fills in and disguises indifference. And all the time giving you money, to imagine myself at peace with my duties toward you. In short, I shall be a father like the others, whereas I only wanted to become a father again in order to be a father different from the others. But why a father like the others? Because you will have been a child like the others, instead of being superior to the others. And you will all the time wonder why I've rejected you, because the reasons I'm giving you you don't understand. And you'll remain my sorrow and my reproach, one of those drowned faces that look at us eternally from the depths of the water. Gilles, my little boy, make me able to love you. Put something of yourself into it. Unless it's I, perhaps, that am lacking. . . . If at the start I'd loved you more, perhaps by force of affection I'd have been able to draw something out of all that is muddled and barbarous in you. . . . [*At this moment Gillou, who, without moving his head, has let his gaze fall on one of the magazines left lying on the stool, then started to read it, turns the page. Georges sees the movement and stops short.*] Ah, you were reading! You couldn't listen to me for five minutes, when perhaps never in my life have I spoken to you so seriously. Well, my friend, that simplifies things. [*He gets up.*] On Monday, at Marseille, I shall start the steps to get your permit. When I've got it, I shall give it to you or not, according to what I think of you at that moment. Why cry? Havre, think of it, chicory at ten sous! Come on, my child, we're going to announce the good news to your mother.—And now begins the reign of mysterious gentleness. I have given up; you'll no longer hear my observations; all that was forbidden becomes permitted. You'll even be able not to take your tonic without my reminding you. To begin with, here's fifty francs. Why won't you take them? Take them, go on. Here, another twenty. With that you'll be able to go to the movies. And congratulations in advance on *Lend Me Your Wife*! Ah, what a lovely Sunday you'll spend there!

CURTAIN

ACT IV

Same setting. Three weeks later [*end of January*].

SCENE I

GEORGES, MARIE, GILLOU

[*When the curtain rises, Georges, Gillou, and Paulette—she is in town clothes—emerge onto the stage, carrying three suitcases. Marie follows.*]

MARIE: I don't know why you wanted us to bring these suitcases down. The porter would have got them from the second floor.

GILLOU: And suppose he doesn't come? You're always saying the people around here aren't punctual. Perhaps we'll have to carry them to the station ourselves.

MARIE: I don't want people to see us carrying suitcases in the street! We should look as if we'd tried to economize on a porter.

GILLOU: Who cares two hoots for the people of Cannes now?

MARIE: That's true, you can be sure this is a part of the country I'll never come back to in my life. But, all the same, we must behave properly to the end. [*Opening her bag*] I'm looking to see I've got the tickets and the receipt for the registered trunk all right. Paulette, why not bring us a little coffee here? We've time.

GILLOU: Why coffee, when we had breakfast an hour ago?

MARIE: One needs fortifying, for the journey. And remind me to buy some mint lozenges at the station.

GILLOU: Wait, one can hear the trains whistling from here. I'd never noticed.

MARIE: *I* heard them from the first day of being here. And I was glad to hear them. Women always think, when a train whistles: "How many disappointed hopes, unrealized dreams, is it carrying away?" But why don't they sometimes think of all the realized hopes it's carrying too?

GEORGES: Your joy is pleasant to see.

MARIE [*with animation*]: See no more in it than a simple nervous reaction against your air of gloom. You are so silent.

GEORGES: All that I had to say to you has been said.

GILLOU: Send us an interzone card tomorrow.

GEORGES: I shall certainly not have more to say to you than today.

GILLOU: Yes, but we'll see your writing.

MARIE: And pay attention. In our postcards, always understand the opposite. If I write: "Food difficult," that will mean: food easy. If I put: "Father ill," that will mean that he's in good health.

GEORGES: The children at play.

MARIE: It's curious, you will not understand that these cards may be read.

GEORGES: Your father's health is of supreme interest to the Germans.

GILLOU: Mamma is right. First, that's always the way they do things in detective stories. And above all, don't forget: if I put my signature on the left, it means we shall have been bombed. (*Gaily*] Zzz. . . . Tac! Tac! Tac!

MARIE: Will you shut up!

GILLOU [*gaily, to Marie*]: Hi! Look here, if we do get bombed —has it at least got a cellar, Grandfather's house?

MARIE: Of course. And I've already told you it's two miles from the town. There there's no risk. Besides, if there were a risk of something, I wouldn't take you, would I? Imagine their bombing us! That would be the limit! A house your grandfather built with forty years' work!

GILLOU [*to Georges*]: Do you think they'll bomb us?

GEORGES: I've already told you fifty times that I think it is probable.

MARIE: You always foresee the worst! At least don't say so, if you do foresee it. One makes things happen when one talks about them like that. And to say it to a child!

GILLOU: You remember? Before the war you scolded me because I said to you: "Every time you talk of war as if it were bound to happen, you'll be fined." And the war did come. That time you were right.

GEORGES: I'm always right.

[*Marie and Gillou laugh.*]

GILLOU: You still haven't told us when we'll see you again. You leave that vague. In three months?

GEORGES: Three months! . . .

GILLOU: What? Still longer? [*Silence.*] You think the war won't be finished in three months? There's a prediction that says—

GEORGES: Oh, shut up!

MARIE: Even if the war lasts longer, one must hope that between now and then the escaped prisoners of war will be given the right to go back to the occupied zone. [*Pause.*] Don't you think so?

GEORGES: Hoping is not forbidden by law.

MARIE: It would be too frightful if one couldn't hope. [*Pause.*] Don't you think so?

GEORGES: I suppose, yes, it would not be very agreeable.

MARIE: And besides, the war's bound to end some day. [*Pause.*] Don't you think so?

GEORGES: I suppose, in fact, the war will end some day.

PAULETTE [*entering*]: Madame, someone's come about the butcher's bill.

MARIE: I'm coming.

SCENE II

GEORGES, GILLOU

GEORGES: Woman's son! You too always making yourself blind, like her. In the three weeks since I began to get busy about your permit, you have still never been willing to see that even if the war were to end tomorrow, today you're seeing me for the last time.

GILLOU: But why? Why? What have I done?

GEORGES: I've told you over and over again, till I'm sick of it. Now it's too late. In an hour we shall have parted forever.

GILLOU: Papa! . . . No, you're not going to do that! Just now you're vexed. . . .

GEORGES: "Vexed"! Always, to the very end, your mother's words, words to one side of the truth.

GILLOU: I don't believe you. For the last time! It's not possible!

GEORGES: There are things that seem impossible and that happen. Woman's son, don't you know that? Will you blind yourself right to the end?

GILLOU: What do you mean by blinding myself?

GEORGES: Not seeing what is there.

GILLOU: In that case you too are blind. There are plenty of things you don't see.

GEORGES: Perhaps. But there are more that I see. [*A woman's voice is heard humming a tune in the entrance hall.*] Who's singing like that, at this moment?

GILLOU: It's Paulette.

GEORGES: No, it isn't Paulette. It's your mother. Her joy will out in spite of her. Her monstrous joy. Her incomprehensible joy. So much joy—no, there's more there than insensitiveness. Could there be— Could there be something

I've failed to see? What makes you say that I'm blind? What makes you say that it's Paulette singing, when you know very well it's your mother? Is there another reason than that of rejoining her parents that makes Havre such an extravagant obsession for her?

GILLOU: A reason? What reason? Here she was ill—

GEORGES: You know something! You know! Your confabulations with her, of an evening, in her room, till after ten, whereas at Marseille, when we were alone, you always used to leave me at half past nine. . . . Have I got to tell you now why a month ago I decided to change rooms? Why I didn't any longer want my room to be next to hers?

GILLOU: You could hear us talking and it disturbed you.

GEORGES: Disturbed me! Always this genius for words beside the truth! It hurt me to hear you laughing too much with her, and lingering with her too long, and talking as if you were all the time talking against me. Your life, at once so neighboring and so foreign. And my struggle not to listen at the keyhole. And my relief when you opened the door of her room and shut it after you, to go back at last into yours! And now what have you learned, what have you guessed in that intimacy? There's another reason for her wanting to go to Havre. Your secret nearly escaped you. Speak! Everything is still possible. If your mother is taking you off lightheartedly to that sinister place, separating you from me forever, and if she's doing it for the reason that I guess, I swear to you, I'll get back the permit from her by force and you shall not go from here. I shall not let her have her abominable joy.

GILLOU: What are you imagining?

GEORGES: I was offering you up to something lofty and pure. But she! And I find that in offering you up I was at the same time offering you to her. I will not have us divided that way! Come! You're going to live with me at Marseille; she will go where she likes. You'll see, I shall be quite different with you. Now I'm sure that I've the power to transform you. Now I know all the things I should have said to you. Speak! Why did she want Havre?

Gillou: To see her parents again.

Georges: That isn't true!

Gillou: Yes, it is true.

Marie [*somewhere in the house*]: Gillou!

Georges: Gillou! Tell me the truth! It may change your whole life, and mine.

Marie [*as before*]: Gillou!

Georges: Gillou! [*Gillou hesitates, then goes toward the door through which his mother's voice comes, and goes out.*] He has chosen once more. Once more I am condemned.

SCENE III

Georges

Georges: I have sacrificed him to the idea I have of man. She has sacrificed him to the need she has of man. Each of us, she and I, kept talking of our own sacrifice. And he alone was the one to be sacrificed. Woman's son? No, no man's son. No man's son, like the others. But let what is begun be pursued without weakening. Whatever else may be, my reasons remain. Let's not give way to this burst of passion that is urging me to tear him away from her, and to tear him away from her so vainly. I had weighed things; I'm not going back on my word. No, it isn't to her I'm offering him up. I'm offering him up to a principle. I'm offering him up to the pride I take in doing so before the judge within me. —Ah, terrible pride! I shan't see his ink-stained notebooks lying about on all the tables any more, nor his stamps, nor his toy bomber . . . God, make me firm! While he is still there for a few moments, before not being there any more forever, give me already forgetfulness of all he was. God of human sternnesses, God of human tendernesses, grant that to the end I may remain hard enough with him to repress on his lips the little word that would overwhelm me and that would plant in me, instead of the peace of things just, an eternal remorse, an eternal horror.

[*Sound of voices outside. Georges goes and sits down at one side, to remain so during the whole of the following scene, as if petrified.*]

SCENE IV

GEORGES, MARIE, GILLOU

MARIE: That child pays no attention to anything. He's packed the eau de Cologne!

GILLOU: But you'll get it out in the train!

MARIE: Perhaps the compartment will be crowded. It's a regular scene, opening a suitcase in a compartment full to bursting. And besides, I don't like the other passengers prying into my things.

GILLOU: But I don't know which suitcase I put it in, I don't! I'm not going to unpack the three suitcases to look for your eau de Cologne.

MARIE: I'm sure I shall be taken ill in the train; that's the way things happen. And I need to have my eau de Cologne this instant!

GILLOU: Oh! you are—! [*He undoes a strap of one of the suitcases violently. The strap breaks. He almost weeps with exasperation.*] Ah! There now!

MARIE: That would happen! Ever since I woke up I've been saying to myself: "He's going to break something!"

Gillou: You break things too. But you don't scold yourself.

Marie: My God! What are we going to do? Go and look for some string.

Gillou: String? Where? I'm fed up, I'm through! It's quite simple, I'm not going! To go to Havre, to be bombed! The whole thing's your fault, you had only to stay here.

Marie: Gillou!—Georges, you might give the child a hand. But there you are in your chair— Where are you?

Georges: I am beyond.

Marie: It's impossible to travel with Gillou. He loses his head. He becomes odious. [*Shouting into the hall*] Paulette! Look in all the drawers. We absolutely must have a piece of string. The strap of one of the suitcases has given way.

Gillou: Now we shall miss the train. It's twenty-two minutes to.

Marie: Twenty-two minutes to! The porter should have been here at half past! [*Paulette comes in again with some string.*] Ah! Thank God. [*To Gillou*] Here.

Gillou: Fix it yourself.

Marie: It was you who broke it.

Gillou: Yes, but all because of your eau de Cologne. Here, there's your eau de Cologne.

Marie: Oh, that string! What *shall* we look like? Emigrants! Gypsies! It's awfully conspicuous! Do you know what you should do? Smear a little shoe-polish over the string; that'll make it less visible.

Gillou: So now I've got to open the three suitcases again to look for the shoe-polish! No, no, no! I'm fed up, I am! What's more, if the porter doesn't come, so much the better, we'll stay at Cannes. [*The doorbell rings.*]

Marie: Ah! that must be him. [*She starts toward the door.*] Yes, it's him. Here, come in.—I believe I'm forgetting something. Yes, I'm sure I've forgotten to put something in the suitcases. Paulette, go up and look in all the drawers. No, don't; I'll go myself.

THE PORTER: I'll put the suitcases in the hall and wait for you there.

SCENE V

GEORGES, GILLOU

GILLOU: Mamma's crazy. I—I'm fed up with living with her. If I'd known, I'd have stayed at Marseille with you.

GEORGES: Known what?

GILLOU: She's crazy! I could still stay, if you wanted. I'm sure she'd leave me all right, provided *she* could go.

GEORGES: Too late. The spring has dried up.

GILLOU: Do at least come back to us quickly! You've only to smuggle yourself across the line.

GEORGES: You don't know what you're saying.

GILLOU: All right, send for me to come back. I'll smuggle myself across. Look here, if I put my signature at the top of the card—at the top, see?—it'll mean: send for me to come back.

GEORGES: Too late, too late.

GILLOU: Why are we leaving Cannes? I'm sure some day I'll be saying: "At Cannes, how happy I was!"

GEORGES: You say, when the suitcases are packed, all that should have been said three months ago.

GILLOU: Going to Havre! And all because there's a fellow there.

GEORGES: Too late.

GILLOU: She had a postcard sent to her general-delivery. He's called Roger. He wrote to her: "Dear Mariette"—

GEORGES: Too late.

GILLOU: You'll send for me to come back at Easter, eh? Promise?

GEORGES: I never make promises.

GILLOU: You must! You must! I want to go back with you. Poor Papa, I know I made you fed up. But now, when I come back, you'll see, I'll be good.

GEORGES: My little, big boy!

GILLOU: Give me a kiss!

GEORGES [*at the end of his strength, pushes him away*]: No, on the platform, soon. . . . Let me go. . . .

[*He goes out into the hall. Gilles, left alone, hesitates for a moment, then goes to look for his coat, toward the right, throws it over his arm, and goes out slowly, through the same door as the others.*]

CURTAIN

TOMORROW THE DAWN

(*The sequel to*
NO MAN'S SON)

⚜

A Play in Three Acts

CHARACTERS

GEORGES CARRION, *aged 47, a lawyer*

GILLES SANDOVAL ("GILLOU"), *aged 17 years and seven months, his illegitimate son (unrecognized)*

A MESSENGER, *aged 20*

MARIE SANDOVAL, *aged 49*

Paris, June 1944.

ACT I

A studio in a bourgeois apartment. Strips of paper pasted criss-cross over the glass of the window. On a table, a wartime meal, very frugal [it must include a bottle of water and a glass].

SCENE I

GEORGES, MARIE

MARIE: What are you punishing me for?

GEORGES: I'm punishing you because you're miserable. Stop your jeremiads. I hate you when you're miserable.

MARIE: So I've got to be happy, in spite of everything, in the face of everything, whenever I'm in your presence!

GEORGES: Yes. A man can't stand a woman who's miserable, unless he consoles her by going to bed with her.

MARIE: You too have been known to arrive home with a gloomy face. But you don't hide it. I've got to force myself to look joyful. You, oh no.

GEORGES: That's right.

MARIE: What's more, if you noticed I was straining to appear joyful, that strain would exasperate you as well.

GEORGES: Probably. As you know, my apartment is pretty austere. And Paris in June 1944 is no fun. When I come to see you, I'd like to find relaxation from my work and from my worries. What I find is other people's worries, I have to saddle myself with them, and to take on a funereal expression so as not to look as if I was insulting your sorrows.

MARIE [*who has just taken a sip from the glass of water*]: Sad, I get on your nerves. Pretending to be cheerful, I get on your nerves. All right, what ought I to do? Yes, I know, I ought not to exist. All the same, you always find your way to me when you're in the least difficulty. I'm the one who must always come to your help over the little things of life.

GEORGES: Because those are all you're good for.

MARIE: You have a damnable skill at choosing the words that can hurt me most. Twenty years ago, with a single one of those words you'd have killed me. Nowadays I find it almost funny, or at any rate I'd find it funny if there weren't, behind it, the child. [*She takes another sip.*]

GEORGES: What do you mean, "the child"?

MARIE: Gillou, your son.

GEORGES: "The child": is he eight years old? So it's Gillou who's giving you the blues?

MARIE: Yes.

GEORGES: The blues he gives you will end by setting me against him. And to think that it's always the same thing: boys who at ten are their mother's joy, and at eighteen are her misery.

MARIE: No, always her joy. Blessed be he who has never caused me a single pang. The one man who won't have disappointed me.

GEORGES: You wait a little, a year or two, for the age of ingratitude.

MARIE: I shall love his ingratitude too.

GEORGES: What's the matter with Gillou this time? That excitement you live in about your son—

MARIE: It's always the same thing.

GEORGES: That Resistance business? I won't have him joining the Resistance. To all the reasons I've already given against it, I'll add this: it's not at the moment when the Americans have just landed in Normandy that one joins the Resistance. He should have done it earlier.

MARIE: You'd have stopped him just as much then. For some

time past, that child's had nothing but disappointments. The exams have been canceled because of the emergency. All that school business would have been settled; now he'll have to spend the holidays in uncertainty and uneasiness. And what holidays! They're fighting on the north-coast beaches, they'll be fighting tomorrow on those of the south, trains are being bombed everywhere: he's going to have to spend the summer in Paris.

GEORGES: In short, he'd like to throw himself into courage, as a pastime for the summer. Idleness breeds a multitude of things.

MARIE: I'm simply saying that it would give him an aim, during these months when he'll have neither pleasure nor even the satisfaction of having finished a task.

GEORGES: He'll have distressing holidays? Well, he'll be like the others.

MARIE: You find it easy, nowadays, to accept his being like the others. [*She takes another sip.*]

GEORGES: Don't drink water like that, without stopping. Your throat's dry because your son's not going to get killed; it's unheard-of. To join the Resistance and risk death in it, in June 1944, when the war will be finished in three months, is an absurd idea. Admit it, come: it's from tiredness that you accept an idea like that. For weeks he's been goading us with it; sometimes insistence and sometimes the sulks.

MARIE: So he didn't wait for the arrival of the Americans as you said he did.

GEORGES: From tiredness, and also from unreflecting indulgence.

MARIE: I live by his happiness.

GEORGES: To the point of consulting him, the other day, on whether or not he wished to go to school, because of the raid warnings! Of course he said no.

MARIE: No part is ever played in your mind by the fact that that child isn't happy. Whereas I, now—my one reason for existing is that he should be happy. The war, current events, all that—I take their temperature by asking him: "At this moment, are you happy?" According to what he answers, the world is going well or badly. And that is how one should behave, when one loves a person.

GEORGES: By yielding to him in the present case, you do perhaps want him to be happy. But you also want him to stop being sullen with you, to become nice to you once more.

MARIE: You're always the same: everything has to be brought down to selfishness. The announcements of births in the papers use the formula: "Mother and child are doing well." When I think of your selfishness, I say to myself: the father is doing well. "Father is doing well": that would make a title for a novel. And yet you love him, that lad. You love him,—and often I see you react as if you didn't love him.

[*A silence.*]

GEORGES: I don't love him.

MARIE: Don't make yourself out worse than you are. You do love him, but you love him as a man does—that's to say only so-so.

GEORGES: I don't love him.

MARIE: You haven't the time! You work without stopping.

GEORGES: A life may be packed and overstrained, but time can be extended infinitely to let in someone one loves.

MARIE: And to think that you adored him when he was fourteen!

GEORGES: That long disappointment he used to drag about after him, which used to stagnate in me for hours on end after he had left me—that too was one of the forms taken by my love for him. To tell the truth, I liked few things about him. But I loved him even in the things I didn't like about him. And at bottom, yes, even when I let the two of you leave me to go to Havre, I hadn't stopped hoping. You lived for two years and a half at Havre, with him more or less under the influence of a man who wasn't his father. Everything led me to believe that that new influence could not do him much good. And yet when, a year ago, you were abandoned by that gentleman and came back to Paris, and when at that stage you asked me to come—when you *summoned* me—I came. In the south I was a shirker; coming up to Paris was like coming up to the front. I returned from the unoccupied zone to the Paris of the occupation, with all the difficulties and all the problems that involved for me, and I did so entirely because of him. For I was remorseful at having let him leave Cannes, I was still hoping, I was unable to adjust myself to the idea of disappearing one day without having given him something of what there is in me. But I found him once more in Paris just as he had been at Cannes—worse perhaps, because solidified in insignificance, if I may put it that way. I regret to confirm to you that Monsieur Gilles Sandoval is not an intelligent person, and never will be. This time, no appeal. I've lowered the portcullis. My son is nothing to me. Well, you can get on with someone who's nothing to you when he's reached manhood, if there are interests and cares in common. But what can there be in common between a man of my age and someone who's nothing to him and is—what is he? Seventeen or eighteen? I don't even know.

MARIE: You know perfectly well.

GEORGES: I swear to you I'm incapable of telling, like that, out of the blue, Gillou's precise age.

MARIE: He's seventeen and seven months.

GEORGES: I either don't know or forget everything that concerns him. How difficult it is to make people understand that they're nothing to you! And yet can't you see that I never *look* at him, that my eyes never come to rest on his face, while you—you even look at him by stealth, for the sake of looking at him a little more, like a woman who wants to steal another look at her lover? Can't you see how listless, absent, bored my looks are when you so much as mention him to me? And how all the cordiality and kindness I manage to show him is only a mask for that indifference? Besides, what sort of kindness? My only kindness toward him consists in scrupulously giving him all the foreign postage stamps I receive on any letters—knowing perfectly well, all the same, that he stopped collecting stamps two years ago.

MARIE: I can't manage to understand why you want to convince me that you don't love your son.

GEORGES: People believe I love him, and I don't love him. What a hostage he'd made!

MARIE: What do you mean?

GEORGES: What a way of taking in the enemy, leaving him as a hostage, something that for you has no value!

MARIE: I still don't always understand you. Some of the ideas you have are so distorted—

GEORGES: My future indifference about him I had foreseen; indeed, I even announced it to him, three years ago, at Cannes.

MARIE: You foresaw it, and that's why you take pleasure in it in so shocking a way. Once again you want to be right. But how is it that so many years of familiarity—

GEORGES: It's harder to give up one's old clothes than to give up people one loves. After twenty years of intimacy people find themselves less united than if they'd met only once. Daily presence, confidence, shared worrics create nothing; what's more, they sometimes separate. Habit separates.

MARIE: I've lived every day with him for eighteen years, and I'm not habituated to him.

GEORGES: Perhaps even it's love that separates. With all the women I've loved there's come a break, and from the day of the break, each has known nothing of the other: the portcullis is down. The ones who've lasted are the ones I didn't love: the friendships, the fellow feelings. . . . What lasts is indifference. Nothing sticks to a tree better than a dead branch.

MARIE: You do say frightful things.

GEORGES: Everything is frightful.

MARIE: Everything is frightful when one makes it so on purpose.

GEORGES: I could say to you: "I don't love him because you love him too much," or again: "He irritates me, but that's my way of loving him," or again: "I hate him, and that hatred is enough to prove that I'm his father." But none of all that would be true. I don't love him, because I don't find this love in my heart. I had a son who disappeared like a dream. Besides, what are you complaining of? You ought to be pleased that I don't love him; that leaves you the field free.

MARIE: If that were so, I should be able to love him enough for two.

GEORGES: That would be only just.

MARIE: I love him, that's enough: I've no need of justice. I love him, and what a strength it is, loving!

GEORGES: But also what a strength it is, not loving! You don't love me: you should know all about that.

MARIE: Oh, enough of this: I should end by believing you. Are you really a monster?

GEORGES: A monster of frankness, perhaps. But not a monster because of this indifference. Or, in that case, we are all monsters. The hen that fusses so much over her chicks later leaves them and doesn't even recognize them. And all fathers are ready to let their sons, at twenty-one, go and settle in the colonies, so that they'll not see them again for two and a half years, and then for a few months only. Does one love a person when one accepts his absence? Come, that's enough joking. I'm not master of what there is in my heart; and what there is in my heart for him is: nothing. If that amazes you when I reveal it to you, it means that this nothingness has never been apparent either to you or to him. That's all that matters.

MARIE: You've been play-acting!

GEORGES: People congratulate me on the way I fake my voice on the telephone. Luckily, I can fake other things. If I fake affection with him, that's a guarantee of your happiness and of his.

[*A noise in the hallway.*]

MARIE: Sh!—Here he is, back.

SCENE II

GEORGES, MARIE, GILLOU

[*Gillou comes in, throws his coat, which was over his shoulders, onto a piece of furniture, and rolls up his sleeves.*]

GEORGES [*playfully*]: Triumphal entry of the son! The son is absolutely determined to show us that he could do with a shave, and also that he has some hair on his arms. The son is absolutely determined on reminding us that he is handsome, that he is seventeen and seven months and has the future before him.

MARIE: It's curious, that undertone of bitterness. . . . One day because somebody has said that he's good-looking. Another day because he's more smartly dressed than you. Poor son! Well, my pet, you won't kiss your mother?

[*Gillou comes up to his mother, who kisses him. Gillou does not return the kiss.*]

GEORGES: The son is kissed, but does not kiss.

MARIE [*playfully*]: Well, if he doesn't love me, what do I care? I think I should love him even more if he didn't love me, because then my love for him would be more disinterested.

[*Gillou sits down at the table and falls to, ravenously, on the food.*]

GEORGES: The son wishes at all costs to show us that he eats with his front teeth, that he has a young puppy's teeth, which are good for anything.

GILLOU [*to his mother*]: Eat!

MARIE: I'm not hungry.

GILLOU: Yes, you are, eat! Can't you see that I'm hungry?

[*Marie starts to eat.*]

GEORGES: It's not credible: he has to be hungry for you to get an appetite! Is it sublime? Is it grotesque?

GILLOU: All nonsense!

GEORGES: Look here, old man, you really are a messy eater. And the way you scour up the gravy off your plate.

MARIE: One has the right to scour one's plate when one's in the fourth year of undernourishment. How I should like to go without something to give it to him!

GEORGES: So it seems you've still got that idea of going into the Resistance.

GILLOU: Yes.

GEORGES: Go into the Resistance, with all the hardship that that means, when you're sick in the summer in the subway!

GILLOU: I wasn't sick last month when I was picking up the bodies after the air raids.

GEORGES: What folly, to risk compromising a state of equilibrium in which, in the midst of the worst storms, people are more or less happy, as we are, the three of us! If you only knew how precious a moment of equilibrium is!

GILLOU: At that rate one would never do anything!

GEORGES: It's three months from now, when peace is here, that France will need you.

GILLOU: You too, at my age, wanted to join up. You've told us so often enough.

GEORGES: Yes, at your age. The age of idiocies. You want to expose yourself just at the moment when the others want to get under cover. I'm thinking of those of my colleagues who, ever since the Germans have been there, have been a bit too active. You should see the way, for some days now, they've started looking for cover! Think of it, Berniquet, who feels he's doomed to prison, has chosen the monastic life: he's becoming a novice! Fear gives wings to fly to God. I, who saw Verdun, I shall never regret having also seen this great reverse test of the French nation. And it's perhaps the same men. Most men conceal in themselves their own caricature. And that caricature comes out one day, unexpectedly, under the power of events. The present period is excellent for making these caricatures come out.

MARIE: You used to reproach Gillou, four years ago, with being "of poor quality." Now he has a fine idea: he wants to serve. And still it won't do. You seem to detest finding again in him the "first fine careless rapture" and even the quite exalted sentiments that you used to have at eighteen. Could this be jealousy of your own youth? Or jealousy of his wanting to do a man's work? Let's be frank: of his wanting to do more of a man's work than you did?

GEORGES: It seems that, on pain of being taken for cowards, we must expose ourselves for convictions we haven't got.

MARIE: I am proud of my son.

GEORGES: And prouder still if he got himself killed. The hero's mother!

MARIE: And you, proud of being odious.

GEORGES: I see at this moment a great conspiracy for getting people killed, and above all, young people. Emulation in useless courage. The women are largely responsible. If a woman is there—a hospital commandant or an ambulance worker—there you have all the little males falling over each other and burning to offer their lives. What terrorizes them is not shells, it's fear of people thinking they feel fear—and a fear that is justified, fear for the best reasons for which one can ever feel fear. Around woman the rhythm of needless death quickens. What lightness—no, what ardor about pushing youth toward death, about stoking up its recklessness and its generous blood! Yes, I confess, you can't imagine how much anyone who despises death can exasperate a person who's reaching his fiftieth year.

Marie: A couple of weeks ago, when Gillou joined the air-raid rescue teams, I remember how impatient you were over his wanting a helmet. "You don't need a helmet. It's ridiculous!" At that moment you weren't reproaching him with taking risks, but with being prudent.

Gillou: Yes, you let me go into the rescue teams, where there was danger. And you forbid me to join the Resistance because of the danger. Does it mean that you don't agree with the Resistance?

Georges: I've too prosperous a legal practice to have time to form an opinion of the various political ideologies. If you had asked me if you could do something dangerous on the side of collaboration—let's say, join the Milice,* or even go on one of those instructional tours of German industry—I should have forbidden it just the same. My part in our little circle is to be the gentleman who pays; you remind me of it often enough. I'm also the gentleman whose advice is asked, but on the clear understanding that no account is taken of his advice. I'm also the gentleman who has to give his permission for his son to be butchered. Very well! No, I'm not giving it. And now, if you want to join the Resistance in secret from us—

Gillou: You know very well I don't do many things in secret from you. I'm not made that way.

Georges: In that case, old man, go on being always frank and straight with us. And if my decision hurts you a little, we'll try to procure for you, in spite of everything, some slight pleasure for these holidays. For example, that famous bike to replace the one stolen from you—

* The Milice was a small but active movement of French fascists who served the Germans. (Translator's note.)

GILLOU: You don't understand. That has no connection.

GEORGES: Parents never understand, as you know quite well.

SCENE III

GEORGES, MARIE

MARIE: He wants to do something clean, something French. And you offer him, in its place, a bike. Yes, you were quite right: all you're good for is paying. Your heart's a checkbook.

GEORGES: Well, that's something.

MARIE: Luckily Gillou isn't resentful. One ticks him off: a minute later, he's as nice as ever. He won't hold this against you. All the same, poor boy!

GEORGES: Poor boy, whose life I may be saving. But don't you think he'll go into the Resistance without our knowing?

MARIE: No, certainly not. You don't know him.

GEORGES: Why "no, certainly not"? Because I've forbidden it?

MARIE: Yes.

GEORGES: It's a funny feeling, being obeyed. All the same, other young fellows wouldn't ask their parents' permission to do something in the Resistance. If they were told: "It's madness," they'd answer: "That's why I'm going to do it."

MARIE: That's the limit: one would think you were reproaching him for being obedient!

GEORGES: A little softy, playing at being hard. When I was a young lawyer and had to do with children who'd gone off the rails, I could tell at a glance the hard and the soft ones, and they were only twelve-year-olds. There were also the ones whose look revealed that they were both hard and soft, the ones with the troubled look. The most dangerous.

MARIE: And you—come, what's your look like?

GEORGES: Me? . . . [*Smiling*] Troubled. But let's get back to our young man. So you like this docility of his?

MARIE: I like it because I love him. If I didn't love him, perhaps it would displease me too.

GEORGES: Excellent short definition of a certain system of education, or rather of non-education. [*Searching in his coat pocket and bringing out some papers*] I've brought you back your electric bills. I've done what I could with the company: the amounts, unfortunately, are correct. I say! I put all my letters in my pocket after picking them up at the concierge's, and I'd forgotten them. Do you mind if I have a glance at them?

MARIE: Of course not.

GEORGES [*having opened an envelope and unfolded a letter*]: Always madmen, certifiable madmen! [*Examining an envelope*] Now, this is certainly a tiresome letter.

MARIE: How can you tell?

GEORGES: I have a flair. I'm never wrong. [*Covering the stamp*] Note: I haven't even seen where it comes from, and I can sense that it means trouble. [*He opens the envelope, glances at the letter, and bursts out laughing.*] That's too absurd! It's from a chap who's owed me eighty thousand francs for ten months and has at last decided to send them to me!

[*Marie and Georges laugh.*]

MARIE: Magnificent! What an incredible flair!

[*Georges, still laughing, opens another envelope, and suddenly his laughter stops, his face changes.*]

MARIE: This time it's the tiresome letter?

GEORGES: Bah! We're living in a time when everyone gets insulted.

MARIE: An insulting letter?

GEORGES: Oh, no, not at all. But still—it isn't an agreeable letter.

MARIE: So what am I to do about the electric bills? There's nothing for it but to pay?

GEORGES [*as if terror-stricken, his voice jerky, clenching his hand on the edge of the table in the effort to get the words out*]: Pay? No.—What did I say? Oh yes! All you can do is pay. . . .

[*Marie having moved a little away from him, Georges stealthily moistens his mouth from the glass of water.*]

CURTAIN

ACT II

Same setting. Next day.

SCENE I

MARIE, GILLOU

MARIE: For three years now I've been having that dream about you, and hearing myself cry out in my dream.

GILLOU: The dream in which you lose me?

MARIE: Yes, the dream in which I lose you.—Oh, I have lots of other dreams about you, but I don't tell them to you, God forbid!—In that one you are ten, I'm holding you by the hand, from time to time you lean over and place a kiss on my bare arm, that gesture of yours as a small child, which you kept up for so long, and suddenly I lose you, and I run to right and to left like a madwoman, trying to find you, and I don't find you. Then I cry out, and my cry wakes me. Last night it took place in a railroad station. You got farther and farther away, in the crowd. And a moment came when I couldn't see you any more. Ah, why do I care so much for you, and why does caring for you bring me always such pain? Always, when affection starts, tragedy starts.

GILLOU: But what could I do to make you love me less?

MARIE: Nothing.—Your father was quite right to forbid you to embark on that adventure. If he had let you, I'd have thought that dream referred to it and was a bad omen.

GILLOU: Always your dreams! I can just hear Papa laughing at you.

MARIE: Since he was made prisoner, and above all since his escape from Germany, in the dramatic circumstances that you know, he too has become impressionable. I told you how, when he was defending Raffenel, he wept hot tears. . . . It's not for him to poke fun at my dreams.

GILLOU: Obviously, it's because he loves me that Papa doesn't want me to take that risk in the Resistance. But if he loved me better—

MARIE: Your father loves you very much. You've no right to doubt it.

GILLOU: I know Papa and you love me a great deal, but—

MARIE: Your father and I! Let's get this clear! It isn't, all the same, the same way of loving.

GILLOU: Papa loathes young people: it's part of his age. But, in his way, he loves me as much as you do.

[*Marie starts, as if stabbed, then:*]

MARIE: Yes, in his way.—You haven't found he's a little cold with you since we've been in Paris?

GILLOU: No.

MARIE: After all, you remember, at Cannes! How affectionate he was with you, how expansive!

GILLOU: What strikes me above all is the way Papa, who was so rigid four years ago, is less so today. To think that it's he who's forbidden me to go into the Resistance! And two months ago, when I was picking up dead bodies in the first-aid team, and when I said to him: "It hardens me, it does me good"—and I assure you I wasn't in the least posing—he shrugged his shoulders.

MARIE: Your father's getting old. It even makes me regret those days at Cannes when he used to scold you about everything and anything: he was the Sunday father, a week-end preacher, or rather a public prosecutor. Yes, from counsel he'd become public prosecutor, always the prosecutor; you were the prisoner. You—you used to talk to him as if he were fourteen. *He* used to talk to you as if you were fifty. The effect was quite stupefying, but still he did put into his oddities such alacrity, such vigor— He was intransigent, but his intransigence was a kind of youth. All the same, I sometimes ask myself if what he was striking at in you, under the name of softness, wasn't the softness he was beginning to feel dawning in himself; and that's why he used to strike at it with such fury: he was ashamed of it, and afraid of it. He felt himself in a state of legitimate self-defense.

GILLOU: It wears people out, an occupation. Four years of letting yourself be kicked in the pants. And yet—you don't think Papa is a bit of a collaborator?

MARIE: What next!

GILLOU: He did defend Winckelmann.

MARIE: If your father was able, though an escaped prisoner, to pass the demarcation line and come back to the occupied zone, it's because the Germans shut their eyes. And they shut them because Routier intervened. When the Germans later asked a service of him, your father, who is a well-bred man, didn't want to refuse. Winckelmann's a very pleasant man. He's a cad, but he's pleasant. But your father's so far away from all that! I was crossing the Pont Neuf with him the other day. He saw some symbols painted in tar on the parapet, and he said to me: "They've got a nerve, the Gaullists! Coming painting their symbols even here!" Well, do you know what the symbols were? The emblem of the Milice! With everything political he's like that. That doesn't prevent him from having saved I don't know how many young men from the forced labor service, or from saying things against the Germans, even in the street: he's sometimes so imprudent. . . . Never mind, I'm very glad he didn't let you go into that underground work. For one thing, you'd have had to start telling me lies, or at least keeping things from me, you who are so open.

GILLOU: "Not to tell lies": it's a thing that's only forbidden to children. People never dream of asking grown-ups not to tell lies.

MARIE: Because we love children; we don't love grown-ups.

But I think that even if I had caught you lying to me a hundred times, I should go on trusting in you. Trust in the night. Trust braced against wind and tide, against everything.

GILLOU: That's a policy?

MARIE: A policy? Already a man's words! And what words! Listen to me. Next year I shall be fifty. A "quinquagenarian." You see the word in the papers: *A quinquagenarian knocked down by a car in the Place d'Italie*. With Roger, the man your father calls "that gentleman," I lived for the last time—what is known as living. I was forty-five. Since then I've changed a lot: you must have noticed. . . .

GILLOU: You haven't changed as much as all that. When you're pleased, you don't look too old. Obviously, when you're sad, you are a bit old.

MARIE: I meant a moral change. I've changed because I loved him, and because he made me suffer. Now there's no longer any man except you that can make me suffer. My first life has been dissolved; the residues of it have gradually been dispersed; all I've kept in my memory is your childhood. All the ways of loving that a woman can have are now concentrated on you alone. Don't take advantage; I feel so weak. And that's why I have to have that trust in you—a magnificent trust.

GILLOU: You know you can have it.

MARIE: Then all's well. And you don't have to think you're obliged to give me a kiss when I kiss you, as you didn't yesterday, to the great joy of you know whom. You may even show a slight exasperation, when I hug you too close, just to remind me that you are no longer the age to be a possession of mine. That hasn't the least importance: I've no need of your kisses. If I have that magnificent trust in you, that's enough, all's well. [*The doorbell rings three times.*] Oh, your father! What's up?

SCENE II

GEORGES, MARIE, GILLOU

MARIE: What has brought us this visit from you? Your normal rhythm is two a week. . . . You're not bringing us an air-raid warning, like yesterday evening? An air-raid warning, and the evening spent by candlelight. What a restful day it's been today! For the first time for how long, a day without a warning, without a raid. . . .

GEORGES: A day of peace which isn't a day of happiness! Ought such a thing to be? What is peace, what is freedom, what is life, what's the sense of them, if they don't mean happiness?

MARIE: Worries?

GEORGES: Worries? Yes, all around me.

MARIE: Worries, when we are going to be liberated!

GEORGES: For most people the war is ending. But for some it's beginning. You guessed right: my visit has a definite purpose. I've thought over our yesterday's conversations, and I should like to go on with them. But first with you alone.

[*Gillou gets up to go, and as he passes points to his* lycée *notebook, which is on the table.*]

GILLOU: Have you read my essay yet—the one my tutor said was "grand stuff"?

GEORGES [*giving a jump*]: What! I've got handcuffs!

GILLOU: No, no, I said my tutor called my essay "grand stuff."

[*Marie and Gillou laugh.*]

MARIE: See what comes of spending your life in the courts!

SCENE III

GEORGES, MARIE

GEORGES: I want to talk over with you again Gillou and his project. But before that, and while I think of it, another question. I said something to you yesterday about some of my fellow lawyers who are afraid of having trouble at the Liberation. If only lawyers in trouble could see, rising to their defense, all the prisoners who owe them their liberty or their lives! Well, one of them, rather a friend of mine, and a good man, has asked me if, in case of need, I couldn't keep for him some papers that he wouldn't like to have about his own place. For me, as a fellow lawyer, that's difficult: I've already enough with my clients' files. But I thought perhaps your mother—

MARIE: Frankly, I don't see why one should mix my poor mother up with this. The man has got friends?

GEORGES: Doubtless. But he said to me, yesterday: "I wonder which of my friends will be the instrument of my destruction." And I do think that, in such circumstances, it's preferable to rely on somebody one doesn't know.

MARIE: You tell me he's a good man. Then, if he's got his conscience on his side—

GEORGES: That's what frightens him. The innocent always make a very bad defense. Besides, believe me, I understand your reaction perfectly. So leave your old mother in peace. Indeed, cajole her a little. There's going to be a difficult time to get through. Let's be nice to everybody. Let's reconcile ourselves with Peter and Paul. Each of us must create around himself a sort of protective *aura*. . . .

MARIE: You're both alike, you and your friend, you seem to me eaten up with distrust.

GEORGES: When one says that one distrusts everybody, that doesn't mean that one believes all of them will give you away from malice, but that one believes one man will give you away from malice, a second from lack of comprehension, a third from carelessness, and a fourth from clumsiness.

MARIE [*enchanted*]: I think it's excellent that lawyers, who live among other people's troubles, and live by them, should sometimes have troubles of their own.

GEORGES: I've never smiled at a man who was afraid of death. Faced by the test, one always has a first impulse of disarray before finding the philosophic position that will enable you to confront it. And besides, the life, the liberty of lawyers, means something. Men have need of us. They know how to find us when it's they who have cold feet.— But let's talk now of the thing that brought me here. Since yesterday I've been thinking, and I too, like you, am upset at seeing that boy so depressed because he's prevented from—

MARIE: Ah, you're not going to go back on your decision, just when I was happy about it. Last night I had a dream. I shan't tell it to you, I know those things put you in a bad mood. But since this morning I've been blessing you for having said no to him.

GEORGES: Mightn't there, all the same, be a way of satisfying him? By letting him join that organization, but without his running risks. In other words, letting it remain in the realm of childish adventures.

MARIE: He'll always run risks. He's seventeen. He'll always dare things a grown-up wouldn't dare.

GEORGES: The resistants are not the only ones who run risks, at this moment, nor are the youngsters. The streets are full of people who are busy only with making money and would do better to get busy saving their skins.

MARIE: You uphold today the opposite of what you upheld yesterday. What has happened?

GEORGES: And with you, who have changed quite as much,

what has happened? Yes, that dream has happened. For me, a reality has happened.—Anyhow, I mean to say I've examined the question in all its aspects. I think this thing could be done, but under certain conditions, about which I should like to have a chat with him.

MARIE: He'll give you every assurance that he'll be prudent. And then he'll let himself be carried away.

GEORGES: He's the opposite of a fanatic. Indeed, I can well imagine him as a moderating influence among his comrades.

MARIE: I beg of you, Georges, don't go back on what you decided yesterday! I know quite well that if you give him permission, everything I may say to him later will be without influence.

GEORGES [*calling*]: Gillou!—I must ask you to be kind enough to leave us alone.

MARIE: Alone? Why? It seems to me I've the right—

GEORGES: To speak in the name of a dream? No, there are already only too many people speaking in the name of dreams just now.

SCENE IV

GEORGES, GILLOU

GEORGES: I appeal to your common sense, to your judgment, to your sense of proportion. These qualities are always rare, and above all in young people. They are rarer than ever nowadays. When everybody is unbalanced, being reasonable is the great originality. And you are reasonable. I'm going back on what I said yesterday. I'm prepared to give you permission to do something in the Resistance, on condition that you do it reasonably. I mean on condition that you do it prudently, and without taking exaggerated risks.

GILLOU: A skulker, in fact.

GEORGES: If you're keen on that word, yes.

GILLOU: The word comes from that 1914 war of yours. All right, no: a skulker, that's not my line.

GEORGES: I'm tired of the commonplaces of honor.

GILLOU: It's you who taught me them.

GEORGES: Times were different.

GILLOU: Now begins the time of honor.

GEORGES: A fat lot you care for the Resistance. You're only out to get killed.

GILLOU: If I join the Resistance, I want to do what I'm told to do in it—in the normal way. I don't want to do the soft job and leave the hard job to the Communists.

GEORGES: The Communists have their reasons for doing the hard job, which the people of our class haven't got. Are you, by any chance, in sympathy with the Communists?

GILLOU: Sympathy? I've no idea. But I recognize objectively—

GEORGES: When people recognize objectively, it means that they're biased. Admit that you've Communist tendencies.

GILLOU: Not at all. I've social tendencies.

GEORGES: I wonder what the *bourgeoisie* can have done to you to make you have social tendencies.

GILLOU: You who, as a lawyer, are always professing to seek justice, why don't you want it for ideas that are not yours?

GEORGES: Let's drop that. In all armies, regular or not, there is staff work, which is essential, and in which, all the same, whether one wishes it or not, one's less exposed than in the front line. . . .

GILLOU: Me on the staff, at seventeen! . . . And besides, in the staff of the underground the risks are exactly the same as for the man who does the fighting. And what do you expect? That I shall consent, every time I'm asked to do anything, to question myself: "Am I taking a slight risk? A great one? An exaggerated one?" That I shall answer my comrades: "Oh no, not that, it's a little too much. My papa has forbidden it." I should be more ashamed to be in the Resistance under those conditions than not to be in it at all.

GEORGES: I'm going to tell you something that will be useful to you all your life: courage doesn't pay.

GILLOU: So you don't like courage?

GEORGES [*lowering his eyes*]: No.

GILLOU: Then you want me to promise you to be a coward?

GEORGES: One can always promise to be a little careful.

GILLOU: Oh, certainly, one can always promise [*with a contemptuous grimace*] to "be a little careful." [*He shrugs his shoulders.*] Excuse me. Perhaps I'm being rude.

GEORGES: I excuse you. Insulting is part of the genius of adolescence.

GILLOU: No, but you do have some expressions—

GEORGES: In short, I talk the language of the typical bourgeois?

GILLOU: Yes, precisely.

GEORGES [*very soberly*]: Do you hate me?

GILLOU [*laughing*]: Oh, Papa, you're joking! . . .

GEORGES: Because it would seem to me so natural that you should hate me. If you don't hate me, it means you're a decent chap.

GILLOU: But I am a decent chap, I think!

GEORGES: You already know some important people in the Resistance?

GILLOU: Some of my friends know some.

GEORGES: The masters of tomorrow. . . .

GILLOU: Why did you ask? You'd like me to start using them to shelter me?

GEORGES: Oh, not at all. I wasn't thinking of that at all. [*Silence.*] So, then, you're going to join that great organization. . . .

GILLOU: You mean, that means, you're going to let me?

GEORGES: I'll let you with the reservations I told you of.

GILLOU: Which, though—so as not to leave things vague?

GEORGES: You know very well: not risking your life uselessly. Nor your liberty. It's never worth while. Playing the hunted man! What lunacy! But men, and even men's children, are made like that: they love to seek out trouble. And yet to provoke fate has in it a touch of the impious.

GILLOU: Impious, to roll up one's sleeves so as to get one's country cleaned up!

GEORGES: Aren't there enough misfortunes others throw us into without our also needing those we throw ourselves into by our own fault? Don't go raising up misfortune aside from your own path.

GILLOU: Let's say I'm volunteering for the concentration camp as you, in your time, volunteered for the front. You change misfortune's key when you turn it into a work of your will.

GEORGES: That's good: "change the key." You found that in a high-brow review?

GILLOU [*fatuously, and lying without skill*]: No, it's mine. . . .

GEORGES: I see you have ideas. Bravo! Youth must have its fling.

GILLOU: If I were your age, you wouldn't worry about whether I'd read the things I said or whether they were mine.

GEORGES: Not bad!

GILLOU: Is it really you who were my father at Cannes? I can't recognize you any longer.

GEORGES: One believed in certain things in the winter of 1940 that one can't any longer believe in in the summer of 1944.

GILLOU: What things? Explain. You keep talking in riddles.

GEORGES: Soon half the French will be no longer talking except in riddles.

GILLOU: If only there were none but men like you in France!

GEORGES: Whether they're like you or like me, in either case the game's lost.

GILLOU: Lost! The game lost at the moment when one's beginning to breathe again!

GEORGES: Lost. It's written in the sky, in letters of fire.

GILLOU: Look here, Papa, I give up trying to understand you. With you, all is always lost. Let me be what I am, it's all I ask of you.—So, really, as regards what I want, we're agreed?

GEORGES: Yes, provided you're prudent.

GILLOU: Thank you.

GEORGES: Don't get worked up: I'm not used to being thanked.

GILLOU: In this house?

GEORGES: In this house or elsewhere.

GILLOU: Does it make you unhappy?

GEORGES: Oh, one's always a bit unhappy about something. . . .

[*Gillou gets up and, in a rush of affection, goes to embrace his father. Georges pushes him aside.*]

GEORGES: I can't let you embrace me when I'm doing what I'm doing.

GILLOU: You're doing what hundreds of thousands of fathers have done in France, thank God.

GEORGES: No, I'm doing something else.

GILLOU: And now, from tomorrow—

GEORGES: You're going to start something tomorrow?

GILLOU: Don't ask me questions.

GEORGES: That answer's a confession. For an underground worker, you're quick to confess.—But do you at least know how to look after yourself? Do you know how to defend yourself? I so dread the jauntiness of the French. To be killed by the Germans, if one must. But to be killed by the carelessness of the French! . . .

GILLOU: Don't fuss, we are as well armed as they are.

GEORGES: Armed? You're not going to be armed?

GILLOU: Them armed and us not? You have got some notions. A man who's not armed is a phantom.

GEORGES: You're going to be armed, personally? You're going to carry a weapon on you?

GILLOU: You bet!

GEORGES: It's madness! They've only to search you at the first roadblock, at once you're arrested, sent one knows not where, worse perhaps. . . . No, never will I be a party to such insane acts. Ah, enough juvenile offenders! Enough juvenile offenders!

GILLOU: You've just given me permission, and now—

GEORGES: I did give you permission to act, but to act like a sensible boy. Not to toy, under the nose of the Germans, with arms you don't even know how to use, and because of which, at some street corner, you may be killed like a dog. Oh, if you want to disobey us, your mother and me, disobey us; it's easy for you; we're not going to keep you always in sight. But if your idea of prudence is to carry a loaded weapon on you, in the Paris of June 1944, then I tell you, for my part, that all you do will be done against my will.

GILLOU: Are you the man who, three years ago, at Cannes, cried: "To think that tomorrow the dawn will come, and with sons who won't be mine!" And now the dawn is coming, and it will, in fact, be thanks to sons who won't be yours.

GEORGES: Did I say that? I don't remember.

GILLOU: You did say it, and Mamma repeated it to me, and I even repeated the phrase to a pal, and he used it for the title of an article for the school's clandestine paper: *Tomorrow the Dawn.*

GEORGES: "Tomorrow the dawn." And what will be done when the dawn does come?

GILLOU: First, the traitors will be punished.

GEORGES: Meaning?

GILLOU: They'll be given over to the justice of the people. And no pity.

GEORGES: Those are words, or is it serious?

GILLOU: You'll see if they're words. There are already chaps in my class who know the man they'll shoot down. The suspects and the more than suspects. And the less than suspects. And after that the French will be masters in their own house. And they'll remake France.

[*A silence.*]

GEORGES [*in a washed-out voice*]: Your father will not stop you from working at that task. You will do as you wish.

GILLOU: Can one, this time, take you at your word?

GEORGES: We'll say no more on this subject.

GILLOU: You must, though, say something to Mamma.

GEORGES: I'll say something to her about it later. I prefer to go away now without seeing her. You will explain to her. She can always ring me up. [*He makes for the door.*]

GILLOU: Well then, au revoir.

GEORGES: Au revoir.—It's really as from tomorrow you begin?

GILLOU: Yes, as from tomorrow.

GEORGES: But, after all—what? Something serious?

GILLOU: Yes.

GEORGES: Something hard? [*Gillou makes a vague gesture with his shoulders.*] Well then, au revoir, my boy.—And besides, you know, you shall have your bike all the same.

GILLOU: Oh, my bike, a fat lot I care about that, just now.

GEORGES: Yes, yes, I want you to have your bike. . . .

CURTAIN

ACT III

Same setting, but in the evening. The electric lights are lit. The curtains are drawn.

GEORGES, MARIE

MARIE: He never comes in late. You know perfectly well one of his qualities is punctuality. It's ten: he should have been here four hours ago. I've rung up the school: he left at six as usual.

GEORGES: Yes, he is sometimes late. And when he is, each time, you imagine him dead. It's ridiculous. You're unceasingly worried about him. When he's in good health, when everything's all right—

MARIE: If I didn't worry about him unceasingly, I shouldn't love him. It was yesterday you gave him permission. Do you think he could have done something rash the very first day?

GEORGES: No, no, that's not likely.

MARIE: And suppose he isn't in by midnight? With the curfew, that'll mean the whole night. It'll drive me mad. My God, make him come back!

GEORGES: It's you who'd drive people mad, with your fits of terror and your piety. When you're happy, you're not unintelligent. But when you're suffering, you fall off badly.

MARIE: I know now why I had that nightmare yesterday.

GEORGES: Well, each of us has his ghosts. I too have mine. They make me silent in company, impotent by the side of the woman I love, they tie my throat in a knot at table, make me jump when the bell rings, freeze me in spite of the heat, keep me awake at night. [*Marie coughs.*] You've got a cold in June? You've got a cold because Gillou hasn't come home at the time he said? No, no, your illness is elsewhere. What an illness love is!

MARIE: Yes.

GEORGES: One ought to burn out love as they burn out the growths of cancer.

MARIE: It would come up again at the side, like cancer.

GEORGES: Gillou will come in with a smile on his lips, and laughing at your scares.

MARIE: If he hasn't arrived by eleven, I'm going to the police station.

GEORGES: An entirely useless step, since you wouldn't be able to tell them the truth.

MARIE: This room which he left at two, in which he'd turned everything upside down, so full of him, so empty of him. . . . At lunch he said to me: "Papa was decent. He understood." Now quite out of reach, whereas a few hours ago I was touching him with my hands. Separated. Separated. This whole night that stands between him and me—Separated!

GEORGES: Me, too, yesterday, when I left him, he was happy, he thanked me.

MARIE: Do at least tell me that you'll go on loving him! What was it I said yesterday—that I would love him for two? It was blasphemy. You can see very well that the two of us are not too many for loving him, for guiding him, for preserving him—preserving him from himself and from everybody.

GEORGES: Preserving him from everybody. . . .

MARIE: You will love him, won't you? He needs you.

GEORGES [*in a very weak voice*]: I'll love him, I give you my word. It seems to me I can now feel how much I should miss him.

MARIE: But you're not going to miss him! He's going to come back! You do say abominable things. You seem to find my distress justified. Is it justified, or is it mad?

GEORGES: Mad, mad.

MARIE: In a few moments he'll be there. I shall be laughing at myself. I shall be telling myself: "Nothing happened. He's there, and always will be." I can already see myself crying with joy. [*She glances at her wrist-watch.*] God, my watch has stopped. It was still going ten minutes ago. It stopped at the moment when something was happening to him. Something has happened to him!

GEORGES: There she goes, the one who let her mind be changed by a dream! [*The electric light goes out. Total darkness.*] That's good, the light's cut off! And yet the warning's not been sounded.

MARIE: In the state I'm in, being in darkness like this is enough to make one howl oneself to death like an animal. . . .

GEORGES: Keep calm, please. I'm going to light a candle. I know where they are. [*He can be felt getting up and groping his way. He can be heard upsetting something.*]

MARIE: It's terrifying.

GEORGES: Yes.

MARIE: What do you mean: yes? You find it's terrifying?

GEORGES: Yes.

MARIE: Ah, you shouldn't have said so. There must be good reasons for showing fear, for you to be ready to show fear at the same time as me!—One can see nothing. If I move, I shall bump into things, hurt myself. . . . I'm going to have to go on all fours like an animal. No, no, I won't stay here. I'm going out, I'm going straight into the streets.

GEORGES: And Gillou will come back during that time, and you won't know.

MARIE: Well then, open the window. I can't bear to stay a moment longer in this blackness. I feel my reason going.

[*Georges opens the window. There is a confused view of roofs and in the serene and starry night sky, quite near by, the campanile and dome of the Sacre Cœur de Montmartre.*]

GEORGES: How freely the air has made its way into this room! How free it is! And the stars have no quarrels. They follow their path, each of them, without knocking into one another. And the sun and the moon yield each other place by turns, and do so without jealousy. Why can't I fly off through the air's night, there to escape from my fellows and from the idea they form of me!—The whole city, millions of people, shriveled up into itself, holding its breath, in the expectation of the first blow. That false calm is more impressive than if the night had been shattered. That mysterious silence, while a hundred and fifty miles away, in Normandy, hell is loose. One would say nothing is happening. And yet here they're watching, there they're hiding, there they're torturing, there they're killing. We are surrounded by things of horror.

MARIE: And he—he is a shade wandering in this night of horror, plunging into it, losing himself in it forever, as in my dream. Ah, may nothing have happened to him, may he not have been killed! Death is something that doesn't concern him. Let him die later on, when he's old, when he has a beard, but not when he's still the little fresh thing he is, when he's still growing! I measured him the other day against the door of my room: he'd grown nearly half an inch in two months. . . .

GEORGES [*half aloud*]: May God exist, that I may beg Him not to let this appalling thing take place!

MARIE: Shut the window. What one sees out there is even worse than the darkness.

GEORGES: That redness in the sky. . . . One would take it for summer lightning, and it is things being blown up. It looks as if it's in the direction of Levallois. Always the working-class districts. Always the working-class districts. It's true, really: always the same people who bear the brunt.

MARIE: Shut the window, I tell you!

GEORGES: City of my soul, city of the things most dear to me—running with blood, built upon blood. . . . Again that reddening sky: the symbols, the words written in the sky. . . . But let there be some noise, after all! We're at war. Let there be some rumblings, some cracklings! Not that silence, no, not that silence! [*Marie shuts the window and draws the curtains with violence. Once more, complete darkness.*] I must find a candle. [*He once more gropes. Once more something falls and smashes.*] Everything's escaping me, everything's fleeing from me, I lose myself wherever I turn. Here I am, entered into the world of suffering; when shall I ever come out?

MARIE: You recognize that yesterday you did wrong?

GEORGES: Did I do wrong? Worse wrong than you have ever imagined. All my life I have done wrong. People accuse me of what isn't true, people threaten me because of what isn't true. But they don't know what is true. Wrong to him. Wrong to you. Wrong to all. As much wrong, more wrong than any of those whom I sent to prison and dishonored. Always doing wrong, and never punished. And now punished in my son.

MARIE: Punished? So you really think something has happened to him? You admit that you're afraid?

GEORGES: Why should I not be afraid, and why should I not admit it? Why should I not be natural? Yes, I'm afraid. Only Fear itself could be fuller of fear than I am. But people mustn't know. If people get to know, I'm done for. Here, look here, look!

MARIE: What? Look at what? It's dark.

GEORGES: Here. At the Liberation, this is where I shall fall, assassinated.

MARIE: Georges, are you mad? Do you think the Germans will come and kill people in their houses?

GEORGES: Here precisely, at the foot of the chest. My body

will stretch from there to there. Ah, of course provided you've let me come in, after opening your door and seeing me covered with blood. And that—that's not certain.

MARIE: You're delirious!

GEORGES: Isn't human nature, when one sees it in oneself, capable of causing you such horror that one would like to die of it? To die, so as to cease knowing oneself. But no, oneself, one doesn't die. The old get away with it always; it's the sons who pay for them. Thirty years of the father's aberrations are punished in an hour's aberration in the son. One deserves prison a hundred times, and it's your little one, at the first folly he commits, who gets arrested. One brushes against death a hundred times, and it's your little one, at the first risk he runs, who gets killed.

MARIE: Gets killed!

GEORGES: The expression he had when he was sleeping on the sofa. . . . Yet another ghost.

MARIE: What sofa?

GEORGES: Punished for the evil I have done. Punished also for the good I've done. Punished for the evil and the good I've done.

MARIE: Punished, always punished!

GEORGES: One action, hardly an action, one word, hardly a word, a *yes* barely uttered, and suddenly, let loose, punishment, terror without remedy. . . . Here I am, entered into the world of suffering. Don't desert me.

[*The electric light comes on again.*]

MARIE: My God! I'm coming back to life. Simply because the light comes on again, I come back to life and hope.

GEORGES: May the darkness return and hide the trembling of my hands. May it hide the staring of my eyes.

MARIE: Ah, tomorrow the dawn will come, won't it? Tomorrow the dawn will come.

GEORGES: Yes, tomorrow the dawn will come. For some people.

MARIE: For us! For him! Assure me that it will! For once in your life, give me a word of hope.

GEORGES: The presages were lying, perhaps. The stars are perhaps with us, they that were so brilliant and so calm.

MARIE: But why did you confess you had done him more wrong than I can imagine? More wrong: what does that mean?

GEORGES: Me, do him wrong?

MARIE: Wretch! I can see your face. Now I know why you let him go.

GEORGES: It isn't what you think, I swear.

MARIE: You understood me too quickly. Wretch! Wretch!

GEORGES: I don't know what you mean.

MARIE: You're lying! You're a lawyer. You're lying! Coward when you deserted him at his birth. Coward when you deserted him at Cannes. Coward and hideous when you killed him, as you've just done, to save yourself.

GEORGES: He was marked from the beginning.

MARIE: There's your only excuse! Wretch! Wretch!

GEORGES [*stammering*]: It's because I loved him that I came back to Paris, and all that that has involved. . . .

[*Savage ringing of the doorbell, abrupt and repeated. Marie hurls herself out of the studio into the hall. The door is heard being opened. She comes in again, accompanied by a young man, livid, gasping, his clothes in disorder.*]

MARIE: My son? What's become of my son?

[*The messenger slightly turns his gaze away. Marie throws herself on the sofa with a terrible cry. Georges remains standing motionless in the middle of the room, his head down, crushed.*]

CURTAIN

POSTFACE

In the year 1946, I dined at the house of some people who had been, notoriously, "collaborators" (economic) and in consequence, at the "Liberation," had had some trouble. The son and daughter of the house, who were about twenty years old, were at table, and nobody addressed a remark to them during the whole meal, nor did they utter a word. When we got up, I saw that the young man had a limp. Our host then appeared to recollect his existence. "I don't know," he said, "if I introduced my son." He pointed to the injured leg. "He was parachuted three times by the English."

When I got home, I wrote in my notebook: "I have the end of *No Man's Son*," and I imagined what would become of my three characters.

Gillou has remained himself. His personality is weak, he is not very intelligent, but he is nice, affectionate, docile. He whom his father heaped with abuse, treated as mediocre, he does what a boy does who is generous and has not much to offer: he offers his life.

Marie has increased her stature. Having abdicated from being a mistress, she has carried over all her powers of affection to her son. Her better part, maternal love, now isolated, transfigures her. Insignificant and often silly in *No Man's Son*, she is the one who, here, will be the most worth-while human being of the three.

Georges has collapsed. He has seen the occupation, and he foresees the aftermath: this has broken the spring in him. What is more, he has nothing left of his love for his son: the source has dried up. The champion of *quality* is to descend to an appalling action. In 1941 he was sacrificing his son to an ideal. In 1944 he sacrifices him to his own fear. And it is the same man.

The human truth of the development of these three characters, the tragedy of the situation in which it might resolve itself, made me immediately certain that one day I would treat this subject. I did so in October 1948.

In treating it, I yielded to four other temptations.

The first: A "rule" of dramatic art (it comes originally, I think, from Aristotle, that absurd rule-monger) has it that it is impossible to interest the public in a theatrical character who is entirely and absolutely odious.

No doubt Georges Carrion has on his side some extenuating circumstances:

(1) His emotionalism, his nervous tension; these are stressed in *No Man's Son* and in *Tomorrow the Dawn* and make his inability to control his fear almost that of a sick man.

(2) The fact—against which, from the moral standpoint, nothing can be said—that his son has become for him an object of indifference.

(3) The fact that it was through love for Gillou, at a time when he did still love him, that he returned to the occupied zone, "and all that that involved." . . . This fact seems to me so important that I wanted the last line spoken by Georges to be a reminder of it. Someone has written of Gillou that in *No Man's Son* he was "a victim of love" (the love his father has for him). He is still that in this play. And Georges, too, in both plays, is a victim of love.

(4) Finally, the horror he has for his crime, and for his whole self; and on this I need only refer the reader to the third act.

But, notwithstanding these extenuating circumstances, this character is obviously odious. I was attracted by the temptation of interesting the public in him, in spite of the famous rule.

My second temptation was to bring on the stage the case of the father who seeks to save himself—or only to push himself forward—by sending his son to do something that endangers his life. The first sentence of the first essay in my first book, *La Relève du matin*, written in 1916, speaks of "those young war dead" whose death "is for their family a guarantee of honorableness, a petty victory rather as if, for instance, they had got into *the career*." The fathers whose business affairs it suits extremely well that their sons should have "fallen on the field of honor," the parents who in letting their sons join up had at the back of their minds the pleasant ring that decorations have when cited in a wedding announcement, those who pushed their sons, rather compromised by a thing called the Milice, to join *in extremis* our armies on the Rhine, at the risk of their dying there—the men of my generation have lived surrounded by all that, and I think it is the same in every bourgeois community. That being so, I do not see why I should not say so, and why I should not exhibit it on the stage.

That brings us to my third temptation.

A play like *Tomorrow the Dawn* is destined to create a sort of unanimity against the author.

First, of the ex-collaborators, who will say that I am betraying my side in the hope of "working my passage home." (I am here recalling that in the eyes of some people I am supposed to have been a collaborator.)

Secondly, of the resisters or Communists, who will laugh at the thought that I could have believed that such a work could help me work my passage home; and will laugh too at seeing me fall out with the collaborators ("Let crab eat crab").

Thirdly, of those who keep their ears to the ground and will consider me stupid to have made the Communist sympathizer the likable character in my play, at the precise moment when, for the first time for five years, the nation is being tuned up against Communism.

Fourthly, of the *bourgeoisie*, shocked not only because the play is "painful" but because it reminds them of the high price they are willing to pay, on occasion, for their privileges, their liberty, or their life.

To publish this work, knowing so well what reactions it will provoke, one needs to be upheld by a powerful reason, and here it is. *Is it admissible that an author should regulate his works according to a false idea that people have about him?*

First false idea about me. Some people who wish me no good have published the statement that I was a collaborator. Should I, because of a calumny, and for a "loyalty" whose only basis would be a calumny, feel myself bound not to render antipathetic an imaginary character who is represented as a collaborator—not even that, but as a man who has laid himself open to a charge of being a collaborator?

Second false idea. Some superficial people have believed that I "was" Georges Carrion. In spite of my constant assertion, *dating from the very beginning*, that I dissociated myself from that character. Was I, because of a misunderstanding, to forbid myself to make that character odious, on the ground that in doing that to him I should be confessing myself to be odious?

Every man of judgment, at these questions, will answer no, a thousand times no. An author should not be a slave in his creations to the mistakes people make about him and about his work. His independence toward the characters he creates, with whose aberrations he is not associated, should go with a selfsame independence toward the public and its aberrations. To proclaim this by an action, once more, was my third temptation. That action is *Tomorrow the Dawn*.

I ought not to end without noting that in publishing this play I yielded to a fourth and final temptation: that of doing what most authors would not do. To come out of one's repose in order to challenge the bull, with foot, with shout, and with cape, is a temptation that recurs periodically in my life.

THE MASTER OF SANTIAGO

⚜

A Play in Three Acts

EL GRECO: JULIAN ROMERO

Commander of the Order of Santiago, being presented to God by the knight with the fleurs-de-lis [PRADO]

". . . But the summit of El Greco's work, at least according to my feeling, is the presentation of Julian Romero by the knight with the fleurs-de-lis. Here, more than anywhere else, El Greco shows himself a "master of elevation." *

That kneeling man and that other person who appears to be raising him up, could they not be Don Rodrigo de Castro and Carranza, Archbishop of Toledo, dancing together the grand pavan of Jesus Christ? The form in which they execute it is so beautiful that I must describe it, even though it is foreign to my subject. The Inquisition has sent Don Rodrigo to accompany Carranza, apparently to do him honor, really to keep an eye on him and to arrest him if he thinks fit. At the moment when Rodrigo finally decides to arrest the Archbishop, he goes down on one knee and asks his forgiveness for what he is about to do. And Carranza, gently, raises him up.

This sublime scene has no direct relation with the one treated by El Greco: the subject here is a certain Captain Romero, who is presented to God—symbolically—by a knight whose identity is unknown. Never, it seems to me, has there been a more poignant rendering of the "Father, into Thy hands I commend my spirit." The imploring expression of the eyes, the abandon of the mouths (in these two captains! mouths to be given the last rites with a little earth and grass), the perfect brotherly gesture of the knight (how well he gathers his candidate to him!), the kneeling man's hands, fine as a fine destiny—all this becomes an arrow that flies to its mark. At last a Catholic picture that flies to its mark! It elevates and it edifies. The artist this time spares us his celestial vision. The supernatural is not evoked here by the coarse means so dear to

* Phrase quoted from the Prince de Ligne. (Translator's note.)

El Greco: that distortion of the human body which not only is an offense against the most beautiful of God's creatures, but is contrary to the dogma according to which the body will rise again in the most beautiful state it attained during its earthly life. The two suppliants of the "Romero" belong to the real, for it is plausible that at some moment they did have those expressions the painter gives them, just as we see them; and at the same time they transcend the real. They are as human as can be; and at the same time they are reflections of the divine. Note, too, that here is no king or prince donning a penitent's robe and applying himself to self-abasement and putting into it, if not ostentation, at least a certain emphasis of pose. Nor is this, like the St. Francis of the Zuloaga collection, a sort, if I may say so, of specialist in humility. It is Captain Romero, in other words Captain Hardy, offering up his small baggage of patriotic exploits, and all his subordinate everydayness, yours and mine. He is not luxurious, his mantle has no gold braid; and something tells me he is not very intelligent. But he spreads out this small offering before the eyes of his Judge with a luminous confidence, and he says, as if there had never been in his life anything but the soldier's candor: "Forgive me, miserable sinner." And the man who is presenting him with so tender a gesture is saying, as the young man in my book *Le Songe* says over his stricken comrade: "My Father, I present to Thee this my brother." And have I not, one day, had on my face an expression like his?

Christians often reproduce, in honor of their relatives who die, pictures of dubious quality. Why have they never thought of having this work reproduced for that? And especially when they want to honor soldiers killed in action?

There is the real and there is the unreal. Beyond the real and beyond the unreal there is the profound. The profound is what is suggested to me by the *Presentation of Captain Romero*.

H. M.—*Croire aux âmes, 1943*

CHARACTERS

DON ALVARO DABO, *aged 47, a knight of the Order of Santiago (St. James) [as are the five characters who follow]*

DON BERNAL DE LA ENCINA, *aged 52*

DON FERNANDO DE OLMEDA, *aged 62*

DON GREGORIO OBREGON, *aged 35*

THE MARQUIS OF VARGAS, *aged 50*

DON ENRIQUE DE LETAMENDI, *aged 19*

THE COUNT OF SORIA, *a nobleman of the Chamber and envoy extraordinary of the King, aged 30*

MARIANA, *Don Alvaro's daughter, aged 18*

TIA CAMPANITA ("*Aunt Bell*"), *duenna, aged 55*

January 1519, at Avila (Old Castile).

The hall of honor in the house of Don Alvaro Dabo.

Walls entirely bare, gray ocher in color, of rather a dark shade: they are walls of pretty clumsy masonry, in which you can almost pick out the separate stones. On the left, a window with heavy crossbars outside it, through which one can see, from time to time, flakes of snow falling. On the right, on the back wall, a great crucifix, near which there is hanging the huge capitulary mantle—white silk, with a red sword, whose hilt has the shape of the fleur-de-lis, embroidered on the left breast—of the knights of the Order of Santiago.

On the frieze of this wall three carved coats of arms topped with helmets make a burst of sudden ornament. They are askew, as if they had been beaten and hustled by a squall. They burst out there, richly, curiously, almost convulsively ornate, on the wall's nakedness, like three luxuriant oases in an arid desert.

In the middle of the stage, a small table, with seven cups and two ewers. Seven chairs. A brazier.

From time to time, at the producer's discretion, there are chimings of bells, but discreet, with no excess. And no bells during the final scene of the third act.

ACT I

SCENE I

MARIANA, TIA CAMPANITA

TIA CAMPANITA: Today only seven chairs. So only six of these gentlemen will be coming? Last month they were eight.

MARIANA: Five only have sent to say they'd be coming. The snow stops a lot of people.

TIA CAMPANITA: Five? Oh, that's true, there's the chair for the unknown guests.

MARIANA: My father wishes there should be always one chair extra, in case some knight of the Order might want to come without notice.

TIA CAMPANITA: But that unexpected visitor never shows up. No, Mariana, it's not the snow that stops these gentlemen. It's a different cold, the kind that slides into a man when he is losing his love for something. Like all the orders of chivalry, the Order of Santiago is declining: it only really burns any longer in the heart of your father. It's not without reason that they nickname your father "the Master of Santiago," even though there isn't any longer a grand master of that Order.

MARIANA: Excuse me, for the last twenty-five years it's the King who's been Grand Master of the three Spanish orders of chivalry. As soon as the Kingdom of Granada had been won back from the Moors, King Ferdinand broke up the great orders which had made possible for him this complete liberation of the land, and took them in hand himself. He no longer had need of them, and he was afraid of them. And besides, that's what is commonly done with those who've borne the brunt.

TIA CAMPANITA: Nowadays the knights no longer have any corporate existence. If your father were not there, I believe the ones in Avila wouldn't know each other.

MARIANA: Two years ago, on our way back from Paular, we stopped the night at what had been the commandery of Isla. Grasses were invading the mouths of the dried-up wells and the stalls of the ruined chapel. Donkeys were tied up in the chapter-hall, where the knights used to hold council. And I could hear the passing of the dark irresistible river in the night, and it spoke to me of all the things that are borne away to be drawn under.

TIA CAMPANITA: Today these gentlemen are five strong; next month they'll be three. Especially if Don Alvaro persists in offering them such austere hospitality. Why doesn't he invite them to supper, as anyone else would do in his place?

MARIANA: My father thinks it is unsuitable that subjects of a certain gravity should be mixed up with thoughts of food. He very much admires the custom of the Arabs, among whom the master of the house, when he is entertaining guests, is present at the meal without partaking of it.

TIA CAMPANITA: All the same, to serve them with water, when, after all, the wine of our cellar isn't so bad! Yes, I know, you've told me before: the symbol of purity. . . . As if the knights of earlier times minded drinking wine!

MARIANA [*drinking out of one of the cups*]: How cool it is! It carries you away. And how I understand my father's not wishing any other drink but that for his knights!

TIA CAMPANITA: Stop drinking that: you'll make yourself ill! More! Gulping down cold water in great mouthfuls when it's freezing out of doors!

MARIANA: I'm not drinking it: I'm eating it! Oh, madame,

it is icy, and it burns me. It's as if I were eating fire. It is the water of San Lucar. . . .

Tia Campanita: Nonsense, it's the water from our patio.

Mariana: It's the water from the spring of San Lucar, do you think I wouldn't recognize it. My father wanted the purest water, for the gentlemen of the Order. [*She drinks.*] More! More! Oh, it has in it something that I adore!

Tia Campanita: The Arabs have a proverb: "Lion and nightingale are always athirst." My God, the dust here! Of course, Isidro can't at one and the same time do the cooking, answer the door, and keep the house clean. As long as Don Alvaro will not engage a second servant— Ah! I'm sure that when your mother was alive, the house was properly kept.

Mariana: My father is not interested in that sort of thing.

Tia Campanita: And that's why you live in a room where one of the walls has lost all its plaster, and nobody has it repaired. And holes in it big enough to put one's fist in; you give the impression of dwelling in a ruin. A pretty little blossom like you!

Mariana: My father doesn't see that, or if he sees it, he likes it. As for me, I assure you that it doesn't worry me at all and that I understand very well that a serious man should consider it unimportant.

Tia Campanita: And what, then, is important?

Mariana: The soul, madame: didn't you know? For my father, the only important thing, or rather the only essential, or rather the only real thing is what goes on in the inside of the soul.

Tia Campanita: In convents they attend to the soul, if I'm not mistaken. And there is no place better kept than a convent. Don Alvaro argues that he isn't rich. But if he isn't rich, whose fault is it? From the meanest to the highest, everyone sponges on him, everyone robs him, and he doesn't care.

MARIANA: You know very well that he gets pleasure out of being despoiled.

TIA CAMPANITA: No doubt he's not rich; at least he behaves as if he were not. And yet, at certain moments, he displays a mad generosity.

MARIANA: He conforms to the oldest motto of our house: *Dedi et dabo*, "I have given and I shall give." Giving, that is his keep and his battlements.

TIA CAMPANITA: You heard, I suppose, the story of the salt-cellar?

MARIANA: The story of the salt-cellar?

TIA CAMPANITA: The salt-cellar that was stolen by the poor nobleman.

MARIANA: I don't know that story.

TIA CAMPANITA: Oh well, then, I will tell it to you!

MARIANA: If it's a story of which my father is the hero, he has kept it from me on purpose, and there is no use in my hearing it.

TIA CAMPANITA: Oh, but I am going to tell it to you, I can't keep it to myself!—A month ago a poor nobleman, whom your father did not know, presented himself at his house to ask him to help him find work. When he's gone, Don Alvaro notices that one of the silver salt-cellars on the sideboard has disappeared. Some days later the nobleman comes back, and your father observes that he has new breeches instead of the worn and patched breeches he was wearing the time before. Thereupon he goes and gets the two remaining salt-cellars, wraps them up, and gives them to him, saying: "I haven't been able to find you work, but please take this away for the love of God, and pray for me." The nobleman, with tears, kisses his hands and confesses.

MARIANA: Madame, if I wished to recite all the stories of that sort that I know about my father, a whole night would pass in the telling.

TIA CAMPANITA: And to think that so good a man can neglect

you as he does, can treat you with that bad grace which is so typically masculine, so chilling! . . . You're looking to see if the gentlemen of the Order aren't arriving?

Mariana: I should like Don Bernal to arrive first.

Tia Campanita: Ah, why didn't Don Bernal keep his son with him! If Don Jacinto were coming here with his father, then, really, you'd be at that window and unable to drag yourself away!

Mariana: You are quite wrong: that is something I would not do.

Tia Campanita: And you so in love with him!

Mariana: I don't feel in love any longer when I hear you say that I am.

Tia Campanita: You are in love, and may it be God's will that Don Bernal and Doña Isabella win the consent of your father to this marriage, and that you may soon be living under the roof of a man who will not say to you every day: "Oh, what is the meaning of this fine dress?" of a dress you have been wearing for two years.

Mariana: Here is Don Bernal. Leave us, madame, I should so much like to have a little talk with him.

SCENE II

Mariana, Don Bernal de la Encina

Mariana: Don Bernal, I am very glad to see you.

Bernal: So am I, Mariana. For our meeting today is going to be important for you. Three of us are taking ship for the New World.

Mariana: You're not leaving? Nor Don Jacinto?

Bernal: My health forbids me to. As for Jacinto, his service with the Council of the Indies keeps him at Valladolid. But we should like to persuade your father to go.

MARIANA: My father! Go!

BERNAL: You, I, Jacinto, with your happiness in view, all of us need that he should go. Oh, not for long—eighteen months, perhaps only a year. You could go and live during his absence in the house of your Aunt Christine. I've good reasons for feeling sure that your father, in that short time, can make a fortune out there; I shall provide him with the means. And I will explain to you another day why, if we want your marriage to take place, it is essential that your condition be made more solid.

MARIANA: I understand very well.

BERNAL: Really, you understand that? How much more reasonable you are than your father!

MARIANA: But you're not going to tell him that he must go out there to make a fortune! You know the horror he has of acting in his own interest.

BERNAL: No, of course, we shall advance other reasons, and there is no lack of them. I shall whisper in the ears of these gentlemen, as soon as they arrive: not a word about money. Not one of them, incidentally, knows that I have any personal bond in this affair. If we fail, then I shall have to speak to him in private and unfold myself to him in all frankness.

MARIANA: For heaven's sake, watch every step. Just at present he is particularly gloomy. The other evening I surprised him in his room; he had fallen asleep by the brazier. His face was quite new, full of misery; he had his head leaning a little on one shoulder, like the head of Christ on the cross. And he was murmuring some phrase, he was almost moaning. I bent over him, I heard the words he was saying—

BERNAL: And what were they?

MARIANA: He was saying: "O Spain! Spain!"

SCENE III

MARIANA, DON BERNAL, DON ALVARO DABO

BERNAL: What snow, my friend! One can only just force a way through it to your door.

ALVARO: Do you know what it reminds me of, this snow? A certain scene from an old German epic. A knight, of the Teutonic Order I think, is standing before the raised drawbridge of a castle. His head bowed, humbly, beneath the falling snow, he waits for the drawbridge to be raised, for he has come to pay the ransom of his little daughter, who is being held prisoner inside the castle. The hours go by; from hour to hour they put off receiving him; they gibe at him, the varletry throws at him snowballs and gnawed bones; and still he waits. He, the proud, he, the fierce, he, the terror of his enemies, he puts up with it all because it's for his little daughter. . . .

BERNAL: And you, my friend, would you do the same, for Mariana?

ALVARO: Certainly!

BERNAL: Really?

ALVARO: Certainly!

BERNAL: I thought as much, but I am glad all the same to hear you say so.

[*Noise of the knocker at the house door.*]

MARIANA: Your friends are arriving.

ALVARO: My friends?

MARIANA: The gentlemen of the Order.

ALVARO: The gentlemen of the Order are my peers, not my friends. [*Putting his hand on the arm of Don Bernal*] Except him.

[*Exit Mariana. Enter Don Fernando de Olmeda.*]

SCENE IV

ALVARO, BERNAL, DON FERNANDO DE OLMEDA. *Later, the* MARQUIS DE VARGAS *and* DON GREGORIO OBREGON, *together. Then, later,* DON ENRIQUE DE LETAMENDI

ALVARO: I was saying to Don Bernal that this snow reminded me of the Teutonic knight before the drawbridge of the castle.

OLMEDA: To me snow always recalls the eternal snows of the Sierra Nevada, which dominated us as we entered into Granada, twenty-seven years ago. The whole sky, that January, was a blue June sky and you might have thought the snows were the winding-sheets of our enemies hung up there in mid-sky. And we were weeping tears of tenderness, because Spain was at last Spain.

ALVARO: On the evening of Granada I beheld God in His mantle of war. He looked like a tree on which, after the battle, the combatants have hung up their swords.

BERNAL: So here we meet again, the three veterans of the siege of Granada, the three who took part in the great action that restored to our country its independence!

OLMEDA: I shall never understand why Don Alvaro, after covering himself with glory, at the age of twenty, in front of Baza, withdrew himself from the profession of arms.

ALVARO: I went on fighting for two years in Morocco. But—Morocco—

OLMEDA: It's there, they say, that, on the eve of the capture of Tlemcen, you uttered that strange saying: "The victory is assured, but is not worth the winning."

ALVARO: I don't remember. It is possible. . . .

[*After a knocking at the house door, enter, together, the Marquis de Vargas and Don Gregorio Obregon. Vargas limps. Greetings, during which Don Bernal whispers to each newcomer:* "Not a word about money."]

OLMEDA: None is missing now but Don Enrique. I've observed that at appointments it's generally youth that is late.

ALVARO: It's very natural: youth is always a bit late.

[*Knocking, then enter Don Enrique de Letamendi.—Greetings, and Don Bernal's whispered warning. Then the knights, each standing in front of his chair around the table, cross themselves and recite aloud the* Veni Creator, *after which they sit down. A silence.*]

BERNAL: I should like to submit a wish to Don Alvaro and to our companions here present. The other day a man whose name I shall withhold, pursued by an agency that I shall also not name, expressed before me a concern as to where he could find refuge. "Why not in one of our convents?" I asked. "They would give me up," he answered me. That's a saying so horrible that it kept me awake all night. And I decided I would never have peace until I could be sure that a fugitive who rings at the gate of one of the convents of the Order, whatever the reason for which he is pursued, will have the *certitude* that he will there be welcomed and protected. If you think as I do, let us do what is needed.

OBREGON: I am going in a fortnight to Valladolid. There I can see the Archbishop and insist that he bring pressure on the priors of our houses.

ALVARO: You will do well.

OBREGON: While I am at Valladolid, I am tempted to intervene in another matter. Don Juan de Anchorena, knight of the Order, has escaped from Oran, where he was prisoner on parole to the King of Oran. What do you think of that?

ALVARO: Had he really given his parole?

OBREGON: Yes, he even confesses it.

ALVARO: Any officer who is prisoner on parole and escapes,

however strong a reason he may give, is not a man of honor. I propose that we ask the King to strike out Anchorena from the Order.

LETAMENDI: And if the King refuses?

ALVARO: It is we of the Order, not the King, who fix the scale of moral values. It is not for the King, who is nineteen years old and is not a Spaniard, to say where lie good and evil in Spain. A nineteen-year-old King, and beardless!—Don Gregorio, we will sign a humble address to the King, and will entrust it to you.

OLMEDA: I speak in the name of all our companions here assembled, who are with me in what I am about to say and ask.—Three of us are leaving for the New World with Fuenleal's fleet, which sets sail next month. Don Gregorio Obregon, who takes up again the rank of quartermaster to the troops detailed for landing, Don Enrique de Letamendi, whose youthful valor, already tested in Italy, will be put at the service of Fuenleal, and lastly myself, who have no longer the strength for fighting, but am going to stop at Cuba, where the King has deigned to promise me the post of governor of Camaguey.

BERNAL: I too should be leaving if my health allowed.

VARGAS: And I too, but for this wretched wound.

OBREGON: One day, Spain was terribly defeated, overrun from end to end by the Moors. While the majority of the population accepted the yoke of the occupier, a handful of men from the beaten army, taking refuge in the mountains, began a struggle against the invaders that, growing foot by foot, in the course of eight centuries ended twenty-seven years ago in the total liberation of the territory. The people had pursued liberation all alone, abandoned to itself, without the help of its masters, and sometimes betrayed by them. In that very year 1492, in which the power of the infidels is broken in Spain, Columbus discovers San Salvador, and it is once more a handful of Spaniards that goes out to the conquest of an empire, just as it was a handful of Spaniards that had formed the kernel of the reconquest of the native soil. Yes, in the same year! The God that reigns in the heavens has willed that there should not be the least break in this superb continuity: link joins on to link. If ever there was anything sublime in this world, it is that.

OLMEDA: Let us come to the point. Don Alvaro, you, whom we call so respectfully and so affectionately "the Master of Santiago," do you not think there would be honor for you in accompanying us to the Indies? You know the proverb: "There is always a crusade in Spain." The new crusade is there.

BERNAL: And let us make things clear straight away: for the man you are, there is no question, of course, of trafficking in gold or in pearls or in lands, or in slaves: I know that, faithful to our great Christian tradition, rather than engage in commerce you would prefer, if necessary, to live on charity. In the Fuenleal expedition, you land as a soldier, sword in hand. As soon as possible you become administrator; I will see to that; take my word for it. If—as would be very natural—you are no longer in the mood for campaigning, a post can be given you without striking a blow in one of the regions long since conquered and pacified. I have heard that there are going to be some important vacancies in Cuba and in Jamaica.

ALVARO: Roll on, torrent of futility!

BERNAL: What?

ALVARO: I am sorry, but in all this business of conquest I have a feeling of the utterly ridiculous.

LETAMENDI: It's stifling, here in Avila. . . .

ALVARO: From the depths of narrow alleys, how beautiful seem the stars!

VARGAS: Isn't glory a thing you miss, you who had so bright a glory once?

ALVARO: If ever I had had a certain renown, I would say of

it what we say about our dead: "The Lord gave, and the Lord hath taken away; blessed be the name of the Lord." My only thirst is for a measureless withdrawal.

VARGAS: That doesn't make our task very easy.

ALVARO: Yes, I know what embarrassment a man who has no ambition can cause in a society.

OBREGON: No ambition, and in the prime of life. . . . But, in that case, what are you doing with your life?

ALVARO: Waiting for everything to end.

VARGAS: Living in obscurity, when a man has it in his power to shine. . . . A man who does not make the best of himself discourages those who wish him well. It's not for me to vaunt his excellence if he doesn't vaunt it a little himself.

ALVARO: I like to be disregarded.

OLMEDA: If your glory weighs heavy on you, there is the glory of the Order, which is engaged out there in a holy war.

ALVARO: A holy war? In a war of that sort the cause that is holy is the cause of the natives. Well, chivalry is essentially the defense of the persecuted. If I did go to the Indies, it would be to protect the Indians; that is to say, according to you, to be a "traitor." You must know the story of that Spanish soldier who was hanged as a traitor because he had given first aid to a wounded Indian. That is even worse than the worst cruelties.

OLMEDA: Numbers of knights from the Order are out there—among them Hernando Cortez, among them Pizarro—who certainly did not think like you.

LETAMENDI: And it is common knowledge that in a certain engagement our blessed patron himself, my lord St. James, appeared to the Spaniards, riding on his white horse.

ALVARO: Yes, I know it is to the cry "Santiago!" that the most odious infamies are committed. I know that when Ovando lured into an ambush the innocent and confiding Queen of the Indians of Xaragua, who wished us nothing but good, the signal for the crime was that he laid his hand upon the decoration he wore as knight of Alcantara, an image of God the Father; the Queen was hanged and the caciques buried alive. Our chivalry in the New World—there are no words strong enough to express how sick it makes me.

OBREGON: Great ideas are not charitable.

VARGAS: How could there not be excesses to deplore when a handful of men was to hold in check many thousands?

ALVARO: But why hold them in check?

OBREGON: The glory of Spain—

ALVARO: The glory of Spain was in reducing an invader whose presence was an insult to her faith, her soul, her spirit, her customs. But conquests of territory? That is so childish—and so absurd. To want to alter something in lands that have been conquered when it is so urgent to reform the home country itself is like wanting to alter something in the outside world when everything needs altering in oneself. And so futile. Princes busy themselves with winning new possessions that they won't know how to administer or how to defend, which, far from giving them strength, will weaken them, and which in the end they will lose pitifully after having had out of them a full measure of trouble. For we shall lose the Indies. Colonies are made to be lost. They are born with the cross of death on their foreheads.

OLMEDA: You forget that thousands, no, millions of Indians would burn through eternity in hell if the Spaniards did not bring them the faith.

ALVARO: But thousands of Spaniards will burn through eternity in hell because they have gone to the New World.

OLMEDA: What!

ALVARO: Everything to do with the New World is impurity and filth. The New World rots whatever it touches. And the loathsome disease that our compatriots bring back from over there is only the symbol of that rotting. Later on, when people want to honor a man, they'll say of him: "He took no part at all in the Indian business."

OLMEDA: Don Alvaro!

LETAMENDI: You are insulting us!

ALVARO: Through the conquest of the Indies there have settled in Spain the passion for lucre, trafficking in everything and for everything, hypocrisy, indifference to the neighbor's life, hideous exploitation of man by man. The Indies are the beginning of the twilight of Spain.

OBREGON: Let us withdraw. Our place is no longer here.

VARGAS: Admit then: you are waiting for it, that hour when Spain will be at the point of despair.

ALVARO: But let us forget the cause of the evil. Whatever it comes from, there exists a condition of Spain in which I wish to have the least possible share. Spain is my greatest humiliation. There's nothing for me to do in a time when honor is punished—when generosity is punished—when charity is punished—when all that is great is brought low and laughed to scorn—when everywhere in the upper ranks I behold rubbish—when everywhere the triumph of the most stupid and of the most abject is assured. A queen, Imposture, with Robbery and Crime her pages at her feet. Incapacity and Infamy, her two sisters, linking hands. Swindlers venerated, worshipped by those they have swindled. . . . Am I making it up? Remember the words of King Ferdinand on his deathbed: "Our contemporaries, who are day by day degenerating . . ."

VARGAS: All the ages have spoken in this way about themselves.

OBREGON: Chivalry at its most exalted moment—that is to say, in the twelfth century—was in need of reform.

ALVARO: True: everything, always, is in need of reform.

VARGAS: You are a Christian: follow your Christianity through to its conclusion. For three thousand years nations have been perishing. For three thousand years peoples have been falling into slavery. The Christian cannot take those misfortunes tragically. If you are logical, there is only one home country, the one that will be formed of the Elect.

ALVARO: I keep the other to afflict me.

BERNAL: You condemn your own time as very old men do. You are not fifty, and you talk as if you were eighty. And you exaggerate a great deal. If you took more part in events, if you were more informed about what is going on—

ALVARO: I know enough about it. Every time I poke my head out of my shell, I receive a blow on the head. Spain is no longer anything for me but something from which I try to preserve myself.

BERNAL: Yes, but by sheer force of cutting yourself off from it, the world appears to you deformed by your own way of looking at it. The next thing, you reject a whole age for lack of seeing it as it is.

OBREGON: Standing on the threshold of the new era, you refuse to enter it.

ALVARO: Standing on the threshold of the new era, I refuse to enter it.

VARGAS: Let us grant it is heroism to consent to be all alone, through fidelity to one's ideas. Wouldn't it also be heroism to play your part in a society that buffets you, so that in it you may make those ideas prevail which, if they find no incarnation, will remain more or less impotent?

BERNAL: And besides, what is humanly fine isn't sulking, it's adapting oneself; it isn't escaping to be virtuous at one's ease, it's being virtuous out in the world, in among the difficulties.

ALVARO: I am tired out with this continual divorce between me and all that is around me. I am tired out with indignation. I thirst to live among people different from the crafty, from the scum, and from the fools. Formerly we were defiled by the invader. Now we are defiled by ourselves; we have simply changed from one tragedy to another. Ah, why was I not killed at Granada, when my country was still intact? Why have I survived my country? Why am I alive?

BERNAL: My friend, what is the matter? You never spoke to us like that!

ALVARO: The collar of the knights of Cyprus used to be adorned with the letter *S*, which meant "Silence." Today all that is good in our country is silent. There is an Order of Silence: of it, too, I ought to be Grand Master. Why did you provoke me into speaking?

OLMEDA: Become a monk, Don Alvaro. That's the only state that could suit you from now on.

ALVARO: I don't know, actually, what holds me back, unless it's some lack of decision and energy.

OBREGON: And let me add that it is more elegant, when one is withdrawing from the world, to withdraw from it without abusing it. Such abuse is supremely vulgar!

ALVARO: Do you know what purity is? Do you know? [*Raising the mantle of the Order that is hanging on the wall below the crucifix*] Look at our mantle of the Order: it is white and pure like the snow outside. The red sword is embroidered on it where the heart would come, as if it were stained with the blood. The meaning of that is that purity, in the end, is always wounded, always killed, that always it receives the blow of the lance that was received by the heart of Jesus on the cross. [*He kisses the hem of the mantle. After a moment's hesitation Olmeda, who is nearest to the mantle, also kisses its hem.*] Yes, the noble values, in the end, are always vanquished; history is the tale of their ever renewed defeats. Only it mustn't be those whose mission is to defend them who undermine them. However far gone it may be in decline, the Order is the reliquary of all remaining magnanimity and integrity in Spain. If you do not believe that, resign from it. If we are not the best, we have no reason for existing. As for me, my daily bread is disgust. God has given to me in profusion the virtue of loathing. This horror and lamentation that make up my life and on which I feed— But you, full of indifference or indulgence for what is ignoble, you compound with it, you make yourselves its accomplices! Men of clay! Knights of clay!

OBREGON [*in a low voice, to Vargas*]: He says that because he is not very intelligent.

ALVARO: Before the taking of Granada, there was at the Frontera, on the top of a peak, a castle where the young knights used to complete their novitiate. It's there that for the last time I heard the song of the Bird. No one will hear it any more.

LETAMENDI: What bird?

ALVARO: The song of the burning Dove, who inspires in us what we ought to say or to do in order not to be unworthy.

OBREGON: The knight of the year 1519 cannot be the same as the knight of the year 1000. There are no longer gnomes and monsters.

ALVARO: There are still monsters. Never have there been so many. We are hemmed in by them, pinned down by them, overwhelmed by them. There they are—there—there. . . . Woe to the honest!

BERNAL: Gentlemen, let us adjourn. . . .

ALVARO [*at the height of his exaltation*]: Woe to the honest! Woe to the honest!

BERNAL: Let us adjourn the conclusion of this meeting to some other time. . . .

ALVARO [*suddenly depressed*]: Woe to the honest! . . . Woe to the best! . . .

[*Vargas and Obregon withdraw quickly and stiffly.*]

BERNAL [*to Alvaro*]: I need to speak with you in private, my friend. Can you receive me tomorrow?

ALVARO: Come at the sixteenth hour.

BERNAL: Till tomorrow, then, God willing.
ALVARO: Till tomorrow, God willing.
[*Exit Don Bernal.*]

SCENE V

ALVARO, LETAMENDI, OLMEDA

LETAMENDI: I am troubled. . . .
ALVARO: Why are you troubled?
LETAMENDI: I wonder if I should go.
ALVARO: Of course you should go.
LETAMENDI: After what you have said?
ALVARO: Go. That is what you want, and you are nineteen. When one is nineteen, one always ends by doing what one wants.
LETAMENDI: You disdain me! You haven't the right to disdain me like that!
ALVARO: Not the right! You decide what are my rights!
LETAMENDI: No, I will not stay in this frightful town, this tomb of tombs. But now I shall have to leave with an uncertain and unquiet heart. You have broken all my joy. Are you at least sure of being in the right, to disturb me so?
ALVARO: Yes, I am sure of being in the right.
LETAMENDI: Ah, you cast me down!
ALVARO: That is what I want to do. [*Exit Letamendi, with a gesture of confusion.*] Youth: time of failures.

SCENE VI

ALVARO, OLMEDA

OLMEDA: Me too—are you going to tell me to go?

ALVARO: Are you too, then, hesitating?

OLMEDA: The youngest and the oldest among us have been unsettled by you. Ah, you are indeed the Master of Santiago.

ALVARO: I am not the master of anyone or anything. I am the servant of the servants of God.

OLMEDA: Why did you advise that boy to leave?

ALVARO: Because he—he—has no importance. The young have not the daring for anything, nor the respect for anything, nor the understanding for anything. Let them have their expeditions overseas, that is what is right for them. But the high adventures are for the men of our age, and the high adventures are within. You, Olmeda, stay!

[*Olmeda makes an impulsive movement toward Alvaro. The two embrace in silence. Exit Olmeda.*]

SCENE VII

ALVARO, *alone*

ALVARO: O my soul, are you still there? O my soul, at last, you and I!

ACT II

Same scene. But beyond the barred window there is no longer snow falling. And one can see in the very limpid gray air that is characteristic of Avila one of the massive towers of the rampart girdling that city.

SCENE I

ALVARO, BERNAL

[*During this scene chickens come into the room from time to time to pick at something or other between the feet of Alvaro and Bernal.*]

BERNAL: . . . At present it's to the father that I'm appealing.

ALVARO: Mariana is what I love most in the world.

BERNAL [*smiling*]: More than your horse?

ALVARO [*serious*]: Much more than my horse.

BERNAL: Does Mariana disclose to you a little of her inner life?

ALVARO: Enough for me to know that she fears God. Although she does not speak to me of Him as much as I should like.

BERNAL: Perhaps from modesty. Anyhow, I was not thinking of her religious life, but of her emotional life. . . . Since he came back from Italy and went to live in Valladolid, Jacinto has seen Mariana only three times, but he has conceived a tender admiration for her, of which Doña Isabella and I approve. And I believe Mariana, on her side, is—well, hasn't—[*Silence.*] She's said nothing to you?

Alvaro: She knows that I have no competence in this sort of thing.

Bernal: If I have come to see you and to discuss this twofold sentiment, it's because we considered, Doña Isabella and I, that the matter must be brought to a head. [*Silence.*] You are very taciturn.

Alvaro: So many things are not worth saying. And so many people are not worth saying the other things to. That makes a lot of silence.

Bernal: I have the impression that our plan doesn't seem to please you.

Alvaro: You take me by surprise.

Bernal: After all, my dear friend, have you not noticed this inclination of your daughter's?

Alvaro: Let's put it that I haven't noticed it because I did not want to notice it.

Bernal: So it displeases you?

Alvaro: Attachments displease me.

Bernal: Have you never thought about Mariana's future?

Alvaro: To try to establish Mariana, I should have had to lose myself. In social obligations and in waste of time. I was not willing. I thought that God would count it in my favor that I was unwilling to lose myself, and that He Himself would provide for her establishing. And that is what has happened, since here you are. If your proposal allows of such a marriage coming to pass without my having to apply myself to it, it's Heaven that has sent you.

Bernal: There's not only you to consider, there's our children's happiness. And isn't it only right that I should think for us both? For it doesn't seem to interest you very much.

Alvaro: Mariana will be happy. My house is not gay. And I too, perhaps, will be happier when she isn't any longer there.

Bernal: Really!

Alvaro: You have no idea how starved I am for silence and

for solitude: something pared away . . . Every human being is an obstacle to the man who is straining toward God. The movements that God in His loving kindness sets up in me do not become perceptible to me except in a complete abstraction, like those who listen to music with their eyes shut. What I ought to have is empty days, so empty— Whatever came into them, even friendship itself, and above all affection, would only come in to trouble them.

BERNAL: Mariana—

ALVARO: I used to hear her walking about; there were even times when she would sing. . . . She often tired me, and now and then made me lose patience; vitality is sometimes a very formidable gift. And besides, it's a responsibility to have a daughter, in a period when all one can do for her is to protect her. Yes, the whole of education reduced to no more than protecting her against the things one sees, the things one reads, the things one hears.

BERNAL: You are trying to isolate her?

ALVARO: Sometimes to isolate her, and sometimes not to isolate her. Just as the Spartans used to show their sons a drunken harlot, there are times when I show her my country, that she may know what she must not be.

BERNAL: She has, I think, been taught some slight accomplishments. . . .

ALVARO: She has a good familiarity with the Scriptures. I have taught her also a little history: she will know how empires die.

BERNAL: In short, Mariana is a wrong note in the life you've created for yourself. It seems to me that, as a little girl, she gave you more joy.

ALVARO: She also degraded me.

BERNAL: She degraded you!

ALVARO: Children degrade. We only saw each other at meals, and from each of those meals I came away a little diminished. As a young girl, her life became something that I had to take seriously and that at the same time didn't interest me.

BERNAL: Something that doesn't interest you, yet interests you enough perhaps for you to be annoyed that it is escaping you.

ALVARO: Annoyed? No. Tired. The effort I made, through charity toward her, to appear to take an interest in that life so foreign to my own used to exhaust me.

BERNAL: Charity again!

ALVARO: All the things that go on in that little head. . . . Later I stopped trying to penetrate them, and, besides, I was sure that very soon they would change and my study of them would have been superfluous.

BERNAL: Do you realize that Mariana complains, gently, that with her you never used to talk about serious things?

ALVARO: I don't talk to her about serious things because she is incapable of understanding them. Would you be able to pray if you knew for certain that God doesn't understand you?

BERNAL: A little more love would settle all that.

ALVARO: A little more love and I should be wanting to direct her, I should be getting upset whenever it seemed to me that she was on the wrong track or inferior to what I expect of her. On the contrary, as I love her within reason, I don't ask of her anything, I don't reproach her with anything, we never come up against each other. And besides, my friend, as you saw yesterday, I'm not one of those who love their country in spite of its unworthiness: I love Spain in proportion to its merits, exactly as I would a foreign country. In the same way, Mariana's being my daughter will never make me go too far in her favor. You must admit, if we were away from each other we should be at once happier and better.

BERNAL: What a picture you're painting for me! Why not

say, in one word, that you cannot put up with her youth?— God willing, very shortly she will have a house in which her singing will make grow in every soul a bunch of flowers. God willing—that is to say, if my dream comes true. For now I'm going to have to speak to you with brutal frankness. I shall do so, thinking of an expression I found in one of our ancient chronicles. A noble is speaking in the name of the order of nobility, and he says: "We who speak out . . ." Yes, we of the nobility, it's for us to speak out, simply because it is beneath us to bother to invent lies.

ALVARO: In the whole of this last year I have only lied four times.

BERNAL: My frankness, this time, has its risks. For I can see, after our yesterday's council, how easy it is to irritate you.

ALVARO: I am severe toward those who offend against my principles, even if they're my friends. And indulgent toward those who offend me simply as a man. If I held my worst enemy in my hands, I would let him go without doing him any harm.

BERNAL: From charity? Or from disdain?

ALVARO: From anything you like.

BERNAL: Once more, you are warned: I am going to displease you. Listen.—You are not ignorant of our conditions. The only legacy, practically, that I received from my parents was honor. For the rest— And I should tell you that my worry has been not so much not having money but knowing that I wasn't clever enough to make money. King Ferdinand did not much like me. Our house declined steadily until the accession of King Charles and the entry of Don Jacinto into the Council of the Indies—two things that have reopened for us the door of hope. Jacinto is doing very well in this post, but it involves an expense that is a constant drain, and the more he advances, the more it will devour. How is he to keep up what promises to be a brilliant career? The New World, where Jacinto is well placed for acquiring very shortly a position of some power? I'm prevented from going there by my health; it's out of the question. His whole fortune for the time being is bound up with his being here; at Valladolid he has men and affairs in his grasp; he must not on any account let go; it's from Valladolid that he draws his life, and he would be finished if he left. Conclusion: Jacinto must marry a girl who's rich. And that's why what we were asking of you yesterday for various reasons, I'm asking of you today as man to man, as friend to friend, as father to father. Go and spend two years, one year only, in the New World, and you will come back rich. In a post of the kind that I have in mind for you, gold will flow into your hands by the most honest means, and as if it were falling from heaven. Herrera, Contreras, Luzan, in similar posts, made their fortunes in eighteen months. There are considerable special perquisites—

ALVARO: I'm sorry. . . . Is it really me you are addressing at this moment?

BERNAL: I imagine it's the word "perquisites" that has shocked you. That's absurd! Herrera, Contreras are men of high moral value, against whom nobody—

ALVARO: To think that it's, above all, my friends who are determined I should defile myself.—Don't go on. I shall not go to the New World.

BERNAL: Not even for your daughter?

ALVARO: I see. All that I am in the eyes of God, all that I am in my own eyes, ought to be compromised, ought to be ruined for the sake of something that only exists because of one of my moments of weakness! Never!

BERNAL: Something that only exists because of— Is that how you describe your daughter? Ah, Alvaro, what a man you turn out to be!

ALVARO: If only I were the wretch you think I am; if only your humiliating remarks could strike home! But no, alas, I am the man everyone ought to be.

BERNAL: Olmeda was right when he spoke to me, yesterday evening, of your "cruelty."

ALVARO: Olmeda, who at sixty-two busies his thoughts with playing the administrator instead of busying them with how to make a good end, shows that he is frivolous.

BERNAL: You're sacrificing your child to yourself, to yourself and to nothing but yourself!

ALVARO: O race of the strict, how unhappy you are!

BERNAL: Unhappy when it finds that, always so ready to judge, it is being judged.

ALVARO: God is the only judge I recognize, and I adore the verdict He will pass on me.

BERNAL: You have retreated into charity. If you had to act—what I call really act—you would get muddy like the others.

ALVARO: Only a supernatural principle can permit me to look benevolently on my compatriots.

BERNAL: Including your daughter!

ALVARO: Last century still, a knight had to place his son, whether child or adolescent, in the house of another knight, so as not to be enchained by fatherly tenderness. I don't want that chain.

BERNAL: Wouldn't the Teutonic knight, in front of the castle drawbridge, accept everything to save his little daughter?

ALVARO: He accepted wounds. He would not have accepted a tarnishing.

BERNAL: Your idea of chivalry is leading you astray. You are one of those spirits, enchanted by their own dreams, who can become so dangerous to a society.

ALVARO: You, for the first time in your life, talk to me of money, and it's because of your son. I shall be brutal in my turn: you won't give him up except against his weight in gold. And I, I'm to perjure myself for the sake of my daughter. There you have what our children do to us! I always had a presentiment of that. But I never expected to receive so striking a proof.

BERNAL: You reproach me with talking money to you. But I hold that to make a parade of never talking money is a false elegance and a mark of a bourgeois. The men I know who come of the best stock are among those who are frankest about their interests.

ALVARO: Some cacique or other, when asked who was the god of the Spaniards, pointed with his finger at a nugget of gold. And when one has seen the King himself, by threats or violence, steal the wealth of our four Orders, one is no longer astonished that today the world belongs to the shameless.

BERNAL: As if, long before Granada, people did not love gold!

ALVARO: People loved gold because it yielded power, and because with the power they achieved great things. Nowadays people love power because it yields gold and because with this gold they achieve petty things.

BERNAL: You're simplifying the whole thing without rhyme or reason.

ALVARO: I was brought up to learn that you should voluntarily make a bad bargain. That you should not stoop to pick up a treasure even if it was from your hand that it had slipped. That you should never reach out your arm to take something. That that, and perhaps that alone, is the sign of nobility. I endure the pain of hearing that at the moment when the eagle of King Charles has no claws except to search for gold, even in human entrails, it's among the Indians that one now finds that high and holy indifference with regard to things.

BERNAL: It's wrong to let go one's assets too easily; that shows just as much self-love as if one disputed them sharply. Besides, the man who doesn't care for money is despised. It's like that.

ALVARO: As for me, during fifteen years God has done me this special grace, of making me poor. But this is nothing; I want to be poorer still. No, you shall not ravish from me my poverty! Even now I live in a perpetual distraction from the one thing necessary. And I would have to spend time—time that could be employed in the business of my soul—in the revolting cares of a fortune that has to be administered! I do not want to be despoiled of my soul. I do not want to be rich, do you hear? I do not want to be rich! I should be too ashamed.

BERNAL: All right! Die of hunger if you think fit. But Mariana?

ALVARO: If Mariana and your son are drawn together by this emotion of which you speak, let them marry as they are. They will be poor, but Christ will wash their feet.

BERNAL: They will be poor: the problem is easily solved!

ALVARO: You who reproach me for not loving Mariana as I should, you would have me give her riches, that sin!

BERNAL: Being rich in itself isn't a sin.

ALVARO: When I act or react as a Christian, I ought to be understood by tens of millions of men. But it's just then that I'm understood by nobody. Sometimes it seems to me that everything that happens inside me happens so far away from any human comprehension—

BERNAL: You cannot insist that all people should find their satisfaction in an absolute that is only made for some people.

ALVARO: I only tolerate perfection.

BERNAL: I was rich for about three years. Money that came to me from the sale of my lands at Juncas. You've no idea how good it is, having a lot of money; how it sets you at peace! How it makes you solid! The confidence in yourself it gives you! How, at last, one can be oneself! With one's back to a wall of hard cash, that's when one can freely be versatile, be insolent, be in the wrong, anything else! But it also makes possible patience, work well done, magnanimity, constance through moral trials, all the virtues of the soul.—Look, for instance, at that charity which you love so much: charity, to be diligent, needs to be well nourished. Ah, my dear friend, to be a millionaire—how that does add to a man's stature!

Alvaro: I, like you, when my father died, heard from the lawyer that I was suddenly the possessor of a sum that, though small to many other people, to me was quite important. What were my feelings then? My only feeling was sadness. I thought: "To think that there are people who work for ten years to gain what I have just gained in a minute!" At intervals for two years I received in that way several sums of money by no means negligible, and each time it caused me the same embarrassment—indeed, almost despair. Before the bag of coins I said to myself: "My God, what shall I do with it?" I gave them to the houses of the Order.

Bernal: And the idea never occurred to you of investing them to provide Mariana's dowry? No, that would merely have been a natural impulse. You had to have the supernatural, you had to have charity. Not to give to one's child, but to give to poor idiots who hate you for having given to them!

Alvaro: Charity only has meaning if it is rewarded by that hatred.

Bernal: Ah, you make charity nauseous to me.

Alvaro: And you make nauseous to me the impulses you call natural. Charity is accounted to me before God. But is it accounted to me before God if I lay up my treasure for my heirs, who after all have no more need to be rich than I have? If I had died fifty years ago, my possessions would have gone to the Order; at that time it was the rule. There is no family except by election and the spirit; the family by blood is accursed. We of the Order, we are a family.

Bernal: There is no Order any more, Alvaro, you know very well.

ALVARO: I know.—But no; if it existed in only a single heart, the Order would still exist. And here come daughters and sons stealing and intruding into our congregation. With great pains one was raising oneself up a little; they come along, they beat us down again, they hold us down bitterly to earth. Treason is always under our roof, and not only in the kitchen, as the saying is. [*Calling*] Mariana!

BERNAL: For heaven's sake, not a scene! What are you going to say to her?

ALVARO: Perhaps it is good that you should know how some fathers think it their duty to treat their children.

BERNAL: Ah, I am tired of hearing you give us lessons.

ALVARO: In the Moroccan stories there is a classic character: the father who considers having his daughter killed because he sees that she is in love.

BERNAL: Are you mad? . . .

SCENE II

ALVARO, BERNAL, MARIANA

ALVARO: They tell me you have developed some sort of feeling for Don Bernal's son. And you have done that in a room of my house, a few paces away from me! Understand that I've a horror of that sort of thing. Of course you believe, doubtless, that you are the only person in the world who's in love, that you contain the universe, and so on. . . . And yet what are you? You are a little monkey, nothing more. And all this love between men and women is monkey play. Understand that there you are caught in mid-antics, in mid-ridicule, and in mid-idiocy.

BERNAL: Alvaro! Aren't you ashamed! You did not always go against nature. . . . So don't outrage it like this, and in the very thing that ought to be sacred to you above anything else in the world.

ALVARO: Mariana, if I have shocked you, forgive me. But you are wounding me to the quick. I try to live a life a little raised up. And it's you who ruin me! You who ought to be supporting me, it's you who are my stumbling-block!

MARIANA: Father, I only want what you want. How could I ruin you?

ALVARO: If you had but once imagined what the face of God is like, you would turn away your head in the street so as not to see the face of a man. [*To Bernal*] Stay with her and console her, you who like to play the father (but is being the father of a daughter really being a father?). As for me, I tell you once more: I shall not go to the New World—never! My pleasure is that it should be so. And it is also God's pleasure. That is enough.

BERNAL: One day you said to me—didn't you?—"When you hesitate between several paths, always take the most painful."

ALVARO: What would become of me, oh God, if I did not suffer?

BERNAL: Yes, only you always choose, in the last resort, the path that is your pleasure.

SCENE III

BERNAL, MARIANA

BERNAL: Stop tormenting yourself, Mariana, and listen. At this moment there is in Avila, for a few days, a powerful personage, the Count of Soria. You know him well by name, don't you? [*Mariana shakes her head.*] Oh, how like your father, not even knowing what is going on! The Count of

Soria, in spite of his youth, is one of the men best placed at court. I have some influence with him. At my request he will pay your father a visit and will tell him that the King has expressed, in public, the desire that Don Alvaro should accept a post in the Indies. I know your father: he talks about the King with a mixture of respect and ill will, but the King is his lord, for nothing in the world would he fail him. Your father claims that at his age one no longer has any personal plans; but at his age there is one thing one can still do: be faithful. Loyalty will raise its voice in him, and also perhaps (why not?) a little self-esteem. Are you pleased? What! You don't say anything?

MARIANA: Blood is silent when it flows.

BERNAL: Tears too, are they not? Come, dry those tears.

MARIANA: Where can you see tears?

BERNAL: There.

MARIANA: Someone else is weeping in me.

BERNAL: You are a little girl. . . . Ah, why wasn't I your father!

MARIANA: But you are not.

BERNAL: You wouldn't like it if I were your father?

MARIANA: God has done well what He has done.

BERNAL: You don't like me!

MARIANA: How should I not like you? You love Jac—[*She stops short.*]

BERNAL: I shall never forgive Don Alvaro for injuring virtue by his excesses.

MARIANA: My father is a man of exceptional uprightness. That is his only luxury, but it is a luxury for which one pays a high price.

BERNAL: Your father is a saint, or not far short of it. All the same, I begin to understand that the saints must have been a bit exasperating for those who lived with them.

MARIANA: He doesn't exasperate me.

BERNAL: You're standing up for him on principle.

MARIANA: It's a very strong thing, admiring someone.

BERNAL: The gentlemen of the Order think as I do.

MARIANA: The spectacle of uprightness only disconcerts people; it doesn't compel them. A little more, and this embarrassment becomes a sort of horror.

BERNAL: You are quite a philosopher for your eighteen years.

MARIANA: I am only serious.

BERNAL: Perhaps there is in Don Alvaro a certain leaning to contradiction. If the society round about us were austere, perhaps he would affect to be a free-thinker.

MARIANA: For how many years have you known him, and you believe that! What is friendship if it can be so mistaken? And how right I have been not to have friends. There is no affectation in my father. He goes straight ahead. His own salvation, and the Order—that is his path: to right and to left, nothing. His crushing indifference for everything that does not carry some mark of the sublime— *Unum, Domine,* "O my God, one thing only is needful": my great-grandfather knew what he was doing when he changed into this motto the more ancient motto of our family.

BERNAL: And so you, his daughter, are "to the right or left." He keeps you aside from his life.

MARIANA: The really abnormal thing would be for a man of his age, and with his preoccupations, to find much pleasure in the society of a mere young girl like me.

BERNAL: Yes, always the "inward eye"—that inward eye with which he gazes less at God than at himself.

MARIANA: If anything is being done against him, he helps. And you pretend he's an egoist!

BERNAL: He acts against himself because that gives him pleasure.

MARIANA: If I did not know you, I should take you for a wicked man, disparaging him like that.

BERNAL: I am not a wicked man. I am a man who wants to see you happy.

MARIANA: I do not seek to be happy.

BERNAL: You don't want to marry Jacinto?

MARIANA: I don't want it for the sake of being happy.

BERNAL: For what, then?

MARIANA: And he—do you think he will be happy with me?

BERNAL: I am certain of it.

MARIANA: Do you think I shall be able to be useful to him in important and serious things? I should not want an easy life. I should want a life in which one would have need of courage.

BERNAL: One has always need of courage.

MARIANA: But do you think he's good at discerning the things that are important and those that aren't? For that's the essential: to give oneself only to the one, and to hold onto it hard.

BERNAL: You will teach him that, if I haven't managed to do so.

MARIANA: I want to enter marriage, and to close the door after me as one does after entering an oratory, and not to look behind me, ever. He will be the only man for me, and I shall be the only woman for him. Lost in him alone for always.

BERNAL: There will, though, be the little children as well. . . .

MARIANA: I think even they will distract me from my husband.

BERNAL: You're not afraid of wealth?

MARIANA: I shall welcome it as a trial and I shall try to overcome it.

BERNAL: Dear Mariana, you are your father, only more sensible. And sometimes in your very words. Your phrase: "Children will distract me from my husband," reminds me of something Don Alvaro was saying to me just now: that he needed a solitude so complete that friendship itself would only come in to trouble it. Yes, how like him you are! . . .

Mariana: I despise myself too much to believe that what I am is like my father.

Bernal: You despise yourself, and yet you are proud as an asp. "As an asp." The expression is Jacinto's.

Mariana: Don Jacinto is very presumptuous to describe me, when he does not know me.

Bernal: And you are very formal to call him *Don* Jacinto in front of me.

Mariana: I am not going to call by his Christian name a man who is nothing to me.

Bernal: Come, Mariana, stop this comedy of coldness. Do I have to reveal to you that two weeks ago he was writing to me: "In my house her sweetness will be like the dripping of water"? That three days ago he was writing to me: "My love for her woke me up the other night. I could hear that starry, far-off voice—"

Mariana: That starry, far-off voice. . . . Is that my voice?

Bernal: It is your voice. Do I have to reveal to you that two weeks ago he was writing to me: "I cannot breathe because of her"? That three days ago he was writing to me: "The parting in her hair is like the path you trace in the snow as you go toward her house"?

Mariana: Truly, did he say to you all that? But no, you are making it up to give me pleasure!

Bernal: God is my witness, I'm not making up a single word.

Mariana: Then, tell this gentleman from the court—the one who is coming to see us—that he will be wasting his time if, to persuade my father, he dwells on the argument of glory; and that my father will show him the door if he speaks of profit. Tell him he must represent to my father that the King wishes to send to the Indies Spaniards of the best type, for the moral authority of Spain. Tell him he must speak of the Order, how the Indians must be shown what is meant by a true knight of Santiago. Tell him—well, tell him that the King commands. . . . Tell him all that, Don Bernal, will you not? And then it is essential he should not lavish upon my father the worn-out compliments he is always hearing; suggest to him something rather special—you will think of something. . . . As for me, while this gentleman is here, I shall pray on my knees before the crucifix that my father may let himself be persuaded.

BERNAL: You are going to pray to our Saviour. But suppose you also prayed your father? After all, have you no right to a say in all this?

MARIANA: I, pray my father? Oh, never that!

BERNAL: If this marriage depended on a word said by you to your father, you would not say that word?

MARIANA: No, never!

BERNAL: Always the "never" of the Dabo family. Ah, how tiring are the extremes!

MARIANA: Forgive us: we have our heart in one piece. [*Through the window a pale ray of sunshine—pearl-gray, the pearl-gray of Avila—filters into the room.*] Oh God, a ray of sunshine! The first for two months!

BERNAL: Oh, Mariana! And I see that, for the sake of that ray of sunshine, the waters of the heart come up once more into your eyes.

MARIANA: It's the smoke from the brazier.

BERNAL: No, my little pearl, you can't deceive me.

MARIANA: The first ray of winter sunshine. . . . So the sun did still exist? Soon the snow will melt, soon it will be spring.

BERNAL: Alas, we are only at the beginning of January.

MARIANA: Spring is approaching! Tomorrow it will be spring!

BERNAL: And it was you who were saying you did not want to be happy!

MARIANA: No, Don Bernal, I do not want to be happy.

ACT III

Same scene. Outside, the snow is falling continuously.

SCENE I

ALVARO, MARIANA

MARIANA [*reading*]:

"When Diego Monzon found himself once more in his prison cell, after his escape had failed,

"Captive again, and wounded, he sank into despair, a despair with no light and with no bottom.

"But suddenly he understood that it was God who was sending him this trial, as a mark of His favor.

"Then he kissed the chains that bound his hands, and he fell asleep, at peace."

ALVARO: That's enough of our old romances for today; if you were to go on, I should be afraid of softening. I know why the war against the infidels was called a holy war: because the Spaniards who were fighting it were saints. Then there was a pure army; the tears come into my eyes when I think of it. But all is disorder in the army of today. Today if I meet a soldier, I feel like shrugging my shoulders. And in all the thirty years it's been going on, there has not been a single romance written on the war of the New World. [*Mariana picks up with a shovel the unconsumed embers strewn over the flags.*] Those embers worry you?

MARIANA: Do you consider it is nice to have embers strewn all over the room when you are going to receive a distinguished visitor?

ALVARO: Let it alone, please. What would Tia Campanita

and Isidro think? That I put myself out for the Count of Soria, one of the popinjays of Charles of Ghent? That that sort of puppets impress me? Come, I know the way people rise in the world: by trampling at every step on something sacred.

MARIANA: There must, though, be at court at least one unblemished man.

ALVARO: No, not one. And the Count of Soria would not exist for me if I did not suppose that he is bringing me some news concerning the Order. Three months ago we requested the King to try to obtain from the Pope one of the privileges that the Templars used to have: that the cemeteries of our Order might receive the bodies of excommunicated people. It is a desire that I have dearly at heart—ah, passionately, if you but knew . . . I cannot imagine why anyone of the court should come to visit me if not to bring me the answer to this request. And, would you believe it, Mariana, I've a presentiment that this answer is favorable.—You will put the book of romance in my room. And you will renew my stock of candles. Yesterday evening I was reading the *Parsifal* of Wolfram von Eschenbach; it is the Song of Songs of chivalry, and I was forced to break off reading it, for lack of candles. Also you will buy some soap, I haven't any more. And you will mend, please, one of the sheets on my bed; it is torn.

MARIANA: If I mend it again, it will go in another place. It is thoroughly worn out.

ALVARO: It is worn out in the places where there are holes. But in other places it is still very good.

MARIANA: Wouldn't you like me to buy you another pair?

ALVARO: That would be a quite useless expense; why not say that mending bores you? [*With impatience*] And anyhow, do as you please, I ask only one thing: that people should not come worrying me with questions of sheets. [*As he goes out, he stops in front of Mariana and lightly dusts her collar.*] You have some hairs on the collar of your jacket. Decidedly, I believe you are growing careless.

SCENE II

MARIANA

MARIANA: O my well-being! Oh, dear one above all men! You for whom I have kept a little of my childhood, and prepared something in the bottom of my heart from the moment I was born, open to me your arms, take me in my pain, and let this pain be the last to have its birth from me alone: let me soon have no more pains but yours. . . . But what is this? A stranger is my refuge, who has never seen me with my hair down, who does not even know my room! And it's against my father that I'm seeking refuge. . . . Against my father! He created me, I love him, and it's he from whom I'm fleeing! [*A knocking at the entrance of the house from the street. Sound of voices outside the room.*] The Count! Oh God! Since it's an unknown person who must find the arguments and the way of speaking on which my life depends, inspire in him those arguments and that way of speaking! It must be so, I wish it so, fall upon the things my father gazes upon and illumine them with a light in which he has never seen them! That is how your divine grace works, so the books clearly say: an imperceptible nothing, and everything has changed place. . . .

SCENE III

ALVARO, THE COUNT OF SORIA

ALVARO: You bring, sir, a breath of something quite new into a house whose life is infinitely remote.

SORIA: I've brought, above all, snow on my boots. By God, what a winter! I had to travel as far as Torral. The country's nothing but a desert of snow; it very nearly foundered our horses. The snow is breaking the boughs of the trees under its weight, and you can see the corpses of wolves caught in the ice of the streams, like big roots wrenched out of the ground. . . .

ALVARO: Avila itself, all covered with snow, is more than ever the city of withdrawal. It's the best cradle for the great things. The thunderbolt can only destroy. But germination goes on in a profound silence, hidden, unsuspected by all.

SORIA: Surely. It may even happen that withdrawal, too, is action, as it is with you. I know that you work for the hospices of Santiago. You have exchanged the sword for the cloth of St. Veronica.

ALVARO: You are still very young, sir, to be able to feel these things: there comes an age when it seems to you that men only exist to be the object of charity. If there were no such thing as charity, I would gladly forget them, just as I desire to be forgotten by them.

SORIA: But *they* don't forget you.

ALVARO: It is an honor to be forgotten in a period such as ours: perfect contempt likes to inspire contempt in what it has contempt for, in order to feel itself justified. May my name be like those huge clouds which in a few hours are obliterated.

SORIA: Unfortunately, it is not at all like that. The remembrance of your lofty deeds is still alive.

ALVARO: I am astonished it should be alive for others when it is dead for me.

SORIA: The rumor made by your silence—

ALVARO [*dryly*]: Oh, that—

SORIA: So you have not a single ambition? Not a single wish?

ALVARO: What is there to wish for when all is dishonored?

SORIA [*sneering*]: All is dishonored! . . . Is it possible!—It must be depressing, not to wish for anything. . . . However that may be, even if you have no ambitions, others have ambitions for you. It is time, I think, for you to hear why I have come to see you. You are not unaware of the expedition that is being prepared by Alesio Fuenleal—

ALVARO: Ah, sir, I must ask you to stop. Certainly, that is not what I was expecting. . . . You are causing me an extreme disappointment. . . . If you have any design for involving me in that business, let us break off our conversation straightway. I have already been persecuted on that subject at great length and with tenacity. You would spend yourself on it to no purpose.

SORIA: Listen to me a moment. His Majesty, in his great wisdom, has understood that the preaching of the gospel to the Indians, if done for the most part by adventurers, was doomed to failure. He desires that there should be chosen, in future, for sending to the Indies, men of weight and integrity, whose personal quality may constitute a guarantee to the Indians and an example to the Spaniards. I can tell you one thing: many remarkable men will soon be found in the Indies at one and the same time.

ALVARO: They will allow themselves to be corrupted by the fatal environment out there. We have already had plenty of examples of that. No, sir, I am unshakable.

SORIA: You can refuse me. But can you refuse the King?

ALVARO: The King?

SORIA: His Majesty has pronounced several names. Among them he pronounced yours.

ALVARO: Someone whispered it in his ear.

SORIA: No one whispered it in his ear. I was present.

ALVARO: What? Does the King know me as anything but an old madman who torments him with petitions and memoranda about Santiago?

SORIA: The flattering words with which he accompanied your name show the esteem in which he holds you.

ALVARO [*aside*]: Approbation among men, what would you of me?

SORIA: And now, sir, I have no need to instruct you in what is meant by a King's wish.

ALVARO: Everything that I am is opposed to such a decision.

SORIA: One can be unfaithful to oneself when it's for the sake of being faithful to the King.

ALVARO: I have not the qualifications that are needed for success in the New World.

SORIA: All that will be asked of you is your presence and the good effect that flows from that.

ALVARO: You say, sir, that His Majesty pronounced several words about me. Do you remember what they were exactly?

SORIA: Hm—exactly. . . . Ah, yes, he said "that noble hearts are quick to undertake desperate enterprises, and that it was really because of that, perhaps—"

ALVARO: Because of that—what? Because of that that I should go to the Indies?

SORIA: Who knows?

ALVARO: Here's a really profound saying—a staggering one—in so young a man. . . . That the King should realize that the Indies are a tragedy without issue . . . and that he should have thought of me because of that. . . . This, truly, touches me to the quick.

SORIA: Well then, sir, your answer?

ALVARO: I ask for time to reflect.

Soria: Does one need time for reflection when the King has spoken? And tomorrow I must leave again for Valladolid.

Alvaro: Ah! you are leaving tomorrow. . . .

SCENE IV

Alvaro, Soria, Mariana

Mariana [*bursting in*]: Father, it is high time I should undeceive you. All this is a terrible comedy. Don Bernal suggested to the Count that he should tell you the King had spoken about you. The King has done no such thing.

Soria: What, young lady, were you not in agreement with Don Bernal? Wasn't it you who told him—

Mariana: I was prostrate. I spoke then in the way one walks in the fog. My voice was so weak that he must have misunderstood me.—No, it's no good. I confess. I too took part in setting this trap.

Soria: Sir, this is a strange turn that the action they've inveigled me into has now taken. Yes, it is at Don Bernal's request that I lent myself to this piece of play-acting. But even if in fact the King did not utter your name, I flatter myself that I have some influence at court, and I shall make it a point of honor, if you at any time desire—

Alvaro: Are you anxious to insult me, after having made game of me?

Soria: I can see that doing someone a service is more dangerous than to expose oneself in battle!

Alvaro: I have nothing to ask from you and nothing to offer you: These are bad conditions in which to be concerned with each other. I think, Count of Soria, our interview is at an end.

Soria: Not without a last word from me. You reproached

me with being rather young. I will tell you this: that the young have abrupt manners, but often modesty in their hearts, while the old, along with every show of saintliness, are hard and proud.

ALVARO: It may equally well be detachment, which, holding its head high, seems to be pride, while vile covetousness goes bent earthwards. Leave us, sir: your world is not ours. Moved as I am, you must even allow me not to show you the way.

SCENE V

ALVARO, MARIANA

ALVARO: Why? Why?

MARIANA: I was in my room, at the foot of the crucifix, trying to pray that that man might persuade you. And suddenly it was you I saw, in the place of the Crucified One, your head leaning upon your shoulder as I had seen you, one evening, asleep in your chair, beside the burnt-out vine shoots in your brazier. And I felt that you were being scourged, as they scourged the Crucified One, and that it was essential that I should go at once to your aid. Broken be my life, and all I have hoped for, rather than that I should see you mocked under my own eyes, and mocked through my fault, making straight for a decoy that I helped to place for you.

ALVARO [*falling on one knee in front of his daughter, and taking her by the hands and leaning his forehead upon them*]: Forgive me, Mariana, forgive me! I have sinned against you many times in my life. At this moment, how clearly I see it all! It's today you are born; it's today I have found out that you are worthy of being loved. But you—so you loved me? You loved me—how strange! Why did you love me?

MARIANA: Is it you asking me to forgive you, me who took part in a plot to trick you? Rise, I beseech you. I feel I am going mad when I see you on your knees before me.

ALVARO: You were all the time keeping your course beside mine in the darkness; I did not even hear the sound of its flowing. And then, all of a sudden, our waters mingled, and we are rolling onward to the same sea. Mariana! Tell me it's not too late!

MARIANA: My father by blood and through the Holy Spirit—

ALVARO: You have clutched me back on the brink of the abyss. When the better part of me was giving way, you, you were my better part. I gave you your life: you have restored me mine.

MARIANA: I could not have borne seeing you cease to be what you are. You reproached me the other day with ruining you. I have wanted to save you.

ALVARO: Alas, the King—those words—I have to admit that for a moment my heart was half open. God be praised, that He has allowed me to catch myself in a wretched and ridiculous posture, and to show myself before the one person in the world who least ought to see me like that: it's you, it's you who saw me straying! But that profound fall is throwing me back toward the heights. From now on I can reach my aim: that aim is not to partake any longer in the things of the earth. Let us enter again into reality. Oh, how I have always aspired to that! How I did drag at my anchors in my desire to scud out into the vast open sea! The time it will take to put my affairs in order, and then I'll shut myself up, never to return, in the Convent of St. Barnabas. You, my child, you'll go and live with your aunt. Unless— Unless— Why not? Let me draw you with me into that God who is drawing me. Leap toward the sun by sinking into my tomb. Before this I could bear to let you go a little your own way. Now how could I want for you anything but the truth? Come nearer to me still: become me! At St. Barnabas's there is a Carmel for women. . . . You will see what it is, to be nothing.

MARIANA: To have some being, however little, in order to be able for the sake of those one loves—

ALVARO: We shall have no being, and we shall be able to do more than anything that has being.

MARIANA: Oh my God, when I was in the arms of human affection!

ALVARO: Now you will sleep in Jesus Christ; fast asleep, enshrouded in the deep abyss of the Divinity.

MARIANA: "Father, unto thee I commend my spirit."

ALVARO: Should I believe you? Can one believe in one's joy?

MARIANA: An imperceptible nothing, and everything has changed places.

ALVARO: What has once moved will perhaps move again.

MARIANA: In a flash, fixed forever.

ALVARO: Tonight, at three o'clock, in all the convents of Spain, thousands of men and women will rise and pray. At that moment you will rise and will come and see me. And you will tell me if you have made a second renunciation.

MARIANA: Yes, Father.

ALVARO: For you are sacrificing yourself, are you not? Generosity is always the sacrifice of oneself; that is the essence of it. You are sacrificing yourself, Mariana?

MARIANA: Yes, Father.

ALVARO: And yet, no tears? Strive, suffer still more. Where there is no battle, there is no redemption.

MARIANA: If I must, I will cry later. Afterwards I will kiss my chains, like Diego Monzon, and I will fall asleep, at peace.

ALVARO: That young man, Don Bernal's son—?

MARIANA: Thanks to him, I know the full measure of sacrifice. How should I not therefore love him forever?

ALVARO: That you should have loved any such thing will one day seem to you incomprehensible. Think, you will never have known the contamination of a man's love. No blood will come to mix with our blood. There will be no man to turn you over and over in his arms. And no children, nobody to defile me, nobody to betray me: with you I go out, in all my cleanness. The last! We shall be the last! What strength in that word "last," opening on the sublime nothingness!

MARIANA: I could wish—

ALVARO: God neither wishes nor seeks anything: He is eternal calm. It is in wishing nothing that you will come to mirror God. [*He takes down from the wall the great mantle of the Order and, with his hand on Mariana's shoulder, wraps his daughter with him in the mantle, which covers them to their feet.*] The flakes of snow are coming down like the tongues of fire upon the Apostles. Do you know?—it's at Pentecost, above all, that they used to arm the knights. By my hand upon your shoulder, I confer upon you Knighthood. And now let us set out for a country where there is no more shame, let us set out on eagle's wings, my little knight! What a journey we have to accomplish—a journey beside which the journey to the Indies appears so sordid and grotesque!

MARIANA: Let us set out to die, with all our sentiment and love. Let us set out to die.

ALVARO: Let us set out to live. Let us set out to be dead, and the living among the living.

[*The darkness thickens. On the stage no more can be seen than the light patch made by the mantle that covers the two of them, kneeling below the crucifix, he with his hands joined, she with her arms crossed on her breast. Beyond the window the flakes of snow are falling more and more thickly.*]

ALVARO: Eternity! O Eternity!

MARIANA: Infinity! O Infinity!

ALVARO: Religion! Religion!

MARIANA: What silence! The silence of the snow. I have

never heard such a silence in Avila. You would think there was no one left but us two on the earth.

ALVARO: Avila? What is that? A city? And the earth? Can you still see the earth? I can see it all buried under the snow, like us under the white mantle of the Order. . . .

MARIANA: Snow—snow—Castile is sinking under the snow like a ship among the waters. She's going to vanish. She's vanishing. Of Aragon, nothing more is showing but the high peak of the Sierra de Utiel. The snow is engulfing all Spain. There is no more Spain.

ALVARO: I've known that for a long time: there is no more Spain. Very well! Perish Spain, perish the world. If I reach my salvation and you reach yours, all is saved and all is accomplished.

MARIANA: All is saved and all is accomplished, for I am aware of a steadfast-gazing Being, who gazes upon me with an unendurable gaze.

ALVARO: Blood of my blood, you were better than I: in an instant, you have overtaken and passed me—you are seeing, before me, the thing I have so much dreamed of.

MARIANA: O rose of gold! Face of a lion! Face of honey! At your feet! At your feet! My forehead on the earth before Him whom I feel!

ALVARO: No, rise up higher! Rise up more swiftly! Drink and let me drink of you! Rise yet more!

MARIANA: I am drinking and being drunk of, and I know that all is well.

ALVARO: All is well! All is well!

MARIANA: I know that one thing only is needful: it is what you were saying—

MARIANA *and* ALVARO [*together*]: *Unum, Domine!*

Paris, March-June, 1945

NOTES ON

THE MASTER OF SANTIAGO

Note I

There is in my work a Christian vein and a "profane" (or worse than profane) vein, and I nourish them alternately—I was going to say simultaneously. This is quite right, since everything in this world deserves both attack and defense, and since we are bound, concerning whatever truth we live in, to say to ourselves what every married man has said to himself at least once about his wife: "Why that one?" To the first vein belong *La Relève du matin*, *La Rose de sable*, *Service inutile*, Costals's letters to Thérèse in *Les Jeunes Filles*, *Fils des autres*, *Port-Royal*, *Le Maître de Santiago*. To the second belong *Les Olympiques*, *Aux fontaines du désir*, *La Petite Infante*, the four books that compose *Les Jeunes Filles*. In *Le Solstice de juin* I have intermingled the two veins at the heart of one and the same book.

The Master of Santiago is the third of three *autos sacramentales*, the others being *Don Fadrique*, four-act play begun and abandoned in 1929, and *Port-Royal*,* four-act play written and fin-

* Early in the seventeenth century the convent of Port-Royal, not far outside Paris, became, under the reforming abbess Angélique Arnauld, the center of the Jansenist movement in France. This movement aimed at reforming the Catholic Church from within, in ways that would take the wind out of the sails of Protestantism. It held that men are saved not by correct theology and diligent churchgoing, but by the love of God and holy living; that this love of God cannot come to a man from himself, but only from God, being either born in him or implanted through conversion; but—and here it marked itself off from Calvinism—"justification by faith" is a snare, for conversion is only the beginning of a long process of salvation, and the personal relation of the soul to its Maker is only possible within the Roman Catholic Church. The first great French exponent of this doctrine was Abbess Angélique's brother, Antoine Arnauld, and it was to defend him against the Jesuits that

ished from 1940 to 1942. (*Fils des autres* is a miniature *auto*, only a few pages long.) I intend to write a fourth play on a Catholic theme, whose action will take place in contemporary France.

The seed from which *The Master of Santiago* entirely sprang is a little phrase I read in 1933 in some historian or other. It ran, more or less: "Some years after the discovery of America, there were many aging Spaniards who judged that this discovery was a misfortune for Spain." This phrase joined onto the thought that had come to me ten years earlier, when I visited Barcelona for the first time and was standing in front of the statue of Columbus: "Here is a statue the Spaniards would do well to knock down on one of their days of revolution."

From that moment I conceived the part of this old Spaniard in its entirety, with the whole of his character and even with some of his lines. After that I waited twelve years before there came to me the plot in which I would lodge him.

From the first I "saw" him as a knight of the Order of Santiago, the emblem of which is a sword with a hilt in the shape of a fleur-de-lis, because of my family's motto, which is: "Only for the fleurs-de-lis." (Let us smile.)

In the plot that I have created all is fiction. There is nothing borrowed. But the part of Don Alvaro has a strong historical truth to life. The Castile of the eighteenth century coined this type of noblemen with rather narrow heads, who, having passed their fiftieth birthday, withdrew from the world: complete with their decisive faith, their contempt for external reality,

---

Pascal wrote his *Lettres provinciales*—with little success, for after a long struggle Jansenism was condemned by Rome and driven underground. At one moment, because of a plague, the nuns of Port-Royal moved to Paris, and their place was taken by "solitaries" or hermits. When the nuns returned, some of these solitaries remained in the neighborhood of the convent and in close touch with its doctrines. They set up a school, one of whose pupils was Racine.

There is a short history of the convent and of the movement by Racine, and a monumental one by Sainte-Beuve. Montherlant's play on this subject is still, by the author's own wish, unpublished and unacted. (Translator's note.)

their taste for ruin, their furious desire for annihilation. The uncle of St. Teresa, who had a certain amount to do with her conversion, was of that kindred.

I have not made of Alvaro a model Christian; indeed, he is at moments a counterfeit, almost a Pharisee. He feels strongly the first impulse of Christianity: renunciation, the *Nada*; he has little feeling for the second: union, the *Todo*. Spain at that period is impregnated with Islam; Alvaro's religion consists almost wholly, like that of the Moors (or that of the Old Testament) in venerating the infinite distance of God: Allah is great. But what of the Incarnation? What of tender intimacy with a crucified Saviour? What of "Emmanuel" ("God with us")? In the final scene of the ecstasy the words that come to his lips are words of struggle, of renunciation, of the *Nada*; the only word of union he pronounces is pronounced only in connection with his daughter.* Besides, his egoism is so strong as to make him say: "If I achieve my salvation and you achieve yours, all is saved and all is accomplished"; whereas the true Christian will sacrifice, if necessary, his salvation for the glory of God, and will say with St. Francis de Sales: "If I cannot love Thee in the other life, let me at least love Thee in this one."—And again, he is rather odious in Act III when Mariana, under his spell, takes the risk of a sacrifice that will be without compensation if it should turn out that she is deceiving herself about the steadfastness of her conversion.†

Just as after *Queen after Death* I was glad to write *No Man's*

* And at the same time I thought it essential that in this scene they should speak more or less the same language: Alvaro through the slow and natural flowering of his personality, Mariana from the sudden unexpected stab of Grace—he in the satisfaction of his nature, she in the sacrifice of hers—arrive and meet at the same point.

† The sacrifice of Abraham is decidedly an obsession in my work for the stage! Alvaro accepts the risk of sacrificing Mariana in the name of transcendence. Ferrante sacrifices Pedro for the good of the State. Georges sacrifices Gillou to his own idea of what a man should be (*No Man's Son*). And at the end of *L'Exil* Geneviève consents to sacrifice her son, if that will first give her back that son's love.

Son, I have found it agreeable, having recently written that ample and thickly wooded play *Port-Royal*, to make of *The Master of Santiago* a short play with a simple and pure line, both of them being abrupt plays. Agreeable, too, to take up again, in a work that is obviously a minor one in proportion to *Port-Royal*, the same subject with situations reversed, since both are concerned with the dealings between man and divine Grace. For example, after having put on the stage the "*journée du Guichet*"—that is to say, a father in agony because his daughter takes the veil—it was interesting to depict a father leading his daughter to take the veil; or again, after having shown the reforming zeal that existed under Abbess Angélique, to show the reserve of the "Knights of Clay," etc.

Are there communicating channels between Jansenism and sixteenth-century Castilian Catholicism? It is for Catholic pundits to find the answer. Doubtless it should be childish to spend time over the Basque origin of Saint-Cyran (emphasized by Unamuno), over the "Spanish-style religion" (Sainte-Beuve *dixit*) of Sister Agnes, that other "*petite Infante*," over the fact that d'Andilly translated St. Theresa and John of Avila, over Nicole dreaming of a congregation that would bear the typically Castilian name "the Order of the Annihilated." . . . But, though spangled with attractive moments, both those communions will always appear to the eyes of the world with the same aspect, both radiant and somber, and will seem like the two black diamonds of the crown of Jesus (only, one of them has over the other the advantage of having been trampled on). And I myself, as I wrote *Santiago*, had not altogether departed from the valley of *Port-Royal*,* so much so that I gave the

* When Alvaro, at the end of the knights' council, realizes that he is isolated not only among his countrymen in general but even among the men of his particular caste—too far ahead of them all—his exaltation is followed by a physical collapse. It was long after I had written this passage that I compared it with the collapse of Pascal when he discovered that Port-Royal could compromise with the truth.

gentlemen of Avila some externals that are not altogether foreign to ourselves: in particular, certain of their tears are French.

Note II: The Romance of Diego Monzon

THE ROMANCE OF Diego Monzon, which Mariana is reading at the beginning of the third act, would be looked for in vain in the *romancero:* it is an invention. Connoisseurs, too, will have detected in it a taste of a sensibility that is less Spanish than French. And, in fact, the deed it describes was taken by me from the recent war: the kissing of the shackles after the failure of an attempt to escape (and with the very sense that "Diego Monzon" gives to it) was reported to me about a young Frenchman who was a civilian prisoner of the Germans. The quality of this act is exactly what one finds in our *chansons de geste.* And it causes in me, only more strongly, the same emotion I assigned to the hero of *Les Jeunes Filles* when, as a child, he came to that passage in a novel of the Comtesse de Ségur where the authoress shows the Maréchal de Ségur (in the eighteenth century), in order to protect himself from a specter that he thinks he sees enter his room, kissing the cross of the Holy Spirit that is hanging on his breast.

Note III: Charity

THERE EXISTS a rule that we can only yield our charity at a certain distance away from us, not quite close, just as the projectile from a firearm can only hit its mark at a certain distance: a father takes part in the Conférence Saint Vincent de Paul, but is indifferent and hard toward his children; a benevolent institution is charitable toward those in whom its business is to take an interest, but exploits disgustingly its own staff; etc. I wanted Don Alvaro not to be an exception to this rule.

While I was making him speak of charity, I came to scribble the following notes in the margin of his lines. They arise from his character. For Alvaro's charity is, I think, artificial. I have already said that Alvaro seems to me as if he were outside the Gospels. Charity, too, has its birds of prey.

Passion is always a kill, its victim the thousand objects outside it. If I could write (in *Mors et Vita*) that indifference had been one of the passions of my life, that is doubtless because I named in the same line another passion, by which that salutary indifference had been created in me. As the tree lets fall its numerous dry barks and reduces itself to one single mass, young and strong, so passion transports a man's being, out of a multiple world where he was dispersing himself, into the oneness of what belongs to that passion, and in this he regains youth and strength.

One of the other good effects of passion is that the states of soul it provokes are denuded of vanity, which is one of the most ridiculous sentiments in this world.

How fine it would be if the soul could be, without passion, what it is in passion! For then it is denuded of vanity, impetuous, hard, ready for all sacrifices and for all generous acts; ingenious too, imaginative; above all, energetic, madly energetic. A man can use, to serve his passion, such an energy, can so utterly drain his resources in its service, that he is left exhausted for all else. The world thinks him apathetic and spineless, and really he is a monster of will-power—only in a domain that the world does not know.

This setting free, by passion, of sleeping forces, this magnetization, by passion, rendering the impossible possible, makes me think of the story of those two old maids who, believing they hear burglars, find all of a sudden the strength—in their terror—to move and make fast against the door an enormous wardrobe, which later it takes four lusty men to put back in place; or of the story of the wrestler who for a quarter of an hour cannot manage to get the upper hand of his opponent, but finds all of a sudden—in his indignation—the strength to lay him out, because the other has just tried a foul on him.

Charity has many of the characteristics of a passion, for in any sentiment of the religious kind, aiming at an absolute, there is some passion. It has all the fire of passion, all its impetuosity, austerity, exclusiveness, tyranny, but a part remains that is contemplative, pure, and disinterested. There are some illnesses that partake of a different illness, though still having the specific elements proper to them. The symptom of charity consists in being a passion, yet capable of suddenly losing sight of its aim. It stops in midcourse, it becomes motionless. It is still identical with itself; it has only turned its face in another direction.

That is the moment when it seems to have turned itself toward heaven and received from there a diamond flash. That is the moment when it reflects that diamond flash. The purity of charity detached from its aim, when it has become ignorant of what it is doing, touching, and wishing, when it is no longer anything but essence. And its fixity. Fixed and fixing you. There is an English expression, "transfixed": fixed and pierced through. That motionless charity transfixes you with its unendurable ray. When one has once been struck by it, one can never again forget it.

It is the memory of that flash that forces you to start all over again on the humdrum run of charitable action, on a task apparently vulgar, wearing and tearing body and soul. It is the moment of motionlessness that throws you back into the "Left, right, left . . . !" The passion is on the march again and will never let you go. It is marching in the hope of finding once more, one day, that instant of its own motionlessness and of its own purity.

Note IV: The Coffin of Philip II

WHAT I AM about to write, the note on which people will shut this book, has no direct relation with anything in *Santiago*. But it closes it well—anyhow, closes it and rounds it off completely. A beam of that very hard wood which is called angelin, or cabbage tree, in the Indies, a beam with which the conquistadors had sheathed the prow of one of their ships, had been washed up on one of the quays of Lisbon, and there it was being used as a bench for the poor. King Philip II, having seen it and discovered its story, had been touched by it and had had it sent to the Escorial, where it was once more used as a bench for the poor. Then Philip II, at the approach of his death, commanded that his coffin be hewn from this beam. The same beam that had been cleaving unknown seas to carry beyond them the Revelation, the conquerors' wood that had later become the poor man's wood—God, war, charity—ends as the ferry of the shadows, ends as the dream ferry allotted for the last journey of the monarch of the world.—That is all. We can shut the book.

BIOGRAPHICAL NOTE ON

HENRY DE MONTHERLANT

1896, APRIL 21: born in Paris, of an old family of Catalonian origin, which settled in Picardy in the sixteenth century.

1910: began bullfighting; killed his first bull in 1911.

1914: wrote his first play, *L'Exil* (not published till 1929).

1916: joined up for auxiliary service, asked for transfer to active service. Three times mentioned in dispatches. Severely wounded in 1918.

1919: published his first signed article in a review (*Écrits nouveaux*, October).

1920: published at his own expense (after eleven publishers had refused it) *La Relève du matin*.

1920–6: sports (100 meters and football).

1922: published his first novel, *Le Songe*.

1924: publication of the two *Olympiques* and the *Chant funèbre pour les morts de Verdun*.

1920–4: secretary of association for constructing the war cemetery of Douaumont.

1925: left France.

1926: grave illness (trouble from war wounds after being gored by a bull). After many months in hospital, forbidden all sports. Published his second novel, *Les Bestiaires*. Wrote *Aux fontaines du désir* (essays).

1929: published *Pour une vièrge noire* and *La Petite Infante de Castille*.

1930: wrote *La Rose de sable* (novel, never published).

1932: published *Mors et Vita.*

1934: published *Les Célibataires* (novel) and *Encore un instant de bonheur.*

1935: published *Service inutile* (essays).

1936: published *Pasiphaé* (play), and the first two novels, *Les Jeunes Filles* and *Pitié pour les femmes*, of the tetralogy *Les Jeunes Filles.*

1937: published *Le Démon du bien* (third novel of *Les Jeunes Filles*).

1938: published *L'Équinoxe de septembre* (essays).

1939: published *Les Lépreuses* (fourth novel of *Les Jeunes Filles*). Tried to join up at outbreak of war, but prevented by pneumonia.

1940: began writing *Port-Royal* (four-act play finished in 1942, not yet published or performed). War correspondent of *Marianne* during German invasion of France, and slightly wounded. Went to south of France after the armistice.

1941: destroyed MS. of *Le Rêve des guerriers* (a book on the defeat of France), but published *Le Solstice de juin* (a book of essays, banned by the Germans in Holland and Belgium throughout the war and at first in France also, then authorized by an official of the German Institute in Paris who had for some years been his usual translator).

1942: *La Reine morte: ou Comment on tue les femmes* (*Queen after Death*) produced at the Comédie Française.

1943: *Fils de personne: ou Plus que le sang* (*No Man's Son*) produced at the Théâtre Saint-Georges. Writing of *Malatesta* (not yet produced) begun.

1944: trouble with the Germans; flat searched by Gestapo.

1945: wrote *Le Maître de Santiago* (*The Master of Santiago*).

1942–5: worked with Swiss Red Cross for French war victims. Has written a book on this (still not published).

1946: published *Un Voyageur solitaire est un diable* and *Malatesta*.

1947: *Le Maître de Santiago* produced at the Théâtre Hébertot with great success (over 500 performances in French, in Paris and elsewhere.)

1948: return of *La Reine morte* to the repertoire of the Comédie Française.

1949: *Demain il fera jour* (*Tomorrow the Dawn*) produced at the Théâtre Hébertot, being played each evening after *Fils de personne*, to which it is the sequel.

A NOTE ON THE TYPE
IN WHICH THIS BOOK IS SET

This book was set on the Monotype in Janson, *a recutting made direct from the type cast from matrices made by Anton Janson some time between 1660 and 1687.*

Of Janson's origin nothing is known. He may have been a relative of Justus Janson, a printer of Danish birth who practiced in Leipzig from 1614 to 1635. Some time between 1657 and 1668 Anton Janson, a punch-cutter and type-founder, bought from the Leipzig printer Johann Erich Hahn the type-foundry which had formerly been a part of the printing house of M. Friedrich Lankisch. Janson's types were first shown in a specimen sheet issued at Leipzig about 1675.

Composed, printed, and bound by Kingsport Press, Inc., *Kingsport, Tennessee.*